PERSONAL LAW REFORMS AND GENDER EMPOWERMENT

A DEBATE ON UNIFORM CIVIL CODE

PERSONAL LAW REFORMS AND GENDER EMPOWERMENT

A DEBATE ON UNIFORM CIVIL CODE

Nandini Chavan
Qutub Jehan Kidwai

Foreword by
Dr. Asghar Ali Engineer

HOPE INDIA

SOCIAL JUSTICE SERIES
VOL. 2

PERSONAL LAW REFORMS
AND GENDER EMPOWERMENT

© **Nandini Chavan**
   Qutub Jehan Kidwai | **2006**

Published in India by
HOPE INDIA PUBLICATIONS
85, Sector 23, Gurgaon – 122017
Tel (0124) 2367308
E-mail : info@hopeindiapublications.com
www.hopeindiapublications.com

ISBN 81 - 7871 - 079 - X

Printed in India by
Nagri Printers, Shahadra, Delhi

FOREWORD

Uniform civil code has been included in the Directive Principles of the Constitution and many people sincerely believe that it should be enforced for ensuring gender justice. The framers of the Constitution believed that all gender just laws should be uniform for All Indians irrespective of caste and creed. This ideal is, of course, admirable. All our present personal laws, no matter of which community, are hardly gender just. Traditional laws cannot be satisfactory as they were evolved centuries ago when gender subjugation, rather than gender justice, was the norm.

The Qur'anic laws were highly gender just but patriarchal society could not put up with gender just laws and took away most of the women's rights through backdoor. Even the *Shari'ah* laws could not fulfil the ideals of the Qur'anic justice and social ethos, where, basically, patriarchal prevailed over Quranic ideals. It is, therefore, necessary even in Islamic societies to approach the Qur'anic ideal rather than justify the *Shari'ah* formulations of eighth and ninth centuries. The tension between the Qur'anic and *Shari'ah* laws should be resolved in favour of the Qur'an.

There were more serious problem areas in the personal laws of other religious traditions. The British rulers did not touch the personal laws of any community (except enacting the Christian Divorce Act). There were good reasons for not touching these laws. One of the reasons of the Revolt of 1857 was a feeling among the common people of India that their religious traditions were being interfered with. Even Sati abolition affected with the support of Raja Ram Mohan Roy led to sour feelings among upper caste Hindus.

The British also enacted a common criminal procedure code which was accepted by all communities including the Muslims who had their own Islamic criminal code. In fact, Maulvi Nazir Ahmed, a traditional 'alim translated the code into Urdu for which he was given the title of Shamsul '*Ulama* (the sun of the learned). Indeed, touching the personal laws was very risky and would have led to another mutiny, perhaps.

Women in nineteenth century India were far from liberated; even today they are not. Women were not even literate—except very few. They had no awareness of their rights. They had internalised their own oppression and exploitation. Thus one can say even women were not prepared for radical change in their status. Also, men would have never accepted any radical change in their personal laws.

The British judges also decided all cases pertaining to marriage, divorce, inheritance, etc. strictly in keeping with traditional and customary laws or religious laws in case of certain Muslim communities (few Muslim communities like Khojas and Cutcchi Memons were also governed by traditional laws until the enactment of the 1937 *Shari'ah* Act). The enactment of the *Shari'ah* Act of 1937 greatly improved the position of Muslim women belonging to these communities. The status of women in traditional laws was far worse than the *Shari'ah* laws.

If in colonial society it was difficult to bring changes in traditional personal laws, it was much more difficult to usher in changes in the present democratic society. The politicians are afraid of facing the wrath of their voters. The vast number of women continue to be illiterate and unaware of their rights as equal citizens and hence it is men who decide what is good or bad for them.

The Constitution makers were faced with a dilemma.

Most of them were educated and believed in gender justice but the vast masses whom they represented did not share this awareness with them. Religious traditions and customs were 'sacred' for them and could not be allowed to be tempered with by legislators. Thus a compromise had to be found. The UCC was included under Directive principles. The state shall strive to enact uniform civil code, it said. No time limit was prescribed. It had to be left to the discretion of the state as to when time was ripe to do so.

Later on, it became increasingly difficult to enact the UCC for a number of reasons. Firstly, no community, including the majority community, was prepared to accept gender just laws. The Hindu Code Bill as originally drafted by Dr. Ambedkar was strongly opposed by conservative Hindus. They *gheraoed* the Parliament and even Nehru's cabinet colleagues developed cold feet. As a result, the Code Bill had to be withdrawn. Dr. Ambedkar, who had worked hard to draft the Bill, resigned out of sheer frustration. Later on, the Bill was enacted in its watered down version in series of enactments on marriage, divorce, etc.

If the changes in the majority community personal laws were so difficult, it was much more so for minority communities like the Muslims, Christians and Parsis. Muslims constituted the largest minority community and it was not possible to ignore their feelings. The Jami'at al-'Ulama-i-Hind had stood by the Congress for united India and had opposed partition tooth and nail and the Congress had given them assurance that Muslims will be free to practice their faith including the *Shari'ah* laws. Going back on the promise so soon after independence could have had severe repercussions.

Thus the Congress had to reassure Muslims that their personal or *Shari'ah* laws will not be tempered with unless they themselves desired. The *'Ulama* continued to be their allies. Secondly, the Muslims were in minority and it is minority fear basically which had led to partition of the country. Minority psychology played an important role in Muslim politics in post-independence period too.

Also, due to partition the educated middle class from U.P. and Bihar migrated to Pakistan leaving behind more illiterate and backward class Muslims who sincerely believed that since the *Shari'ah* is divine it could not be changed at all. They had no idea that *Shari'ah* had several Arab traditional and customary laws as well and the Islamic jurists could not ignore those Arab institutions and practices while formulating the *Shari'ah* laws. Thus the *'Ulama* used their mass base to oppose any changes in *Shari'ah* laws.

Minority status, poverty, illiteracy and sense of insecurity due to repeated communal riots all combined together to make any changes in *Shari'ah* laws impossible. On the other hand, the communal forces politicised the issue and began to propagate that the Congress does not enact UCC to 'appease' its Muslim vote bank. During sixties and seventies genuine secular elements were demanding UCC on genuine grounds of gender justice. But by the end of eighties the UCC became a part of the Hindutva agenda, knowing fully well that Hindus themselves were not prepared for it.

In fact the Hindu society is bewilderingly diverse and no uniform law can smoothly work. Also, among Hindus there are a large numbers of illiterate and backward sections for whom their traditions are very sacred. Even today child marriage, though outlawed since thirties of the last century, takes place openly and unabashedly. The Sati and Dowry Acts are violated with impunity. Thus advanced laws and backward society work in conjunction.

No wonder, then, that the NDA Government led by BJP, though elected on the Hindutva Agenda which among other things, included UCC, never tried to enact any such law. It conveniently ignored it. It was used only as anti-minority measure to arouse middle class Hindus against Muslims and get their votes. Such crass politicisation of the issue killed its very secular spirit.

However, in view of all these difficulties the issue of gender justice cannot wait and women cannot continue to suffer. If UCC is not possible then one should work for reforming personal laws of all communities to empower women. In a democracy women are equal citizens of our country and they must enjoy equal rights in matter of marriage, divorce, inheritance and property. This can best be achieved through reforms.

Since our Centre for Study of Society and Secularism is committed to gender justice our two scholars undertook this study of Hindu and Islamic laws to explore the potentiality for reforms in their respective laws so that women could enjoy equal rights in personal sphere within the framework of traditional laws. This book is the labour of their love and readers would find it quite informative and useful. Both the scholars Qutub Jehan Kidwai and Nandini Chavan have good grasp of Islamic and Hindu laws and have studied these laws closely. This study shows clearly that it is possible to bring healthy changes in the status of Hindu and Muslim women by invoking the true spirit of their religious faith.

Thus it will be seen that much can be done without waiting for enactment of UCC. The women of both the communities are becoming increasingly aware of their status and are vocally demanding necessary changes. Muslim women are also now much more educated and would no longer be satisfied with their traditional status. They have formed their own personal law board and are challenging the unjust laws and practices and are interpreting the Qur'anic provisions from a gender perspective.

These are indeed signs of great change and time is not far off when more and more gender just laws will be enacted and UCC through other means will gradually come into effect though without shedding the religious imprint.

Asghar Ali Engineer

CONTENTS

INTRODUCTION

Uniform Civil Code (UCC) is a very controversial issue in Indian politics. It is incorporated in the Article 44 of the Constitution, which lays down that the state is bound by this Constitutional mandate to secularize and homogenize the family laws. The enactment of UCC is a goal to be achieved through a gradual process. This is a directive principle of governance. The controversy over the UCC has been there since independence, but, it has received very much importance now. Communal politics has also played very important role in the matter.

Basically, UCC has its own dilemmas. It is understood in various ways through national integration, majoratisation of the issue and concept of modernity, gender justice including Hindutva ideology and religious identity. These are the mainstays of the issue.

The basic objective of the research project under which this volume has been prepared is to explore the possibilities of reform in Muslim Personal Law and Hindu Personal Law from women rights perspective. In order to found that effort on the most factual and least controversial information we have attempted to collect and organize very convincing material in this volume. It has got two sections, one on Hindu Personal Law and the other on the Muslim Personal law. To understand this material in relation to the underlying objective of the project as a whole, we present here an overview of the controversy of Uniform Civil Code and Hindu and Muslim Personal Law

A lot of research has been conducted on the controversy

of Uniform Civil Code. The demand for a Uniform Civil Code has got contradictory origin and diverse implications. In fact, it is, as indicated above, now one of the most controversial issues in contemporary politics. The two groups who consider it as a priority are the women's organization and Hindu fundamentalists.

To understand the debate on Uniform Civil Code and Personal laws, views of Dr. Asghar Ali Engineer are very significant. We have made a big use of them in the study. The main points raised during the course of the debate are as follows:

- It is argued that it is a constitutional provision under Article 44 and hence must be implemented. It is more than 40 years since the Constitution was framed and yet UCC has not been enforced. This is what has essentially been the argument of the judges in the recent judgment.
- It is often argued that there cannot be different laws for different communities in one country. How can Muslims be allowed to marry four wives and divorce them at will whereas the others must follow a different set of laws.
- It is highly necessary to have a uniform law in order to strengthen unity and integrity of the country.
- It is argued that UCC is needed in the interest of gender justice. The Muslim personal law in particular is gender unjust as it permits polygamy and unilateral divorce. It is only UCC, which can ensure gender justice.
- The Hindus have accepted reforms in their personal law right after independence and it is only Muslims who are resisting change and modernization in their laws. In modern secular India no one can be allowed to practice archaic laws.

We have examined these points at length here.

The focus here is basically on gender issue. The issue of UCC is always politicised and communalised by communal forces in the name of religion. But we see through the lens of gender equality. The communal forces portray the issue of UCC in the light of Hindu law and stress that Hindu laws are very secular and gender just. Within the concept of identity politics a support to the demand of a UCC is being construed almost as a betrayal of the community not only by the religious leadership but also by secular, progressive sections of the community.

The first section portrays 'Hindu Personal Law' and 'Uniform Civil Code'. Nandini Chavan analyses in her research the position of women in the Hindu Personal Law during the ancient, medieval and colonial periods including the post-Independence period in India. It is necessary to understand the personal law in its proper perspective as the current debate on UCC is linked with gender justice, which can only be understood through social status of women through the ages. The status of women has been analyzed through various dimensions like socio-economic condition, political condition, religious norms and values, cultural diversity and social stratification.

Chapter 1 deals with Feudalism and Patriarchy. There is no one to one relationship between feudalism and patriarchy, but these two concepts determined the role and the status of women in society. It is in this perspective that the issue of UCC has found its roots. Chapter 2 examines women status since *Vedic* period as it was in the *Vedic* period when women's role formation began. This chapter is a comprehensive text on women's role and status in the context of customary laws, regional practices and reforms in Hindu society, from *Vedic* period to colonial period. Chapter 3 analyses Hindu Code Bill, which is a landmark in Hindu legal history and also towards the empowerment of women. The Chapter comprises debates, discussions and controversies over Hindu Code Bill. Chapter 4 deals with Reforms in post-Independence Period, viz. Hindu Marriage Act, Hindu Divorce Act, Hindu Succession Act. These personal reforms were the first legal steps in the direction of providing gender equality in Hindu society. Chapter 5 is a detailed discourse on Hindutva and UCC. It explains misinterpretation of Hinduism, emergence of Hindutva, Hindutva Ideology and Politics, origin of Hindu-Muslim conflict, politics and UCC and BJP's gender perspective. Chapter 6 discusses Women's movement and UCC. In some recent decades women's movement gave a different dimension to this issue, that is, that it will not be discussed on the communal grounds, but since all women are equal, they must be provided equal rights. Thus, the gender consciousness gave a different dimension to the issue. Women's movement insisted that the talk of UCC must be based primarily on women justice and security.

In the last decade the Hindu fundamentalist groups, specially the Sangh Parivar, were successful in generating hatred against the minorities in general and Muslim minority in particular. Specially, the BJP has, in these days, always been on the lookout for a cause that might reflect adversely on the Muslim community and thereby help it consolidate its 'Hindu' vote. They were the first to declare that in BJP ruled state UCC will be implemented. The current demand for UCC is motivated by reasons other than the protection of women's rights. UCC is a weapon to attack the Muslim community. In and after math of the demolition of the Babri mosque in December 1992, and the communal riot that rocked the country specially the city of Mumbai, BJP is on the lookout for an issue to further attack and alienate the Muslims and to consolidate its 'Hindu' votes. All those who are for UCC without worrying about the larger conspiracy are falling in the trap of

BJP. This includes feminists who are for a UCC. The whole politics behind the UCC is a mere propaganda against the minorities, specially Muslim minority.

The second section deals with Muslim Personal Law. In Chapter 1 the 'Muslim Personal Law or *Shari'ah* and Uniform Civil Code' and some other aspects of Islamic law beginning with the bases of its formation like the Quranic principles. The other sources of *Shari'ah* law are *Hadith* (Prophet's Tradition), *Ijma* (Consensus) and *Qiyas* (Analogy). Among these the first two are accepted by all schools of laws, while the other two are either considered lesser important or rejected by some schools.

Chapter 2 discusses the beginning of distortion in Mohammedan law during the British period and explains how a very humane and just law got transformed into anti-woman and anti-progressive law. Are we really practicing true Islamic law? Are our *'Ulama* aware that the *Shari'ah* which they consider divine and immutable is actually framed by the British?

The third Chapter deals with the debates against and in favour of UCC whether it is truly concerned about empowering woman or to bring integrity among the citizens. In the fourth chapter, which is very interesting, is has been shown how Muslim countries where women are aware of their rights, have, time and again, brought reforms in Islamic laws to suit their needs. One cannot ignore the fact that the *Shari'ah* laws can be changed and reformed unless if they negate Quranic values.

Further it has been discussed here the difficulties or rather impossibilities of introducing UCC in the matter of Family Laws in view of huge diversity of our society. The laws of all religions not only differ sect-wise but they also differ from region to region, from caste to caste and from community to community.

In sum, this is a humble attempt to understand the Islamic law in general and laws relating to women in particular. With our limited understanding of Quranic Law we have tried to bring out what actually is the essence of Muslim Law for this can be helpful in living as a minority in a secular country. We feel that by taking more initiative to educate our Muslim masses about the true laws regarding marriage and divorce we can create more awareness among our women and enhance their status. Our ignorance about Islamic law is leading to a situation that is ambiguous and conflicting.

Nandini Chavan
Qutub Jehan Kidwai

SECTION ONE

HINDU PERSONAL LAW AND UNIFORM CIVIL CODE

1

FEUDALISM AND PATRIARCHY

Feudalism in India differs from European feudalism. Its forms are different and are not a product of an agrarian era. Under Indian feudalism, no private property in land existed. In ancient times, 'the land belonged to the village community, and was never regarded as the property of the king'. The king or his intermediary claimed only a part of the produce of the land, a claim that was met by the village committee as the representative of the village community. The structure of agricultural production in Indian village thus remained un-interfered with for centuries. No king or his viceroy ever challenged the ultimate customary right over the village land by the village community. Pre-British Indian society almost completely subordinated the individual to the caste, the family and the village panchayat. 'Even at the end of the eighteenth century, the Indian social order was, for the most part, equivalent to the discharge of obligations to the family, to the caste and the village panchayat's working on the basis of an economic self–sufficiency in the rural units, and in addition, to the guilds and corporations on the basis of trade and commerce between urban areas.'

Within the village, the economic life based on primitive agriculture and artisan industry was on a low and almost stationary level. In this type of economic existence, helplessness before natural catastrophes and a state insecurity were bound to develop the outlook of the village population on lines of superstition, religious mysticism and the crudest form of worship of natural forces.

The caste-stratified social organization of the village population was also not conducive to any development of individual initiative, adventure or striking out of new paths. Caste system assigned to the individual his space in the social and economic structure of the village life. The village population thus continued to live for centuries, the same sterile, superstitious, narrow, stereotyped social and intellectual existence. In other words, the same group of superstitions, the same pantheon of deities, the same narrow village and caste consciousness, the same local perspective not transcending the limited miserable village existence, held in their grip the Indian humanity almost wholly concentrated in autonomous, self–sufficient, self–absorbed villages, which were no less than the citadels of economic stagnation, social reaction and cultural blindness. The only change that we witnessed there used to be the transfer, from time to time, of land revenue from the old to the new monarch when one succeeded the other. In rest of the things, the villagers continued to live by caste and village committee codes with a low level of socio-economic existence.

The, village panchayats and caste communities performed all judicial, administrative and even economic functions in the legion of villages. The village intelligentsia was almost exclusively composed of the village priest and schoolmaster who were the servants of the village community and looked after the religious-cultural and secular-cultural interests of the people. Actually, the feudal society has its own identity where the land centralizes the economy. That was feudal economy.[1]

With the emergence of agricultural economy the question arose as to who owns the land, which manifested the beginning of patriarchal society. As private property created the problem of inheritance, the consequences led to male dominant society. Clearly, feudalism and patriarchy go hand in hand as patriarchy is firmly established in land relationship. Feudalism has its origin in the term *'fief' (feodum, feudum)*. 'The classical fief was a piece of landed property held by a vassal from a lord in return for military service, or giving of aid and counsel.' The relationship between lordship and vassalage based on loyalty, service and counsel was the main basis of Feudalism. This is the economic dimension of feudalism but equally important are the political and ideological dimensions of feudal society that give us the perspective of social formation.

During religious upheaval, for example, the rise of Buddhism, the preachers of the new religion gave a fresh interpretation of the old religion and spread out to the villages with a view to converting the people. Such startling changes in the religious outlook of the people in the villages however did not bring about any fundamental change in the consciousness of the people; or in any national consciousness. The same narrow village perspective continued to dominate the outlook of the villager. The villager never developed the consciousness of being Indians, which the growth of the national sentiment had signified. Even during the call for unity of India all response was only in a religious sense, i.e. India as a land of the Hindus who were united by the common religion of Hinduism but not that of the Indians who inhabited the Indian territory and who were economically and politically welded into a single unit.

BASIC FEATURES OF INDIAN FEUDALISM

Regarding the feudal nobility, the ruling monarch gave them only the right to collect and appropriate land revenue over a specific number of villages. The nobility was not the owner of these villages but only the revenue collector keeping the whole or a portion of the land revenue. Since the king was not the proprietor of the land, he could not create a class of

nobles with proprietary rights over it. It was only his reve-
nue-collecting power that he bestowed upon and transferred
to the noble. The very fact that under all types of kings, be-
nevolent or despotic, Hindu, Buddhist or Muslim, no attempt
was made to deprive the village communities of the land and
establish a class of landowners over them, is the testimony to
the fact that the land was not regarded as the property of the
king, that the village community was the de-facto owner of
the village land and that the state or the monarch had a claim
only over a share of the realized annual produce from it. On
the other hand, there did not exist individual peasant proprietorship over land either. This means that there did not exist in pre-British India any form of private ownership of land.

During the Moghul rule, innovations were introduced,
but these in no way affected the fundamental land relations
in agriculture. The system of cash payment of the land revenue due to the state from the village was introduced but the
village possession of and its customary right over the land
was not interfered with. The village as the unit of revenue assessment also continued as a rule.

EMERGENCE OF THE CONCEPT OF PRIVATE PROPERTY

The British conquest of India led to a revolution in the existing land system. The new revenue system introduced by the
British in India superseded the traditional right of the village
community over the village land and created two forms of
property in land: landlordism in some parts of the country
and the individual peasant proprietorship in others.

The permanent *Zamindari* settlements prevailed in Bengal, Bihar and sections of North Madras and enveloped about
20 per cent of British India. The temporary *Zamindari* systems covered the major portions of the United Provinces, certain zones of Bengal and Bombay, the Central Provinces and
the Punjab and constituted about 30 per cent of the British In-

dian territory.

Considering that the *ryotwari* like the *Zamindari* was based on private property in land, unknown to pre-British India, it was as much exotic to the Indian tradition as the *Zamindari*. Both were points of departure from the traditional Indian economy, which excluded the economic category of individual private ownership of land. The *ryotwari* system, although it was advocated as a closer approach to Indian institutions in point of fact by its making the settlement with individual cultivators and by its assessment on the basis of land not on the proportion of the actual produce broke right across Indian institutions no less than the *Zamindari* system. Thus the private property in land came into being in India. Land became private property, a commodity in the market, which could be mortgaged, purchased or sold.

The British conquest of India brought about an agrarian revolution. It created the prerequisite for the capitalist development .of agriculture by introducing individual ownership of land, namely peasant ownership and large-scale land ownership. This transformation of the land relations was the most vital link in the chain of causes, which transformed the whole pre-capitalist feudal economy of India into the existing capitalist economy.

The practice of the new land and revenue system logically and inevitably brought in its wake the phenomena of the mortgage, the sale and the purchase of land. When a landholder could not pay the land revenue due to the state out of the returns of his harvest or his resources, he was constrained to mortgage or sell his land. Thus, insecurity of possession and ownership of land—a phenomenon unknown to the pre-British agrarian society—came into existence. The new land system disastrously affected the communal character of the village, its self-sufficient economy and communal social life.

Previously, the village owned the land, looked after and

supervised agriculture carried on by different peasant families among whom it had distributed the land according to the customary law. Along with this agricultural-economic function, it also performed, through the village panchayat, the judicial functions of settling disputes arising among the peasants in connection with agriculture.

The emergence of new social classes in India was the direct consequence of the establishment of a new economy, a new type of state system and state administrative machinery and the spread of new education during the British rule. The Indian people were reshuffled into new social groupings, new classes, as a result of the basic capitalistic economic transformation of Indian society. Hence new social classes came into being earlier in those zones, which came under the direct British influence earlier.

The moneylender in the old Indian society played almost an insignificant role. The village occasionally lent money to the village agriculturist or artisan, the interest strictly fixed by the village panchayat. Further, the moneylender could not annex the land or livestock in case a farmer did not meet the interest claim since the land belonged to the village community. Similarly, the village merchant, in old society, only reinforced the village with a few articles, which it could not produce. His role, was, however, magnified, even became transformed, when land became private property and agricultural produce became a commodity. The merchant became indispensable to the peasant as an intermediary for the sale of his crop in the Indian or world market.

FEUDALISM – IT'S CRITIQUE

Karl Marx visualized a feudal society as one of the pre-capitalist modes of production. The economic structure of capitalist society has grown out of the economic structure of feudal society. The dissolution of the latter sets free elements of the former. The feudal exploitation is transformed into capitalist exploitation. But Marx and Engels observe that the feudal lord appropriated rent in an agrarian society from the peasants who could barely meet their subsistence needs. Peasants were treated as serfs. They did not enjoy property rights, and had to surrender their labour or the product of their labour to the feudal lord. The notion of feudal society is not simply exploitation of peasants by landlords and their movements against such exploitative devices: feudalism is an epoch in the historical evolution of modern capitalist society.

Marx subscribes to the existence of an Asiatic Mode of Production (AMP) in India, but decries a unilinear view of development. The AMP is different from feudalism, and there is no unilinear mode of production and transformation. But the AMP highlights the state, not the feudal lord as the principal appropriator of the surplus product. The AMP focuses on the stagnation of the forces of production and the absence of classes. The state is seen as a repressive force. The emergence of 'classes' marks to a phase of transition from the AMP to capitalism. Marx thus observes predominance of one mode of production (in all forms of society) over the rest.

Feudalism in economic terms can be equated with serfdom or slave economy. In political terms, it is a method government signifying relation between lord and vassals. Opinion regarding feudalism in India is sharply divergent. According to Ashok Rudra, the AMP characterized by the Indian society, whereas a host of historians such as Kosambi, Sharma, et al, argue that feudalism was the predominant social formation in India, and Harbans Mukhia talks of the prevalence of self-dependence of the free peasant production. Kosambi also refers to a process of 'feudalism from below' while distinguishing the Indian feudalism from the European, as the latter was characterized by a process 'from above'. Caste hierarchy was an inseparable part of feudalism too as Brahmins paid low taxes on the same amount and quality of land, and also faced lower punishments for offences.[2]

Godes conception of feudalism excludes the role of 'patrimony' and patron-client relationship (through the *jajmani* system). Both theses institutions gave a distinct character to feudalism in India, but even then it was despotic as a political and administrative system. In Asia, and particularly in India, the state was despotic and it superimposed itself on the communities engaged in agriculture and handicrafts. Max Weber considers patrimonilism and feudalism as the two major variants of traditional domination. He uses the term 'patriarchalism 'to explain the authority of a master over his household. Drawing his clue from the authority of the head of the family, Weber observes that their patrichal authority can characterize the despotic regimes of Asia. All other structures, political, economic and religious, become typical patriarchal structures. The patrimonial authority exorcizes arbitrary and personal power in the name of 'tradition'.

Paternal authority and filial dependence are the basis of patrimonial government and the latter paves the way for feudalism. However, Weber makes it clear that patrimonial officials can acquire personal independence on the basis of hereditary land grants, while landed nobles who possess this independence may lose it. The distinction between the patriarchal structure and the state–structure of traditional domination, despite being blurred, remains analytically important.

In India Feudalism in terms of *jagirdari, zamindari, ryotwari* and other systems of governance, those systems were in operation in different parts of India, and they have had differential impact on social stratification and land reforms. There was no single model of feudalism in India. The first divide was between British India and princely India, and then there were several divides in terms of *jagirdari, khalsa. bhai-*

bhaichara, etc within the latter, and *zamindari* and *ryotwari* systems in British India. Therefore, feudalism with its nexus with caste (particularly with the upper and functionary castes), was a social formation in terms of dominance over peasantry, artisans, and craftsmen, wage-workers, traders, etc it dominated the entire social system, including the caste system.

In India feudalism has existed along with colonialism, and the latter can be taken also as a form of 'dependent capitalism' in the Indian context. Today neo-colonialism and 'capitalism' co-exist along with the remains of feudalism. Feudal or semi-feudal relations in the agrarian system have found a place for themselves despite the 'capitalist mode' and democratic polity.[3]

PATRIARCHY

Patriarchy looms large in feminist debate. It implies that power is imperative in producing and maintaining gender relations. Contemporary Feminist Scholars have used the word 'gender' after two decades of intensive thought and research. According to them gender is a social and political construct, related to and not determined by, biological sex difference. Two major theories of gender prevalent today—the psychologically focused theory of gender; and historically and anthropologically focused explanation of gender. The second theory of gender proclaims that in most societies across the cultures, so far, gender has been a socially constructed category rather than biologically determined. However, the proponents of this theory have also stressed that the nature also and this social construction differs from one society to the other. Actually patriarchal structure of the society reflects the construction of gender relation and status of woman in the society.

The basic value of the term patriarch and importance of

its use is that it denotes a structural system of male domination. The term 'patriarchy' has double meaning: 'rule of men' and 'rule of father', the latter being its literal meaning. Its original use was to describe a specific type of male-dominated family, the large household of a patriarch, which included women, junior men, children, slaves and domestic servants, all under the rule of this dominant male.

There are several theories regarding patriarchy. Aristotle and Sigmund Freud believed that biological differences between men and women determined male superiority. Engels (19th century) attributed patriarchy to class divide and evolution of private property looking at the concept in economic terms. For radical feminists patriarchy was rooted in the contradiction in the sexes rather than in economic classes. Socialist feminists argued that while sex was biological, gender was social. For them man –woman relationship was always dynamic and changed with changing modes of production.[4]

MARXIST VIEW OF WOMEN

In the German ideology, Marx and Engels had incorporated crucial insights about women. Engels' major contribution was to bequeath to the working class movement a conceptualisation that women were not naturally second sex; that they were in fact exploited within an oppressive family structure and that this exploitative system was historically created and would historically disappear. Though he used the term father-right, this was essentially a conceptualisation of patriarchy.

Contemporary feminist theories of patriarchy emerged primarily in reaction to and in confrontation with the mechanical materialist form of Marxism. This was because it was within the Marxist tradition that concepts such as patriarchy were retained in however inadequate form. It had a theory of patriarchy, though it is inadequate. It has avoided biologism and retained the notion of a separate, male dominated family/

reproduction systems.

Many theorists have moved in the direction of defining women's labour as a special kind of labour, and patriarchy in terms of male control of that labour. Patriarchy can be defined as a set of social relations among men, which has a material base and which, though hierarchical, establish or creates interest to dominate women. The material base on which patriarchy rests lies most fundamentally in men's control over women's labour power. Characteristic of this approach is that it not only adds reproduction to the concept of production, but also very often makes it basic.

It is significant that nearly all versions of 'women's labour' or 'production of life' approaches to patriarchy involve a two-tier structure of exploitation with male hierarchy at the top, structured by the exploitation of women.

Karl Marx was to point out one problem forcibly in the mid- nineteenth century: abstract notions of equal rights and force of reason failed to consider the actual economic and social inequalities among individuals, which greatly affected how rights could be exercised. Principles might be very fine, but the poor had to live in the meantime. Some advocates of women's emancipation from the 1820's noted another difficulty; to say all individuals could acquire reason ignored that reason itself was culturally formed. They began to argue that men had the power to set the terms of culture and to make reason thus in their own image. Women's emancipation consequently required the transformation of culture, not just gaining access to existing culture.

Women to reveal and illuminate aspects of their oppression could apply Marx's thought, but in his own work women's relations to men and women's capacity to shape society and culture are extrinsic. Man in his early thought is the maker of history and woman the passive indices. True women could claim inclusion within the general concept of humanity. Later as the Promethean struggle of the workers against capital consumes him, women are admitted as proletarians but otherwise left dangling. Although Marx was formally committed to the legal emancipation of women and the right to work, his intellectual passion was not directed toward the relations between the man and women, but toward class. When it came to business of changing society it seemed women's interests were assumed to be safely included with those of men.[5]

PATRIARCHY AND WOMEN'S SUBORDINATION

Uma Chakravarty in her book has analysed that the subordination of women and the control of female sexuality are crucial to the maintenance of caste system. The book highlights the interface of gender and caste.[6]

Nur Yalman, an anthropologist, has argued that a fundamental principle of Hindu social organization was to construct a closed structure to preserve land, women and ritual quality within it.[7] These three are structurally linked and it is impossible to maintain all three without stringently controlling female sexuality. Neither land nor ritual quality, that is, the purity of caste, can be ensured without closely guarding women who form the pivot of the entire structure. There is thus a close connection among class, caste, gender and the state laid down in the religio-legal texts of Brahmanic Hinduism.

CONTROL OF FEMALE SEXUALITY

The shift to an agricultural economy and the second urbanization between B.C. 800 and B.C. 500 were marked by the emergence of class divisions and an incipient though as yet tentative attempt at caste-based hierarchies. The Brahmans as a group were a force to reckon with as they staked a claim to the ritual and ideological leadership of society even though this was being challenged at least by some segments of society, while birth-based hierarchy was not yet in place, patrilineal succession and the emergence of private control over land was already in place. The establishment of private control over land-held and transmitted within a patrilineal succession to kingship was the context where a sharp distinction was required to be made between motherhood and female sexuality.

Women's sexuality, their essential natures, their maternal power had to be organized and ordered by paternal power in the emerging class/caste based societies to serve the new social and political arrangements organized by men of the dominant sections of society. Women's general subordination was essential at this stage because it was only then that the mechanism of control upon women's sexuality could actually become effective. Both in terms of economic autonomy through a denial of control over productive resources and autonomy in law, women were made appendages of men. Indeed women themselves were the property, both in terms of their reproductive and their productive labour of men. The general subordination of women was thus the basis of the specific controls that the patriarchal structure placed upon them. It was one of the most successful ideologies constructed by any patriarchal system, one in which women themselves controlled their own sexuality and believed that they gained power and respect through the codes they adopted. *Pativrata* may be regarded as the ideological '*purdah*' of the Hindu women as chastity and wifely fidelity came to be regarded as the means to salvation: it was also the means by which the iniquitous and hierarchical structure was reproduced with the complicity of women. The actual mechanisms and institutions of control over women's sexuality and the general subordination of women were thus completely masked: patriarchy could then be more firmly established as an ideology since it came to be 'naturalized'.

Stridharma or the *Pativratadharma* was an ideological

mechanism for controlling the biological aspects of women. Through the *Stridharma* the biological woman can be tamed and converted into woman as a social entity. The structure of social rules also provided for a third level of control to ensure the perpetuation of the patriarchal structures: the king was vested with the authority to punish errant wives. The patriarchal state of early India viewed adultery as one of the major crimes in society along with theft as the other major crime in society.[8]

The archaic state was both a class/caste state and a patriarchal state: a close linkage existed between caste, class, state and patriarchy. Together they provided the structural framework of institutions within which gender relations were organized.[9] So the society had given such types of ideal formation for woman and they ruled by patriarchal structure. These types of structure arise from the problem of subordination of woman and this affects the rights of woman in the societyAmong the various means of maintaining the purity of the caste two are specially stressed: the ban of commensality among members of various castes and the strict observance of rules of endogamy and exogamy as applied with reference to caste. The rules of marriage were rigidly enforced and marriage was primarily a social institution. The lower the status of women the stronger was the legal tie of marriage. The patriarchal system tended to keep the status of women at a low level, and the emergence of the joint family with special property rights for the male members reinforced male dominance. The family was recognized as a basic unit of society and enjoyed the right to protection by society and the state. This was accentuated in the case of families who owned land and who worked on the land. The concept of property in the Hindu tradition was usually associated with the ownership of land. The right to own property was granted to those who could afford it.[10]

CASTE STRATIFICATION AND PATRIARCHAL PRACTICES

There exists the pyramidal structure of the caste system. The most valued attributes are associated with the top and the least valued attributes with the lowest rungs of the caste system. Among the key elements that distinguish these rungs are occupation and foods eaten—in terms of pure and impure— and marriage practices in terms of the most tightly controlled sexual practices—the highest forms of rituals and sacraments for the uppermost castes, and the more 'flexible' practices for the lower castes. The tight control of the sexuality of women of the upper castes is an aspect of the larger 'rationale' of pure and impure. The pre-pubertal marriage of upper castes girls so that the unpolluted womb of the wife was the sexual property of the husband before she began to menstruate, immediately after the *garbadhanam* or consummation ceremony would be completed, were necessary elements in the notion of caste purity.

Widowhood in India among the upper castes was a state of social death, though physically alive. In contrast the lower caste widows did not suffer social death, apart from differences according to the caste there are wide regional variations in widow remarriage practices. Among castes like *Jats* in Haryana and the Marathas in Western India and in many other intermediary castes across India, a secondary marriage with distinctive rituals was permissible. Similarly among the lower castes studied by Pauline Kolenda in Uttar Pradesh, the marriage practices were a total contrast to the Rajputs of the same village.[11] While enforced widowhood was the norm as well as the practice of Rajputs, enforced cohabitation was the rule among the 'untouchables'. There is not so much recognition of widow's sexual needs but an arrangement to utilize the productive and reproductive labour of widows. While maintaining land structures intact for the patrilineal household, levirate marriage among *Jats* and other servicing castes ensured the full reproductive potential of a woman to provide for the maximal replenishing of the labouring and servicing castes. The insistence that each caste should observe its own customs ensured that they continued to maintain their privileged high ritual status. Patriarchal formulations for women of the high castes and women of the lower castes were structurally integrated into the ideology and the material relations of the caste system.

The apparent difference in widow remarriage and widow mating patterns between the high castes and the low castes can lead to the conclusion that there were different patriarchies according to the respective caste status of a group. Despite major differences of practice in relation to women, brahmanical patriarchy was a single framework, which linked caste, gender, land control and demography together. It held within its ambit both the brahmanized upper cases and the less brahmanized middle and *dalit* castes.

Nevertheless, the wide range of marriage practices in accordance with the caste, it needs to be remembered that this diversity does not in any substantial way weaken the endogamous basis of marriage in Hindu social organization. The structure provides for marriage within the endogamous caste unit for the primary marriage and leakages in the system pertain mainly to the secondary unions or liaisons which are tolerated or permitted if they are between the higher caste man and a lower caste woman. These are congruent with the power of some men over others according to their class and caste locations, and of men over all women; the patterns of marriages within the caste system upholds the structures of class, caste, and gender stratification.

WOMEN IN SOCIALIST THEORY

Socialist theory in its understanding of society presented the first and most comprehensive historical analysis of gender oppression. In challenging the hitherto dominant and idealistic notion of social history, the Marxist theory of historical materialism demolished the understanding that existing social hierarchies, including male superiority/ female inferiority, were a preordained, permanent, natural order which had existed from time immemorial and are eternal.

Marx and Engels, the founders of revolutionary theory, traced the 'enslavement' of the female sex and the development of patriarchal society to a particular stage of social development, to the growth of class society and private property. Women, according to the Socialist theory, were not always considered 'weaker' or 'inferior' by virtue of their sex. In his seminal work in collaboration with Marx, though published after Marx's death, the origin of the Family, Private property, and the State, Engels drew the links between the development of class society, the changing forms of the family and the oppression of the women. The crux of his theory is the understanding of the sexual division of labour (reproduction of the human race and production of the means of existence). The first division of labour in human history was the sexual division of labour between man and woman for the procreation of the human race. Along with the centrality accorded to women's reproductive role and the line of descent being decided through the woman, historical evidence of the woman's central role in the nurturing of the family, in food gathering, and at later stage in the practice of agriculture, indicates women's control over the means of production at the stage of human development. Women held a place of high respect, and indeed were at the centre of early structures. In such 'mother-right' societies, kinship ties were decided through the mother.

The development of private property and the struggle for control of the surplus led to the formation of classes, bringing a fundamental change in social relationships and in the relations between men and women, which in turn found expression through the changing form of the family. The owners of property required the identification of progeny for inheritance rights. This meant the control over the female to ensure her 'chastity' and the 'purity' of the line of descent. Thus, it was the development of private property, and the question of inheritance rights which had its logical outcome the development of the monogamous family and the establishment of male control over the female. In other words, the 'historic defeat of the female sex', as Engel has described the overthrow of mother-right, was a result of the development of class society and of private property through a period lasting several million years.

Historically, it was class society that gave birth to patriarchal ideologies and the subordination of women. In contrast to current feminist theories, Marxism does not see patriarchy as an autonomous system, unconnected to the basic organization of a given society. It is only when women are reintroduced into the sphere of socially productive labour on an equal footing with men, and with equally shared domestic responsibilities that they can advance and the present unequal sexual division of labour is abolished. Marxist theory holds that the abolition of private property and the establishment of a socialist society are essential requirements for women's emancipation from her unequal status.

Marxist theory believes that human consciousness is determined by social being. Further, the development of class rule necessitates the development of class ideologies not just for the ruler but for the ruled as well. The control of women could not continue only through the use of force, but by becoming the accepted norm of social relations through the domination of the idea that women were by nature weaker and therefore, inferior. It is the ideology of the ruling classes, which determines through a conscious effort, using the power of the state, the major trends and levels of social consciousness in any given society, over a period of time. The exploitation and oppression on grounds of gender/caste/community can be changed provided the crucial link of class ownership and control of the means of production is identified and transformed.

In gender specific terms this would mean that with the creation of a society based on social ownership of the means of production (social, meaning male and female) which would eliminate class, and therefore the material basis of gender discrimination, women would be equal in the processes of social production. Marxism subsumes gender by class it cannot be considered a theory sensitive to women. Again, production in ancient societies is used by feminist scholars to show that women did have control over the means of production, and they were still oppressed, and therefore, gender oppression is not linked to socio-economic structures as understood by Marxist theory.[12]

CONCLUSION

There is no one to one relationship between feudalism and patriarchy, but these two concepts determined the role and the status of woman in their society. Feudalism has its social and economical roots in India with its own lens, which reflects the caste strata and position of woman. Feudalism and its relationship with private property encourage the male dominant society. Patriarchy is responsible for the subordination of women, which has immense impact on society. The issue of UCC becomes more complex and confused as the communal forces link it with the patriarchal norms, though, implicitly. So the basics of patriarchy are a very important thing in this whole debate on UCC.

NOTES

1. Desai, A.R. (1948), *Social Background of Indian Nationalism*, Popular Prakashan, Mumbai, p. 18-21.
2. Sharma, K.L. (1998), *Caste, Feudalism and Peasantry –The social formation of Shekhavati*, Manohar Publishers, p. 30.
3. *Ibid.*, p. 27-36.
4. Gopalan, Sarla (2000), Empowerment of Women in *50 Years of Indian Republic*, ed. M.K. Santhanam, Publication Division, Ministry of India, New Delhi, pp. 330- 331.
5. Sinha, Niroj (1999), Patriarchy: Politics and Women in *Women in Indian Politics*, Gyan Prakashan.
6. Chakravarty, Uma (2003), *Gendering Caste Through Feminist Lence*, Street, Calcutta, pp. 66-78.
7. Setaketu Jataka, *The Jatakas*, vol. 1, ed. E.B. Cowell (London: Pali Text Society, 1957).
8. *Ibid.*
9. The preceding paragraphs are drawn from Uma Chakravarti's article, *'Conceptualising Brahmanical Patriarchy'*.
10. Thaper, Romila, (1978), *Ancient Indian Social History*", Orient Longman, Delhi, p. 32.
11. Kolenda Pauline, (1987) 'Widowhood Among the 'Untouchable', Chuhras' in *Regional Difference in Family Structures in India*, Rawat Jaipur, p. 289-354.
12. Karat, Brinda (2005), *Survival and emancipation--Notes from Indian Women's Struggles*, Three Essays Collective, New Delhi, pp. 34-37.

2

DHARMASHASTRA AND FORMATION OF HINDU LAW

The analysis of women's status in *Vedic* period is necessary in view of the fact that it is in the *Vedic* period when, for the first time, women's role formation began. However, the whole discussion regarding women was, then, based on philosophy and spirituality. Women's socioeconomic status was altogether ignored. This was the reason which necessitated gradual declined of women's role and status in society, till *Dharmashastra* period. Although there had been talks over issues like women property (*Streedhan*), Marriage (Vivah), adoption (*Dattaka*) but not to enhance the status of women. Women's issues centred around women's sexuality, glory of motherhood and idealistic image of women. Consequently, women found themselves under many restrictions and bindings, which did not allow them to have their identity and freedom. Factor of Casteism and patriarchy added fuel in deteriorating women status in the society. Nevertheless, it cannot be said that women's position was similar in every section of society. As there had been some customary laws, which favoured women as far as their rights are concerned, such as marriage and divorce. In the colonial period women's positions in general became more and more prisoned in the hands of cruel practices like child marriage, dowry, widowhood, etc. This undue situation demanded immediate attention. As a result, subsequently many reformers came in the Hindu society.

VEDIC PERIOD : SOCIO –ECONOMIC STATUS

In the *Vedic* period there are details to be found regarding donations and purchases of land, although property rights were to a large extent subject to the 'will of the tribe'. Cultivated plots were made over to individual members of the tribe, and this step in its turn paved the way for the further development of inequality stemming from the differences in property rights or social status. Questions of inheritance became important and land was contested by individuals and by tribes. Gradually certain members of the tribal groups grew rich and came to constitute a privileged class in what had once been an untied community owning slaves. At the same time, impoverished members of the community lost their independence and became dependent members.

Slavery is a clear pointer to the growth of the economic and social inequality. Slaves were basically prisoners of war. *Vedic* tribes lived in the *ganas,* which constitute the clans or tribal groups and later units with a class structure. Women were not entitled to be present at the meetings of the *gana,* and were deprived of all political rights. The *ganas,* which consisted of large patriarchal families (*kula*). Clan ties were strong and the influence of the same *gotra* was it felt in all spheres of life.[1]

On the caste system the question as to the origin of *Varna* is most complex, but it would seem logical to connect the appearance of the social estate the *Varna,* with the break-up of primitive communal relations and the development of inequality based on differences in property ownership and social status. In the later *Vedic* period there arose within the *Varnas* smaller rigid subdivisions based on occupation, which later took the form of castes. According to Dr. N.C. Gupta, "there is no trace in the ritual literature of the *Vedic* times of joint families of married sons and grandsons living in the same house with the father. The *Vedic* family consisted of the husband, wife and immature sons and daughters but we find some restraints to this. The text of law bearing on the subject which were doubtless developed in different stages of the society and the different environments are an interesting study, that show a tendency to restrain the father's free dealings with the property till at last we reach the climax in a theory of the acquisition of ownership with the father of sons and grandsons from the moment of their birth." [2]

Rigvedic society is essentially a pre-urban society with copper and possibly iron technology. It evolved from nomadic pastoralism dependent on cattle to an agrarian form with more settled communities. Barley (*yuva*) appears to have been the staple food. There is a strong sense of tribal identity and the basic social unit is the patriarchal family.

The Rigvedic deities no longer have the pre-eminent position, which they had earlier since equal importance is now given to more recent incorporated deities. The four-fold *Varna* structure mentioned rarely in the *Rigveda* is now a recognized feature. The geographical and philosophical connection with West Asia has weakened. There appears to be a greater assimilation with local cultures. In comparing the early and later *Vedic* literature, it would seem that the major characteristic of continuity remains language, Sanskrit. In the analysis of social structure there is need for redefining social relationships. To see caste only in terms of the four-fold *Varna* does not take us very far. One would like to know how tribes and social groups were adjusted into the caste hierarchy and assigned a caste status. The theory that the caste-structure was initially flexible but gradually became rigid and allowed of little nobility is now open to question. There is enough evidence to suggest that there have been in all periods' deviations from the theoretical concept of caste. We also know that there was a continual emergence of new castes for a variety of reasons. Furthermore, social change presupposes social tension and at times even conflicts between groups, and these are referred to in the sources. The origin, nature and consequences of these constitute another significant area of study.[3]

VEDIC RELIGION AND CULTURE

The Aryans accepted the authority of *Vedas* and followed the *Vedic* rules. These rules consisted of moral, ethical and religious injunctions. To the Aryans whatever was contained in the *Vedic* texts was *'Dharma'* and the *'Dharma'* in the simplest sense meant law to them.

'Varna Dharma' and *'Varna Ashrama'* governed *Vedic* society and a Hindu was born in the then society for fulfilling the four great missions of his life, viz. the *Dharma, Artha, Kama* and *Moksha.*

The *Rigveda* referred to only two classes of the people, the 'Aryans' and the *'Dasas'*. The 'Aryans' were white complexioned and the *'Dasas'* were black-skinned. The Aryans were religious minded who worshipped the Supreme Being, performing different *Yajnas* (sacrifices) the *Dasas* were not religious-minded people and did not submit to the authority of the *Vedas*. The *'Dasas'* merged into the 'Shudra' community at a later stage. The *Vedic* texts assigned each *'Varna'*, their academic or professional duties. The *'Dasas'* or the 'Shudras' were categorised into the class of servants and were asked to serve the class of Aryans.

The Aryans were a prosperous community—kind of people leading a holy life, and following *Vedic* injunctions. They worshipped five elements of human existence, viz., *Kshit,* (Earth), *Jal* (the water), *Vayu* (the air) *Agni* (the fire) and *Akash* (the sky), which represented great five gods.

Among the Aryans the Brahmin was the repository of all known or revealed knowledge and for that reason alone held semi-divine authority. As the *Vedic* culture flourished and progressed *Vedic* religion grabbed many non-Aryans into her fold resulting in the growth and the development of Aryan race beyond the Indus valley.

The authority of *Vedas*, as a sacred Hindu text, is claimed to be the first source of orthodox Hindu law even to-day and all the *Smritis* and Digests and Commentaries on the *Smritis* owe their origin to it. Now, it is a judicially acknowledged view that whoever believes in the authority of *Vedas* and in the philosophy of Hindu way of life is a Hindu.

POSITION OF WOMEN IN THE VEDIC SOCIETY

The status of women in the *Vedic* society is a matter of some debate. While there had been a consistent tendency to idealise their position, it is likely that reality may have been more complex. That women played a certain part in the productive process is evident from the term *duhitr*, as noted earlier, as well as from their involvement in activities such as weaving. Further there are references to women seers of *Vedic* hymns, which would indicate some access to ritual and spiritual traditions. Besides, certain practices such as child marriage seem to have been organised patrilineally and while there were prayers for the birth of sons in particular and for praja or off-spring in general there was none for the birth of a daughter. Further, most of the major deities in the early *Vedic* pantheon temple are male, which could possibly indicate male domination on the human plane as well. Moreover, while early *Vedic* society was by and large relatively undifferentiated, there are no indications to suggest that women could occupy the highest positions of authority and prestige those of priests or the raja. Thus, a certain degree of social stratification along gender lines is discernible.

Vedic women had neither property nor the right of inheritance and their status was on a level with that of the Shudra. But other evidence tends to show the opposite. The wife as a companion in conjugal life in *Vedic* society was not an unusual feature.

The basic social unit was probably the patriarchal family. The four-fold *Varna* system, on the other hand, was virtually absent. There are only fourteen references to Brahmans, nine to Kshatriyas and one to the Shudra, the last named being referred to only in the context of the *purushashukta* hymn, which occurs in the tenth *mandala* of the *Rigveda* which is commonly regarded as late.

There are four *Vedas* but comparatively, in the Rig *Vedic* period the women enjoyed a high position in society. Many women made a mark as renowned scholars and philosophers like Visvavara, Ghosala and Apala. Saunaka in Brahmadevta mentions 27 *Brahmavadinis*, great scholars who contributed Shuktas in the *Rigveda*. Women were married at a mature age, participated in religious ceremonies and had freedom in the choice of husbands. Polygamy was rare.[4]

Kumkum Roy questions whether in the *Vedic* period women position was really high? She states that women composed only about fifteen of the more than thousand shuktas in the *Rigveda*. And while we have the names of dozens of men who participated in philosophical discursions, the names of only two women, Maitrayi and Gargi survive. Clearly, such women were exceptional.

The later *Vedic* texts, especially the sutras, are categorical in denying women and shudras access to *Vedic* learning. As such large section of the population would not have been able to learn and chant mantras.

Kumkum Roy pointed that the historian uses the *Vedas* for some purpose. She says that *Vedas* contain rules. There are historian have used the *Vedas* to provide us with an account of the past.

We can have different types of histories:

- Histories of economic processes, such as the spread of pastoralism, agriculture, craft production and trade toralism, agriculture, craft production and trade

- Histories of social developments: we may want to know how the system of *Varna* emerged, or how gender relations were shaped
- Histories of daily life: we may be interested in what people ate, wore, their houses, and modes of transport
- Histories of religious and cultural ideas, beliefs and practices.

We analyse *Vedic* period on the basis of the histories of social developments. Hence our concerned area is mainly social developments and religious and cultural norms.

We are, by and large, familiar with the perception that women held a place of honour in *Vedic* society. This perception is supposedly based on the existence of women seers in the early *Vedic* tradition, and their participation in philosophical discussions in the later tradition. Hence, it is argued we can be certain that women had access to education. Other arguments advanced are that the age of marriage seems to have been relatively high and we do not have instance of *Sati*. There was some provision for widow remarriage. And finally, we are told that women had rights to perform rituals: in fact, no sacrifice was complete without the presence of the wife. However, the number of women seers recognised in the early *Vedic* tradition is abysmally low: around one per cent of the total number of compositions compiled in the *Rigveda* is attributed to women. The figure does not allow us to generalize about women's access to education in general, and the composition of the sacred tradition in particular.

If we examine the question of marriage, it is true that the analogies used in early *Vedic mantras* seem to indicate relatively flexible sexual relations. However, by the time we come to *Dharma* Sutras, norms are laid down for ideal marriages. These indicate that marriages were ideally to be arranged between men and women who belonged to the same *Varna*, and that the best form of marriage was that of *Kanyadan*, which involved the gifting of *kanya* (daughter). In this, 'ideal ' form of marriage, the woman was denied any say in the matter, and was treated as an object, although definitely a valuable one, to be given away and to be received in a transaction that was surrounded with and sanctified by rituals.

The question of women's participation in rituals is as problematic, as we have seen earlier, women probably did not have the right to chant mantras. In fact, women seers were the exception rather than the norms. Yet the wife of the sacrificer was regarded as a vital presence in the ritual. So the *Vedic* tradition does not necessarily indicate that women had a high status in terms of access to education, marriage, or rights to perform rituals.[5]

POST-VEDIC PERIOD

However, this was short-lived as the position of women declined steadily from the later *Vedic* period onwards. The injunctions of Manu merged the wife's individuality with that of her husband and recommended strict seclusions for women and rigorous discipline for widows. While glorifying motherhood and allowing women all freedom in the management of the household, he permitted child marriage and polygamy. In the *Dharma Shastras* women are unambiguously equated with the Shudras. Even the *Gita* places women, vaishyas and shudras in the same category.

SOCIETY AND LAW IN THE HINDU AND BUDDHIST TRADITIONS

The relationship between law and Hindu society involves both the actual and the ideal. To the extent that particular laws are related to a particular society, they can be regarded as a reflection of its value system. But law (both customary and codified) were also seen as a means of controlling society and, as such, an attempt has been made to perfect the legal framework, which then becomes a reflection of the aspirations of society in which these laws were evoked.

In the Hindu and Buddhist traditions this framework can be deduced from a number of texts and documents, most of which were composed in the period between 400 B.C. and A.D. 500. Much of the later literature is in the nature of commentaries on the earlier works, which reflect relevant changes in both society and its laws.

There are two approaches to an attempt at understanding humane in these traditions. First of all, the metaphysical aspect provides a framework of a rather generalized kind emanating from a small group of thinkers. Metaphysical thought certainly contributes to the ethos of a society, but this contribution becomes fairly diluted by the time it reaches the concrete reality of a legal code. The second and more significant aspect of the study is provided by the law books themselves, which draw a more distinct picture of the legal framework. However, reliance, even on such definite sources, is not without its dangers. The Law books are both a reflection of early Indian society as well as attempts at working out what was believed to be a perfect social system. Therefore, the aspirations of the lawmakers are also to be considered. Nevertheless, the danger can be mitigated somewhat by testing from historical sources the actual validity of the legal systems codified by lawgivers.

Hindu law was first formulated in a tribal society and it was based on customary practices and relationships. As is frequent in kin-societies, social control had the force of law. The central problem at this stage was to maintain peace between the tribes rather than to protect the rights of the individual. The acceptance of a monarchical system by these tribes introduced two new features. The political structure required by kingship encouraged an element of authoritarianism

ism amongst the lawmakers. The close association of kingship with divinity was projected into the realm of law and provided a supernatural sanction for it whenever necessary. The status of the individual in society came to be conditioned by these new factors.

THE BUDDHIST TRADITION

The Buddhist tradition originated at a time when tribal loyalty was changing into territorial loyalty and there was a sharper awareness of political organization. Buddhism began as one of a number of heterodox sects whose common feature was their breaking away from Brahmanical orthodoxy.

According to the Hindu tradition, men in a state of defencelessness and social disorder, appealed to the gods and the latter appointed a king in their own image, who would protect the people and maintain law and order and in return take a share of one-sixth of the produce. The social order of castes also emerged from a divine source.

The Buddhist theory relates to a different sequence of events. It postulates a golden age, which gradually decayed through the institution of private property and other social evils. Finally, the people gathered together and elected one from amongst them to rule over them and maintain an orderly society. He was given a sixth of the produce as wages. In the Buddhist theory the emphasis is on the quasi-contractual nature of the beginnings of government and on the sovereignty of the people. The latter idea remained central to Buddhist political thinking but it was never taken a step further and developed a theory of the rights of the people. There was no attempt to provide a divine origin for the evolution of the social structure in Buddhist thought. People tended to keep together in groups based on their crystallizations and these occupational groups gradually crystallized into castes.

DHARMA AND LAW

Dharma was essential because it promoted individual security and happiness as well as the stability of the social order. Each man's *dharma* had its own role in the larger and more complex network of the social structure. Therefore, by observing the rule of his own *dharma* a man was showing an awareness of others in society as well. If individual members of society tried to formulate their own rules of *dharma* the result would be a chaotic society. *Dharma* was the foundation of individual and collective security since a state of nature without law was equivalent to anarchy. The fear of anarchy led to the elevation of *dharma* to divine status and this in turn gave it even higher status than the king and the government. To further safeguard the position of *dharma* another concept was introduced that *dharma* is protected by danda (literally a rod or staff, signifying punishment).

The lawmakers who were by and large members of the Brahman caste and who naturally tried to maintain the superiority of their caste formulated the rules of the *dharma*. Inevitably since they were the ones who gave definition to *dharma*, the innate superiority of the Brahman was expounded. As a complement to this, it was necessary to formulate a system of social hierarchies. Social and often economic and legal privileges decrease with each descending step in the social hierarchy. Certain categories of Brahmans were immune from the more extracting labours of routine living such as paying taxes, and could on occasion be regarded as above the law. The concept of *dharma* rooted in caste was extended to every aspect of human activity. It was logical therefore that the equality of all before the law was not recognized. According to the law books judicial punishments were required to take into considerations the caste of the offender. Rights were extended primarily to the privileged upper castes. The lower orders had only obligations. The burden of society fell almost heavily on the shoulders of the shudras and the untouchables who could claim hardly any privilege of rights.

An important characteristic of caste is that an individual is born into a particular caste and cannot acquire the status of any other caste. This resulted in a check on individual social mobility. It also came to be associated with a basic religio-philosophical concept of Hinduism, that of *Karma* which maintains that one's deeds and activities in one's present incarnation determines ones status and happiness in the life to follow. Thus a man's caste status was entirely of his own making and he was in a position to improve it by conforming to *dharma* and being reborn at a higher status in his next incarnation. It also acted as a powerful check on nonconformity through the fear of worsening one's condition in future incarnations.

Among the various means of maintaining the purity of the caste two are specially stressed: the ban on commensality among members of various castes and the strict observance of rules of endogamy and exogamy as applied with reference to caste. The rules of marriage were rigidly enforced and marriage was primarily a social institution. The lower the status of women the stronger was the legal tie of marriage. The patriarchal system tended to keep the status of women at low-level, and the emergence of the joint family with special property rights for the male members reinforced male dominance. The family was recognized as a basic unit of society and enjoyed the right to protection by society and the state. This was accentuated in the case of families who owned land and worked on it. The concept of property in the Hindu tradition was usually associated with the ownership of land. The right to own property was granted to those who could afford it. The Law books maintain that property is founded on virtue and that the king has a right to confiscate the property of the wicked, of which, however, there is no record in historical record.

The Buddhist tradition was a striking contrast. The Buddhist monasteries were open to persons of any caste. The syllabuses had a wider range and included disciplines of more practical interest. The Buddhist tradition protested against the institution of caste. It recognized that in the routine working of society there was bound to be social distinctions, but maintained that these should not be exploited to the point of rejecting the concept that all human beings are equal. The Buddha was frequently asked about the relative purity of the· four castes and invariably replied that all castes were equally pure. An offender brought before justice must be judged and punished according to his offence and without any concession to immunities or privileges relating to his caste.

Arising out of its stern and unwavering ethical code, the Buddhist tradition supported the unqualified supremacy of moral law over politics. Law is for the welfare of all mankind. It saw in Brahmanical law the conditioning of society according to the requirements of a powerful elite. The same idea of the application of a moral law and the equality of human beings were extended to all living beings, and this resulted in the concept of ahimsa (non-violence). Everything that has life has a right to live; and to destroy life, no matter what its form, is a crime. It may be argued that the Buddhists (and more than the Buddhists, the Jainas) made a fetish of non-violence, yet the intellectual and moral assumptions of the concept arose from a healthy tradition.

Whereas Buddhism preached non-attachment to worldly possessions, and property was regarded as an evil (precipitating the decay of the world in the days of its pristine purity), in actual practice the acquisition of property was regarded as a normal activity. Entrepreneurial activities in particular were encouraged and were open to anyone with sufficient foresight and resourcefulness. In its attitude to women, the Buddhist tradition showed greater liberality than the Hindu tradition, as for instance in permitting women to become nuns.

That the imposition of the Brahmanical pattern in its totality was rarely a historical reality can be deducted from the fact that the heterodox tradition throughout the centuries was opposed to it in greater or lesser degree. The heterodox sects often drew their following from the lower castes that were numerically larger than the upper castes. The heterodox tradition emphasized the equality of human beings, the equality of all before the law, disapproved of slavery, encouraged the acceptance of a higher status for women and placed greater value on empirical thinking and education than on the formalism of the Brahmanical system.

In accordance with their own vision of society they enunciated laws on caste. These laws were by and large observed by the upper castes and were familiar in areas where orthodoxy played an authoritarian role. Elsewhere and amongst the lower castes, customs and usage made a substantial contribution to the formulation of laws. The fact that caste was never confronted with the shadow of its decline can be traced to the structure of the institution itself. Each caste or sub-caste formed its own independent social unit, with its own laws of survival based on the economic possibilities to which it could aspire. As long as the Brahmans could maintain their position as the pre-eminent unit—which they did by appropriating the administrative, educational and religious functions—their ascendancy was almost a foolproof concept of *dharma*. But the actual working of society was not strictly in accordance with this plan. Castes and sub-castes as social units did have some mobility and frequently sought to better their status, even if such improvement was denied to individual member. Economic necessities for instance could lead to a change on the status of a particular caste. Invading foreigners had also to be accommodated and their caste status defined. The objection of the heterodox groups was thus not to the system (which was a workable, socio-economic system) but to the Brahmanical interpretation of it.

The Buddhist tradition is not available in a single code of laws. Much of it consisted of regulations, which grew put of custom and usage, conditioned by the professions of those who supported Buddhism. The republican background nurtured an individualistic tradition in Buddhism with a strong support for the kind of social and moral attitudes implicit in human rights. Despite the tradition having to contend worth a caste society, the rights of the individual are given due stress.

The Hindu tradition is in comparison far more complicated and can be analysed from two perspectives. There is firstly the overall framework of Hindu society where the emphasis is on duties judging by the Law books, access to rights is limited to the privileged classes. The second perspective is that of the localized group or caste where the concept of rights did exist although to a limited extent. The functioning of each small unit was controlled by its own mechanism and within this unit the individual member could claim rights of equality and self-expression. The balance of rights and duties was fairly equal. Rights within such a group were not thought of in any total or irrevocable sense. The member of a sub-caste for instance could claim economic and social security from his sub-caste and the right to equality and to protection from violence, provided he observed the rules of that particular group. This is in a sense the key to the functioning of the Hindu tradition. Freedom lies in belonging to a group because the group can claim rights, as for example, the rights of the caste, the rights of the family, the rights of the guild, etc. The individual as an individual has no identity in a societal sense.

The Hindu pattern did not see man and society as antagonistic to each other. The two entities had mutual obligations and a commitment to these obligations would ensure

the welfare of all. The Hindu vision was that of an orderly society with each man attending to his appointed task, which
would infuse a people with a sense of community and which
with its intense loyalty to the social group, i.e. caste would
provide both economic and psychological security. The careful classifying of all degrees of social relationships into a well-
ordered system was partly to meet the requirements of this
vision and partly due to normal tendency of Hindu theorists
to classify everything to its minute detail. This carefully
worked out socio-legal framework reflected the Brahmanical
vision of the perfect society. Those who were opposed to such
a vision could take a nonconformist stand by opting out of
society perhaps by becoming ascetics or mendicants or by
joining a dissident group.

SOCIO-ECONOMIC STATUS IN BUDDHIST PERIOD

During the time of Buddha a major change took place in the
agrarian structure – it was the emergence of the large estates
owned by individual kshatriyas families. The criterion of
wealth came to be associated more with land and money and
less with cattle, which had been the measure of riches in earlier *Vedic* literature. The transfer of land took place largely
within the same social group that had earlier maintained joint
ownership. As an adjunct to this development of a landed
class, there is a noticeable increase in the categories of wage
labourer, hired labourer, and slave.

The rise of political authority as symbolized in systems
of government and the concept of the state were explained in
a variety of ways. *Vedic* literature had connected the emergence of kinship with the emergence of government and
stressed that the qualities of leadership in battle and elements
of divinity were essential to kingship. By the middle of the
first millennium, the tribal egalitarianism had surrendered to
the evolution of a system of government that, whether oligar-

chic or monarchical, was explained as concerning itself with the problems of social disharmony, the need for authority and the justification for revenue collection.

The complexity of the new society is clearly reflected in the need for codifying the laws of the various social groups, which is what is aimed at in Brahmanical *dharmasutras*. The purpose of the laws is to differentiate between the various social groups generally identified as those of *Jana, Jati, and Varna*. These, however, are made part of a cohesive view of society. There is an implicit belief that the demarcation of differences would lead to a resolution of tensions, an attitude that could only have been feasible in the absence of a situation of a conflict. Also implicit in the *dharmasutras* is the Brahmans claim to being the arbiters of the law. There was no overt challenge to this claim since the codification did not aim at uniformity of laws, but on the contrary, to the recognition of their diversity. [6]

BUDDHIST PERIOD

A dichotomy is evident throughout ancient history. The two major heterodox religions, Buddhism and Jainism supported greater freedom for women. In South India, women enjoyed a higher status because of the prevalence of the matriarchal system.

The social organisation rested on the family, which was of the patriarchal type. Polygamy was practiced, at least in the princely families. There was no polyandry, nor child marriage. The prohibitions on marriage in addition to the ban on incest alluded to in the *Yama-Yami* hymn were, in the Brahmanas, within the gotra and in the domestic sutras, within the agnates and cognates. It was not clear, whether remarriage of widows were allowed, except in the case of levirate. It is observed that marriage by purchase was then known though it is not certain whether it was the normal form and the price, shulka, paid to the father was usually a hundred cows and a carriage. The burning of widows was not prescribed in the liturgy, though it must have been known in *Vedic* times, and was not in the form of sacrifice in the direct sense.

POSITION OF WOMEN IN THE EPIC PERIOD

The dawn of puranas witnessed a significant change in the role of Hindu women which was limited and restrained to the basic ends of human existence. The men wanted their dominance making their women folks subservient to them. Neither they were left with freedom of choice nor they became only the means for Hindu men to attain their end. The women lost their past status and glory and subjugated to men's whims. The concept of dual existence and rhythm of cycle of birth and death and rebirth and theory of pinddan threw the Hindu women to a place of subservience. Whatever they received in the *Vedic* period, they began to lose in the Puranic period. They became dependent on men. The marriage lost its independent value. It failed to secure a firm grip in the changing events of Hindu life. Hindu women began to be confined to the kitchen and producing a son. The Daughters were unwelcomed. Freedom to Hindu women was not recognised. They were just physical machines of production of the Praja for the family. Where they failed their life became hell. Son became important to them because through son the Hindu began to find their salvation. The Hindu pantheon god became figurative than supernatural power in the mind of the Hindus and everything began to be understood in the light of attaining *Moksha* through son.

Marriage began to be treated as *Sanskar* and a religious act and obligatory to marry. The freedom to marry or not to marry was disallowed. The question of choice also lost its meaning because that period attached no significance to consent of the girl in a marriage. The martial life was tagged with religion and religion made her dependent. Marriage alone was her granted salvation. This virtually degraded the position of Hindu women in the Puranic era. Whatever independence she enjoyed in *Vedic* period she now began to lose. The concept of sonship was affiliated to the theory of pinddan and for offering the pind to the deceased the presence of the son was essential. Therefore, the women who could not beget a son for the husband suffered indignity and hollowness of her physical existence. One can then find a significant change in the attitude of the men towards women. The story of desertion, cruel treatment, hostile and callous attitude began to show the seeds on Hindu women.

The legal position of women according to Manu, the earliest exponent of law was definitely unfortunate. They were always dependent on somebody either the father, or the husband, or the son. A woman is not entitled to independence; her father protects her age in her maidenhood, her husband in her youth and her son in her old age. They were treated in law as chattels and a non-entity in the family. A wife, a son, and a slave these three even are ordained destitute of property whatever they acquire become his property whose they are.

RIGHTS OF WOMEN

The foremost rights of a wife and the corresponding obligation as a husband, is the provision for her support and maintenance. It has always been repugnant to Indian feeling that a husband should let himself be supported by his wife, as instanced by Sita's contemporary reference to actors living on the vice and earnings of their wives.

The *kanya-dhana* or bridal gifts offered by parents at their daughter's marriage became her *stridhana*. This property must have remained at the disposal of wife. Besides, kings occasionally transferred property and gifts on their wives who then acquired absolute rights over their use and disposal.

As far as conjugal right is concerned, it emphatically laid down that the husband, during the proper season must visit his wife and that it would be a sin for him not to fulfil her wishes then.

The association of wife in the coronation rituals further establishes the status of equality accorded to her on some of the most essential ceremonies. A widow took part in the funeral ceremony of her husband. The wives of Vali are described as joining his funeral procession along with men. Women often led the way on such occasions. They also participated in offering water libations to their deceased relatives.

Normally, husband and wife performed religious prayers and sacrifices jointly. If the husband's participation was not available for some reason or the other, his wife could perform the rites alone. In the absence of her husband she had the right of attending to the daily agnihotra. Worship of the gods and performance of Sandhya were not denied to women. Kaushaluya performed all alone the svasti-yoga ceremony to ensure felicity for her son evidently because Dashrath was engaged in assuaging Kaikayi. These instances show that a women's participation in sacrifices was real and that very often husbands used to leave the affair to the exclusive charge of their wives when busy otherwise.

GLORY OF MOTHERHOOD

Motherhood occupied a high pedestal of honour of love in the estimation of her sons. She was the centre of family life. The custom of sati, or self-immolation by the widow on the husband's pyre has little sanction in the Ramayana. The women were generally treated as a property, the owner having naturally the authority to do what he liked with her. Polygamy was almost the order of the day among kings and this was in its turn a frequent cause of family feuds, squabbles of jealousies, succession troubles, court intrigues and plots.[7]

DHARMASHASTRA PERIOD

Landownership: In the second half of the millennium B.C. the system of private landownership was further developed. The lands were divided into several categories—private, communal and royal. In the *Dharmashastra* period, property rights' were protected: illegal appropriation of the land belonging to somebody else was made subject to large fines and such violators would be publicly branded as thieves. Stratification based on property ownership was already firmly established; apart from the members of the village community who worked on their own plots there had evolved a village community elite who used slaves or hired labours to work their plots.

THE FAMILY AND FORMS OF MARRIAGE

In several regions apart from monogamous relationships, there were also more archaic forms of marriage to be found. The husband was the head of the family. Gradually certain changes came about in the position of women who eventually became fully dependent upon their sons and spouses. Marriage was turned into a sort of property deal. The man purchased his wife and she became his chattel. Source materials tell of wives being sold or lost in the course of gambling.

The women's position was extremely hard one. In childhood, she was expected to be completely in the power of her father, during her youth in that of her husband in the old age in the power of her sons. This is how women is placed in *Dharmashastra*. Wives have to be patient unto death and strictly observe their obligations. The *Dharmashastra* demanded of a wife to respect her husband as a god even if he possessed no virtues. Only husbands were able to divorce their spouses. A wife was unable to abandon her family. Even if her husband sold her or left her, she would still be regarded as his wife. An unfaithful wife would be subjected to most terrible punishments, including death. A man could have several wives and would not be considered sinful. A wife had to belong to the same *Varna* as her husband. Only in rare cases were women allowed to marry a man from the lower *Varna*. The most serious crime was held to be a marriage between a Shudra and a Brahman woman. A father's power over his children was decisive and final.

IMPORTANT SOURCES OF HINDU LAW

The term *Dharma* has been used in the sense of *Dharma* literature including the *Dharmashastras*, the *Srutis* having practically very little of secular or positive law. In ancient India, there was no arrangement for law reports and hence no decision could be preserved in the modern sense of the term; all the customs also are nowhere exhaustively enumerated in any literary form, though certain conditions were laid down for the recognition and operation of certain customs. Lastly the king's edicts also were more in the form of judicial decisions than in the form of legislative enactments, their fate being analogues to adjudications in general. Thus, the literary source alone occupied the most important position, so much so that in later literature, by sources of the Hindu law was meant the literary source. Hence, in enumerating the ancient sources of Hindu law, only the different kinds of literature were enumerated; in more recent times, of course, adjudication and legislative enactments also were referred to as important sources of Hindu law.

Thus, the expression literary source, as used in connection with the Hindu law, comprised the *Srutis*, the *Smritis* and the commentaries of which the first played a very insignificant part, as source of secular law or 'lawyer's law' and the last could not be foreseen by the authors of the *Smritis*, as they were produced much later. The positive law they were produced much later. The positive law that was to be found in the scriptural texts in general and the *Smriti* literature in particular was binding on the kings and the judges as well who were to decide cases abiding by their enjoinment, though, of course, the provisions of these so-called codes could be supplemented by the application of reason and the principles of justice, equity and good conscience. It has also been provided by the *Arthashastra* that in case of conflict between the *Dharma* and *Dharmanyana* (equity) the decision may rest with the latter, it being superior to the scholastic logic of the *Smritis*. This ruling of the Arthashastra is also admitted in the *Dharmashastras* themselves, the edicts of Asoka, the later digests, and commentaries and compendia of the Hindu law as well the writers of the extant treatises like the *Sukranitisara*.

VYAVAHAR

Vyavahar or adjudication must have been a very important source of ancient Hindu law. The different tribunals, including the king with original and appellate jurisdiction, used to decide disputes among the litigants. These decisions must have served the purpose of precedents and principles-however rudimentary for guiding the tribunals in any subsequent dispute or similar or analogous circumstances. An account of the constitution and function of the different judicial units in ancient India has been very lucidly given by Prof. B.K. Sarkar. It is out of this homogenous gathering of the primitive tribes with its all round function that judicial tribunals in Sakyan and post-Sakyan India must have been differentiated through ages of evolution in much the same manner as the modern courts of justice in West European countries and in America are historically speaking descended from the folkmoot described by Tacitus in his Germania.

CHARITRA OR CUSTOM

Due to different subjective and objective conditions, different rules of human conduct grow in different places among different kinds of people. Hence there is nothing curious, if in certain parts of the country, certain people observed some rules of conduct, which were different from those observed in other parts of the country.

MARRIAGE

Regarding the nature, form and history of the institution of marriage, the most competent observations have been made by Dr. N.C. Gupta. The forms of marriage are very largely dependent on environments and as these differ in different societies in their origin as well as their later development, the actual forms of marriage have varied greatly both in their origin and their later growth. It is therefore not possible to construct a single course of evolution, which will account for all the various forms of marriage. On the contrary, people in ancient India came to believe that daughters, given in marriage with adequate gifts, add to the religious merits of their fathers. In order to acquire this merit, Hindu fathers would become anxious to include bridegrooms for their daughters. In the *Rigveda* also it is found that the daughter of the son got rich presents from her father at the time of her marriage. The sages further support this when they are found to discourage any amount of consideration—however small it might be—to be accepted from the bridegroom. Manu also asserts with the same amount of emphasis that if out of greed, a father accepts anything in lieu of giving his daughter in marriage, he commits the sin of killing a cow. The elaborate treatment of *Stridhana* indicates the well-established practice of giving presents to the girls at the time of their marriage.

The Raksasa and the *Paisacha* forms of marriage could not be sanctioned or encouraged by the regular laws of any civilized society of any time. There might be stray cases where girls were captured either in battle or in lesser disputes and taken as wives. But the Raksasa form of marriage could not be conceived unless absolute lawless-ness prevailed in the society. Similarly, regarding the *Paisacha* form of marriage also, it could not be conceived to be a general rule of the society for it only related to some girls ravished while asleep or intoxicated. These two forms were, however, not as prominent as the remaining forms of marriage. All the approved forms of marriage are but the variants of the Brahma form with slight variations. The *Asura* form of marriage existed in early times and it exists even today. The ancient sages depreciated the *Asura* form of marriage but now even the Brahmins are found to celebrate marriage in this form.

HINDU LAWS UNDER MUSLIM PERIOD

There were two parallel systems of personal law in India during the Muslim period. But minimum influence was exerted by one upon the other. A closer look at things would show, however, that the two personal systems of law though widely different, they were, on doctrinal basis, essentially identical. Both systems had a religious conception of law in the sense that they were ultimately supposed to have been based on divine revelation and that the law bound the kings, the judges, and the subjects alike to carry them out. Both in the Hindu law and the Muslim law the rulers themselves administered justice as far as possible and the exceptionally honest and learned judges appointed by them after serious deliberations and mature considerations did the rest. The adjudication by the rulers was often sought by the people for their quick and impartial decisions. Clearly, both the systems of Hindu and Muslim laws were largely governed by the law. Thus the doctrinal similarities between the two systems played a very important part in avoiding major conflicts and frequent clashes in administration of the law in the country as a whole. The analogy between the Hindu law and Muslim law does not end with the points of similarity regarding the fundamental doctrines. In the developments of these two systems of law as well as in the consideration of the different sources to which they owe their existence also there were essential points of resemblance.

The important sources of Hindu law are the *Vedas*, the *Smritis*, the *Nibandhas* and the commentaries and customs and equity. The Muslim rulers did not interfere with the personal laws of the Hindus. On the contrary they adopted many time-honoured principles and institutions of the Hindus.

BRITISH RULE

The powers in the courts of British India to apply the personal laws of the Hindus and the Muslims were derived from and regulated by the statutes of the British Parliament and the central and provincial legislatures of India. The personal laws of the Hindus and Muslims were applied only in some and not all matters. The questions regarding succession, inheritance, marriage and religious usages were decided according to the personal laws of the Hindus and the Muslims, except in so far as some laws were amended by legislative enactments. There were certain other matters in which the personal laws of the Hindus and the Muslims were applied sometimes by the application of the principle of soft justice, equity and good conscience.

In civil disputes between two persons of the same religion, their personal law was recognized, but the disputes were usually referred to their *Pandits* or (Panchayats) or jurors as was the procedure adopted by the *Abbaside* Caliphs of Baghdad. The purely Islamic code of governing the laws of inheritance, marriage and other analogous matters of the Muslims did not apply to the Hindus. The Hindus were allowed to be governed by their own laws on these topics of civil law. But criminal law was applied more or less equally to both the Hindus and the Muslims alike for guaranteeing security of life and property. The Hindus in a sense generally enjoyed self-government and the rulers did not interfere with their personal laws and local affairs.[8]

DIVERSITIES IN HINDU LAW DURING *DHARMASHASTRA* PERIOD

Every member of the coparcenary has a right by birth in the property of the coparcenary. This right is not determined until partition is made; it is liable to fluctuations; it increases with every death in the family and decreases with every birth. The persons constituting the coparcenary own the property of the family as a joint tenant with the right of survivorship and they leave the management of the family and its properties in the hands of the manager, who is clothed with some special powers. But even these special powers do not justify the alienation by the manager of the property of the family unless the transaction is supported by legal necessity. On the other hand, under the *Dayabhaga* system of Hindu law coparcenary is unknown. The father is the absolute owner of the property so long as he is alive; his sons can claim no share in this property by their birth and on his death his property devolves by succession amongst his heirs, each one of whom takes his share as his separate and absolute property and all of whom together own the property not as joint tenants, but as tenants in common.

Yagnavalkya states that the father is master of the gems, pearls and corals and of all other movable property; but neither the father nor the grandfather is so of the whole immovable property. Then he refers to the Manu's texts in which Manu says, "the support of persons who should be maintained is the approved means of attaining heaven; but hell is the man's portion if they suffer. Therefore (let a master of a family) carefully maintain them."[9]

Jimutvahana states that in Bengal it was quite common for the father to sell ancestral immovable property without any objection, and he naturally wanted to bring that practice within the framework of Hindu law. In fact, this part of Jimutvahana's reasoning shows that he was attempting to adapt and adjust the principles of Hindu law to the changed and altered practices that had become popular in Bengal.

At a time when and in the territory where Vijaneshwara lived the popular usage and custom had clothed the sons with the right in the ancestral property by reason of their birth. There are texts, which support both the views of both *Mitakshara* and Jimutvahana. The text of Devala unequivocally supports Jimutvahana because Devala says, "the father being dead, the sons should divide the father's wealth—since there cannot be ownership in them, while the father is living-- being faultless. The text of Gautama says: "From the very moment of birth, one obtains the ownership of wealth—thus say the authorities". "The material text of Manu reads thus": After the father and the mother, the brothers having assembled together, should divide the paternal inheritance. Of the immovable property, and the slaves, although acquired by one's own self, there is neither a gift, nor a sale, without assembling of all the sons. Those who are born, those who are unborn, and those who are laying the womb, they wish for sustenance. There is neither a gift, nor a sale". He says the land apportioned by the grandfather, or corrody, or property, therein the ownership of both the father and the son, should be alike. Jimutvahana wanted to confine the absolute and unrestricted power of alienation of the father to his self-acquired property.

According to the authors, *Dayabhaga* and *Mitakshara* differ radically in their treatment of joint family property, each one of them propounds the thesis that his view is based upon ancient Hindu texts.

DAUGHTER'S PROPERTY RIGHTS

Two distinct tendencies are clearly discernible in the ancient Sanskrit literature dealing with this question. The protagonists of the view that the daughter must be excluded can take comfort from the thought that their view receives the support of a passage from the *Rigveda* itself. The famous 31st hymn in the third Mandala of the *Rigveda* as explained by the Sayana provides: "the son does not vacate the inherited wealth for his sister, he makes her the repository of the issue of him who takes her; although the parents procreate both the males and the females, the one is a worker of good deeds, the other is graceful. In ancient *Vedic* times where the strife and struggle were the order of the day, it is not surprising that the warrior should have monopolized succession to the estate and the female should have been treated as merely the repository of the issue of him who takes her.

Both Manu and Yajnavalkya do not seem to subscribe to this unqualified and absolute prohibition against the daughter's claims to succeed to a part of their father's estate. Manu in chapter IX, verse 130, says: Just as a person is born through his son, so is he through his daughter: the daughter and the son are equal. If the daughter is alive, how can anyone else take away the estate of the father? Verse 118 in the same chapter says: "To the maiden sisters let their brothers give portions out of their allotments respectively: to each one-fourth part of his appropriate share. Those who refuse to give shall be degraded." Yajnavalkya in chapter II, verse 127, says, "And sisters should be initiated into marriage giving them the fourth part of ones own share. It is somewhat surprising that though the *Dayabhaga* school is of later growth than the Mitakshara, the views of *Dayabhaga* on this question are more retrograde than those of Mitakshara. In commenting on verse 127 of Yajnavalkya Vijnaneswara noticed a contrary view and severely criticized it. "If it is said that here also, the speaking of the

fourth share is not intentional, that the real intention is to declare the payment of only as much wealth as is required for
the sacrament of marriage, this is not so. Because there is no
authority for saying that both the *Smritis* (Manu and Yajnavalkya) have spoken of the fourth share to be given, without
really meaning the same; and because we hear also of there
being a sin in case of non-payment."

Therefore, after the death of the father, the unmarried
daughter is entitled to get a share; before, however (i.e. before
the father's death), whatsoever the father gives, she gets. Thus
it becomes unobjectionable. Says Yajnavalkya, "Those not religiously initiated should be initiated by brothers previously
initiated—and sisters also—giving however, one-fourth share
from the self-appropriated share". He is speaking of the in-
dispensableness of initiating the unmarried daughters;
(which means marrying); not of their right. And when there is
much wealth, wealth requisite for the marriage should be
given; there is no invariable rule for one-fourth share. This is
the conclusion.

As to the nature and extent of the rights of women over
property obtained by them, the texts of Yajnavalkya and
Vishnu, which recognize the rights of the widow, the daughter, the mother, and other females as heirs, do not make any
distinction between the character of the estate taken by them
and that of the estate taken by the male heirs. The words used
in reference to both the estates are the same, and reasonably
construed they do not justify the distinction made by judicial
decisions between the two estates. The same is the position
with regard to the text of Manu, which says that the widow of
childless man, keeping unsullied her husband's bed and preserving in religious observances shall present his funeral ob-
lation and obtain his entire share. On the other hand both Ka-
takana and Narada seems to negative the absolute estate of
women. Katyayana says: "The childless widow preserving

unsullied the bed of her lord, and abiding with her venerable protector, should enjoy with moderation the property until her death. After her the heirs should take it."

According to *Mitakshara* all kinds of property in the hands of a female, howsoever it might have been obtained by her, is her absolute property. The text of Yajnavalkya, on which Vijnanaeswara has built his theory, speaks in these terms: "Whatever is given by the father, the mother, the husband and the brother and whatever is obtained near the nuptial fire and at the marital procession and the rest is known as *Stridhana*." Vijnaneswara has interpreted the word '*adyam*' as including all other kinds of property, which a woman may obtain. Vijnaneswara puts his thesis succinctly by emphasizing that the word *stridhana* is used in its literal sense and not in its technical sense. This interpretation of Vijnaneswara is consistent with his view that women are entitled to inherit. According to *Dayabhaga* the property inherited by a widow from her husband is not her absolute estate, and it must be conceded that the courts in India have in effect imposed the *Dayabhaga* view on the followers of *Mitakshara* school. Even so, it is perfectly legitimate if the Hindu Code seeks to make women's property absolute, as Vijnaneswara did in his Mitakshara.

Regarding the daughter's property rights under the schools of Hindu law, which do not admit a daughter to share in the property of her father, it is well recognized that at a partition between the members of the joint family, provision has to be made for the maintenance and marriage expenses of the daughter.

Scholars are divided to the genesis of this right. One view is that the provisions for the maintenance and marriage expenses of the daughter have to be made because the father is liable to maintain all his children and he is bound to get his daughter married before she reaches the puberty. On the other hand, this view is not accepted by a large number of scholars of Hindu law who think that the better reason for this rule is really the historical remnant of her larger right.

According to Justice Ramesam, under the early Hindu law the rights of both the sons and daughters were imperfect rights in the property, which could not be materialized by compelling partition against the wishes of the father. Gradually however the son's rights developed into a right to compel partition, whereas the daughter's right first became a right to compel partition against the brothers only and not against the father and later on degenerated into merely a right to maintenance and marriage expenses. In other words, a study of the historical development of this branch of the Hindu law shows that it is wholly inaccurate to say that the daughters were always treated as being inferior to the sons in the Hindu law. It may be that for some centuries past their rights had gradually decreased and now have crystallized into a claim merely for the maintenance and for marriage expenses. If the Hindu Code seeks to confer upon the daughter somewhat larger rights than she enjoys today, it can well be claimed that the Hindu code has in that behalf the authority of ancient Hindu texts. If out of two undivided brothers one dies leaving behind him his daughter, she would get no share under the orthodox view of Hindu law but the daughter of the survivor would get the estate solely because her father was the last to die.[10]

WOMEN'S RIGHTS AND CUSTOMARY LAW

Custom was an important source of law. Its validity under *Smriti* law and its relevancy to castes and tribes, who were not governed by the *Smriti* law, is there.

Local customs were held in high esteem and were acknowledged as an important source of law under the *Smritis*. Gautama, Manu and Brihaspati granted special recognition to custom. The local customs varied from region to region. The Southern states granted women greater rights. Both Yajnavalkya, and Vijnaneshwar who had expanded the kya, and Vijnaneshwar who had expanded the parameters of women's right to property, hail from the Southern (Dakshina) region.[11] The Southern, and predominantly Dravidian regions, followed various pro-women practices of property inheritance even under *Smriti* law. The liberal construction of *Stridhana* under the Bombay and Madras schools is an indication of this. A custom of handing over a piece of land to the daughter at the time of her marriage prevailed within the Madras presidency.

A woman's right to one-third of the property upon her husband's remarriage was also recognized within certain lower castes of Madras Presidency and was termed as Patnibhagam. In Andhra Pradesh there was a practice of giving land to the daughter at the time of her marriage, which is known as Katnam. In the Karnataka region Virasaiva women inherited twelve per cent property in the form of land from their mother and this property customarily passed on only to daughters, even when boys did not inherit from their fathers. The Buddhist literature also indicates that women could own property and gift property in their own right.

The Brahmanical–Aryan customs followed by the upper castes of North India exercised a strict control over women and their sexuality and the status of women among them was low as compared to women from the lower castes and the Dravidian regions. The Shudras, considered to be out of the caste system, were not governed by the code of *Smritis*, applicable only to '*dwijas*' or the twice-born that had the sanction of the sacred texts.

Shudra women worked and contributed to the household and hence were not totally dependent upon their men. Most of the lower castes practiced the custom of bride price, where the father of the girl had to be compensated for the loss he suffered by the marriage of his daughter. Although the *Smritis* shunned this practice, as it amounted to sale of a daughter, the fact that it is mentioned in most *Smritis* and commentaries indicates its wide acceptance by the various castes including the Brahmans. It continued to be followed by several castes in the southern region, northern Himalayan region, and various tribes right up to the pre-independent India.

Marriages among the various lower castes were less sacramental and more contractual. In the Deccan region remarriages of women whose husbands had been absent for a long time was permitted. If the first husband eventually returned, the woman had a choice to live with either the first husband or the second husband but who was deserted had to be reimbursed his marriage expenses.

The custom of divorce and remarriage was also prevalent among Lingayats of Karnataka, Kapus of Telangana, Jats of Punjab and Haryana, certain castes among the Maravars, Namoshudras of Bengal and the Banias of Bihar. In the northern parts of Bihar, Orissa, Chhota Nagpur and Assam all castes and tribes permitted remarriage. It was also accepted as a universal custom in the Darjeeling and Manipur regions. As a community progressed economically, it took upon Brahmanical practices and exercised a stricter sexual control upon its women.

A casual glance at the customs of the lower castes is sufficient to indicate an absence of a strict sexual code and correspondingly wider scope for negotiating women's rights of divorce, remarriage, property ownership, etc. among them.[12]

CULTURAL AND CASTE DIVERSITIES AMONG HINDU LAW

Even in the *Srautasutras* a kind of Ksetraja—the *dvyamusyayana* or *dvipitr*—is often mentioned; he is regarded as the son also of his natural father and the *Dvyamusayana* is mentioned also in the Srutis. Now, if not Niyoga, at least marriage with the widow of a deceased brother is of common occurrence. Probably it is most popular in the Punjab where so much of what is ancient has been preserved: there it is called *Karewa* and very often causes a man to have two wives at the same time.

Sonship and adoption: The twelve kinds of sonship which to some extent are based on the illicit connections of the mother and for the greater part have nothing to do with the blood-relationship of the son with the father, are probably the most striking feature of Indian family-law. The cause of this abnormal importance being attached to male issue is to be sought, according to the *Smritis* in the offering of sacrifices to the manes which depends upon the male issue: yet, however, originally an economic motive, that is to get for family as many powerful workers as possible, was perhaps a more important factor in it. The children belong to the husband, the owner of the wife, even though he is not their father. Also, through adoption he could take into his patria poteestas other children out of that of another person.

The *datio in adoptionem* (giving away in adoption) of a *Dattaka* is a ceremony in which the parents or father alone or the mother with the permission of the father gave away their son before witnesses to the adoptive parents so that he leaves his own family forever to enter the family of his adoptive parents. The giving away of the son by his own parents is based on their right of disposition over the son by force of which they can give him away, and sell him or turn him out of the house; in this connection the *Smritis* refer to the well known legend of Sunahaepa in the Aitriya Brahman.

The rule that the adoption must take place in early childhood before the sacred ceremonies, viz., shearing of hair of the child and his initiation (upnayanana), or when he is not more than five years of age, is based in fact only on a text of the Kalikapurana, the authenticity of which has been questioned by various commentators. The son to be adopted was required to be of the same status and caste as those of the adoptive father; the nearest blood relations would in particular be chosen for this purpose. According to the commentaries first of all the brother's son and eventually a distant agnate relative was to be selected, but never the son of the daughter or of the sister. Of the adoptive parents the mother alone had the right of adoption only if the father gave permission and that no son of theirs was living at the time of adoption.

THE SYSTEM OF HEIRS IN THE PUNJAB CUSTOMARY LAW

The customary law of the Punjab has various points of agreement with the *Smritis* although it recognizes no connection between the law of inheritance and the funeral sacrifice. The succession of heirs is arranged strictly agnatically according to generations and with unrestricted right of representation. The family never goes out of the *got.* If there is no male issue then the widow inherits the property, but she cannot sell the family-property because after her death it reverts to the *agnates* of her husband and she is on the whole more or less controlled by them in her dispositions of the property. The daughter may claim only maintenance until her marriage though a tendency to allow a share of the inheritance to the daughter is quite perceptible, but elsewhere, on the contrary, even the widow is given only sustenance.

In the *Smritis* the remarriage of widows has been considered only in connection with the five cases of necessity (apad) in any one of which a woman may marry another man, namely, if her husband has disappeared or is dead, if he has joined an order of monks or is impotent or is excommunicated out of his caste. (Nar, 12, 97; Par. 4, 28). This passage is often turned to account by modern defenders of widow marriage in Indian and which is used even in a Jaina work of 1014 A.D. (Bhandarkar Report, 1884-87 (Bombay 1894) 15).

Thus in the law of debt too we find that a wife or a widow who has lived with another man binds him under certain circumstances to pay the debts of her former husband but nothing has been said about their relation being legalized by a fresh marriage. Therefore statements like these hardly affect the general validity of the principle that the *Mantras* of the marriage are for virgins alone. It is normally the case that the daughter is given away in marriage only once.

CULTURAL- REGIONAL DIVERSITIES IN HINDU LAW

The widow marriage—the widow proper or the bride whose husband died at the very beginning of the conjugal life—is indeed allowed by the old law of 1856, but there is a lot of cultural diversity. Take, for example, among the *Lohars* and *Sainis* a bachelor is allowed to marry a 'widow' after his symbolic marriage with a *Sami* tree or a cotton puppet so that he too may thereby be stamped as a widower. Among the *Jats* of Ajmer he who marries a widow must make good to the family of the deceased husband the cost of his marriage. Among many castes in Mumbai, the widow may marry only at night or has to come out of her parent's house by the back door, etc. There are evidences in the Bombay Gazetteer that among the Brahmans and in almost all the higher castes the widow marriage is forbidden. It takes place only among the lower castes.

Marriages between men of lower castes and women of higher castes are universally disapproved and the sons born of those unions are held in very low esteem contrary to the natural order (*pratiloma*). Only the wife of equal position is regarded as the dharmapatni and the mixing of *varnas* is generally a grave sin which the king must prevent. In later texts the marriage of Aryans (*dvija*) the women of unequal position is mentioned among the usages no longer permissible in this age of sins (*kalivarjya*).

The local usages too are to be taken into consideration in this connection: thus Bauddh 1, 2, 3 and Brh 27, 19 declare that marriage between cousins is prevalent in the South—

such marriages still take place in the Deccan among various Brahmanical sects and some other castes.

The prohibition of marriage within forbidden degrees of propinquity, particularly inside a gotra, is mentioned even by Alberuni 2, 155 and is now universally observed at least among the Brahmans, Rajputs and the other higher castes. Among the various Brahman sects of Tamil Nadu marriage between persons of the same gotra is never allowed. Among the Brahmaksatris of Poone marriage cannot take place if the gotras are the same but if the surnames are same it is no hindrance to marriage. In some places in Maharashtra where the similarity of the surname or devak, i.e. the insignia or fetich, is regarded as a hindrance to marriage, it is to be traced back to the same principle, for many gotras are denoted by the same surname or the same insignia. In Uttar Pradesh marriages within the gotra are universally forbidden. It is a universal rule in Punjab that no man can marry a woman of his gotra. Among the Rajputs of Gurgaon in the Haryana, marriage with the relations of the mother or the grandmother of the paternal side as well as with any such person who may be proved to be a relation of the paternal side is forbidden. The exogamy perhaps first came into fashion among the Rajputs (Ksatriyas) in Rajasthan. The practice reflects primitive character, that is, carrying away the women by force.

THE POLYGAMY, CONCUBINAGE AND DIVORCE

Although a second husband for the wife 'is nowhere prescribed', not even after the death of the first, the husband may marry anew after the death of his wife without any delay. But even in the lifetime of his wife it is not forbidden for him to get, besides her, any number of married wives or concubines that he may wish for. Polygamy is in evidence in the *Vedas*: e.g. in MS 1, 5, 8 the ten wives (*jaya*) of Manu are mentioned. Yet in such passages of the *Vedas* and the Srautasutras chiefly the princely or noble families alone seem to be referred to. But the dual dampatisamanasa 'a harmonies couple' and the presence of one wife (*patni*) at the sacrifice prove that monogamy was regarded as the usual and natural state of things. The heroes of Mahabharata had many wives, but there is also a real or chief wife, the Mahisi, mentioned in the *Vedas*. One single wife is ascribed to the princes in several later inscriptions. Even among the Brahmans of the Mahabharata, although they have several wives, the Brahmani appears to be proper and the legitimate wife, the dharampatni.

Generally, a man was required to marry at first a woman of his own *Varna* and only afterwards he could proceed to take wives from the lower classes in the order of the *Varnas*. Only a Shudra is restricted to a single wife of his own caste. The Mahabharata endorses the view that the Shudra woman can never be taken as wife by the higher classes. The analogues teachings of the *Smritis* on this point have already been discussed above. Though four, three and two wives are allowed to Brahmans, Ksatriyas and Vaisyas respectively, only the wife of one's own *Varna* was the dharampatni and the others were regarded as wives of lower grade or concubines and for this reason their children too were at a disadvantage in the law of inheritance.

Even in modern times polygamy is as common as is permissible and separation, at least among the higher castes, is rare. The number of castes in Maharashtra among which, according to the data in BG, "polygamy is permitted and practiced" is very large. They include many Brahmanical and aristocratic communities. There are similar data about other states too. Nevertheless, the percentage of people actually practicing polygamy is nowhere high. Thus in Tami Nadu, where polygamy is most popular only 4 per cent of the men had two wives in 1890s. (*Madras Census Report,* 1891, 138). In Punjab the number of men wedded to more than one wife

did not go above 1 per cent. (*Census of India,* 1891, 19, 223).
Sterility of the first wife is usually said to be the cause of polygamy in the census. The practice is in conformity with the
principles of the *Smritis.* According to the Census report for
Tamil Nadu, separation was allowed by Brahmanical law of
marriage only on account of the adultery of the wife. In Punjab all the Hindu sects answered on the negative when the
question was put before them whether divorce was customary among them; yet sometimes the *tyag* (*tyaga* of the *Smritis*)
took place among them, i.e. the husband turns out the wife on
account of adultery. But a marriage once consummated was
never dissolved even on account of impotence or any other
physical defect. Separation was very common among all the
Dravidian tribes as the Census report for Tamil Nadu shows.
In Maharashtra too, among the lower castes separation from
the wife frequently took place, not only because of adultery—
in which case she was treated as a slave, though she still remained in the house of her husband as laid down in the *Smritis* referred to above—but also on account of impotence,
twelve years absence, disappearance or excommunication of
the husband. In these latter cases the wife could also marry
afresh. Perhaps even in ancient times there were several tribes
who cherished such principles.

WIDOWHOOD

The practice of widow-burning, Sati, which went with the
Brahmanical law of marriage was a sharpened form of the severe demands made by the Brahmanical lawgivers on the
matrimonial fidelity of the widow. Nevertheless, this custom
was hardly ever mentioned in the whole range of the *Vedic*
literature and the *Sutra* works, although the elaborate descriptions of the funeral ceremonies in the *Srauta* and *Grhya
Sutras* offer excellent opportunities for their treatment. Only
the late *Vai-Gr.* refers to the *Sahamarana* in which the hus-

band and the wife are burnt on the same pyre (3). According to the commentators at least the word *Sahamarana* is a usual designation for widow-burning. Even the widows of a king, are said to be maintained by his successor according to the *Vas* 19, 33, although from other sources it is known that the widow-burning often took place in royal families.*M, Y, Nar* too are reticent about the Sati in their metrical *Smritis* (discuss the other duties of the widow. Only later authors such as *Daksha*, 4, 18, Par.4, 30 f., *Vyasa* 2, 53, the *Puranas* and their fragments of *Brh.* (25, 8, 11) *Angiras, Usaanas, Ap.*, etc give us more or less particular references and descriptions of the Sati. Various commentaries and digests of law from *Mit.* (on *Y.1*, 86) up to Jagananatha's *Vivadabhangaranya* (1, 917 ff. of my Ms. = *Colebrooks Dig. 42*), contain collections of these passages and on this material. Colebrook's well-known essay 'on the duties of a faithful Hindu widow' is based. Sati is a rare occurrence in view of the enormous bulk of the *Mah.*

A great contrast of this is the reference to Satis in historical works and fictions. Thus in the *Rajistar* it appears that at the death of a king one or several widows of the same should burn themselves with him. After the death of king Samkaravarman his chief queen and two other widows as well as four faithful servants of the king mounted his funeral pyre. The Ucchvasa of the Harascarita describes in details how even before the death of the king Prabhakavardhana his consort Yasomati, along with other queens, prepares to follow him in death as Sati. She could not be swayed from her determination even by the persuasions of son Harsha. Widow-burning was originally practiced only by the royal families and was spread only gradually among the mass and at last received into the official law of Brahmans.

The widow has to live in a very bad condition. She should live under the protection of her son and the relatives who have absolute authority over her. Even to this day the widow calls for the sympathy.[13]

LAW REFORMS IN COLONIAL PERIOD

The rights of most Hindu women were governed by the *Mitakshara* and *Dayabhaga* systems of law. The *Mitakshara* system made the distinction between the two kinds of property, joint family property and separate property. The first included ancestral property (namely property inherited from upto three generations in the paternal line) as well as any property that had become part of the joint property. Only male members of the family, upto four generations, were coparceners of this property, a right to which they were entitled from birth. Despite strict observations on its alienation, especially when it was immovable property such as land, every coparcener had the right to demand partition, without affecting the right of the others to stay undivided. On the other hand, under *Mitakshara* law, a man had absolute right to sell his self-acquired property, and if he had no male heirs up to the fourth generation, he could treat his share of ancestral property.

In the case of Dayabhaga, man enjoyed absolute right over all property, whether ancestral or self-acquired, including the right to gift, sell or mortgage it. Unlike the *Mitakshara* system, which conferred coparcenary right at birth on sons, and where the interest in the property varied according to the number of survivors, the *Dayabhaga* system ensured no birthright, and defined a fixed and non-fluctuating share for each heir.

Women's rights were extremely restricted under both systems. While systems recognised the absolute control of a woman over her *Stridhana*, this recognition was more or less confined to movables, and there was considerable confusion, of a textual or a practical kind, about whether it could include immovable properties such as land. Under *Mitakshara* law, women only had a right to maintenance as wives, widows, or unmarried daughters, while the expenses of a daughter's marriage also devolved upon the family. On the condition that she remained chaste, a widow could enjoy a limited (lifetime) interest in her husband's property but only in the absence of male heirs upto the fourth generation. This meant that the widow could not alienate the property except in dire times of necessity. The daughter figured as an heir only after the widowed mother was dead but she too enjoyed only a limited estate. The chances of a woman inheriting property under *Dayabhaga* were slightly better, since women inherited both ancestral and self-earned property, although here, too, widows and daughters followed male heirs upto the fourth generation.

The earliest effort to effect changes in the Hindu Miatka-shara law was made through the Hindu law of Inheritance (Removal of Disabilities) Act of 1928 and the Hindu law of Inheritance (Amendment) Act, which further extended the Act of 1850 and put women in the line of succession. Further advancing the claim of women to property was the Hindu Women's right to Property Act of 1937. This was by far the most important single piece of legislation, and was well known as the Deshmukh Act. The Deshmukh bill, introduced shortly after Sharda's bill to grant Hindu widows a share in their husband's property had suffered a resounding defeat in 1932. In order to enhance its chances of being passed, it confined itself only to the Hindu widow's inheritance rights. The Bill, passed in 1937, did substantially improve the inheritance rights of Hindu widows and introduced as heirs a man's widowed daughter-in-law and widowed grand-daughter-in-law. Even so the more radical aspects of the Deshmukh Bill were not included, and daughters were completely excluded from its purview.

The advocates could not successfully speak for Hindu

women with much confidence and ease in the 19th century when women had little access to the public political space. A discourse of women's rights as opposed to a discourse of women's duties to home and nation was slowly, if hesitantly, being articulated. If the discourse on women's duties to the home and nation had provided the only acceptable, indeed legitimate, basis on which to demand reform, the ideology of equal rights was gaining ground.

The piecemeal nature of the proposed legislation greatly disappointed members of the All India Women's Conference, who clearly recognised that the overwhelmingly male legislative assembly was unlikely to initiate the changes that would undermine their existing privileges and powers. Lakshmi Menon declared at the 1933 conference of the AIWC: "If we are to seek divorce in court, we are to state that we are not Hindus, and are not guided by Hindu law. The members in the Legislative assembly who are men will not help us in bringing any drastic changes which will be of benefit to us".

The call for comprehensive reforms was premised on recognition of the entrenched and formidable power of Indian patriarchy; only comprehensive legislation could tackle the tightly interlocking questions of monogamous marriage, divorce and inheritance. In late 1920's and 1930's the nationalist women's organisations failed to sustain pressure for changes, which would most certainly have divided the nationalist women's movement.

Basing themselves on the Karachi Congress resolution, which guaranteed sex-equality, the women's sub-committee called for a uniform civil code to replace the separate personal laws. The Deshmukh Bill put some pressure on the government and it appointed (1941) the B.N. Rau committee to enquire into the need for a Hindu civil code.

The B.N. Rau committee, which had no woman member, affirmed that the time had arrived for a uniform civil code, which guaranteed more equal rights to women in keeping with the modernising trends in Indian society but "the main emphasis of the first HLA (Hindu Law Committee) report was to legitimise the project of reform by reference to ancient Hindu traditions". There was neither an attempt to rigorously read and cite the *Smritis* nor to revamp the traditional legalities to make them consonant with modern judicial systems. The opponents and supporters of the codification bills framed their arguments in terms of scriptural validity. The debate of the pre-independence years continued the practice of scriptural referencing. At the same time, at no point did women themselves make similar use of the scriptures in their favour.

In the past, religio-reform movements like Buddhism tried even partially to elevate the status of the Indian women but it was only during the British period that big movements were organized to destroy the social and legal injustices from which they suffered for centuries. The social reform movements, which arose out of the new conditions of social existence, set itself the task of removing the social and legal injustices and inequalities from which the Indian women suffered.

The subjection of the Indian women in the pre-British period was rooted in the social and economic structure of the society of the period. Birth determined the status of an individual in that society. The disabilities of a woman arose from the fact that she was born a woman. This inferior status of woman in society was made sacrosanct by religious ordinances.

Women had to strive hard for their rights in different spheres of life. The hesitation of the British government and the reactionary resistance of the orthodox sections of the society had to be combated before legislation was enacted such as would increasingly make woman man's equal in matters of civic rights. Among the organizations, which worked for the social, political and educational advance of .the Indian

women, the All India Women's Conference stood in the forefront. Orthodox India and old social and psychological habits
were arrayed against it. However, the movement scored important success, though slowly.

There were barbarous customs in the past as Sati and infanticide from which the Indian women suffered. The widow
had to throw her living body on the pyre with the corpse of
her husband when he died. Parents killed girl babies for the
marriage of a girl was too expensive for poor parents. Even
when the custom of Sati was abolished, widows were prohibited from remarrying. Infanticide was also subsequently declared a crime. Yet it continued at many places. Child marriage had been one of the principal evils from which the Indian women, more than even men, suffered. Owing to the efforts of Ishwar Chandra Vidyasagar, the Act of 1860 was
passed raising the age of consent for married and unmarried
girls to ten. It was also due to the efforts of the same social re-
former that, in 1856, the remarriage of widows was legally
permitted. However, it was only in 1929 that a decisively legal
step was taken to strike a blow at the harmful custom of child
marriage. The Child Marriage Restraint Act passed in that
year raised the age of marriage age for girls to fourteen and
for boys to eighteen.[15]

CONCERNED GOVERNMENT REFORMS

The Hindu Law Committee, set up in 1941 to look into the
anomalies of the 1937 Act, recommended a comprehensive
code of marriage and succession, which led to the setting up
of the Second Hindu Law Committee in 1944. After soliciting
opinions of jurists and the public, the Committee submitted
its report to the Parliament in April 1947. The recommendations were debated there between 1948 and 1951 and again
from 1951 to 1954. Finally, a diluted version, in the form of
four separate acts could be passed only in 1955-1956.

Several provisions including the provisions of monogamy, divorce, abolition of coparcenaries and inheritance to daughters were opposed. It was felt that the Hindu society would receive a moral setback if women were granted the right to inherit property. The reforms were opposed even by the then President and constitutional head, Dr. Rajendra Prasad, senior Congressmen like Pattabhai Sitarammayya, Sardar Patel, the President of the ruling Congress, P.D. Tandon among others.

The representatives of Hindu fundamentalist parties termed the effort as 'anti-Hindu' and 'anti-Indian' and raised the demand for a uniform civil code as a delaying tactic. At this point, the women parliamentarians who had initially propagated a uniform code reversed their position and supported the Hindu law reform. This was a significant political move, since an uncompromising demand for a uniform civil code would have meant an alliance with the most reactionary and anti-women lobby and would have caused a further setback to women's rights.

In the early Hindu society, women had no legal status. The Hindu law of inheritance had deprived women of the right to property (except the right to their *Stridhana*). As a result, their economic security was completely dependent on the pleasure of the man—husband, father, and brother. The movement to strengthen her position in society began from the second half of the 19th century. The earliest attempts may be traced back to 1865. The Act X of that year was the first step towards conferring economic security upon Indian women. The Indian Succession Act 1865 (Act X of 1865) laid down that "no person shall, by marriage, acquire any interest in the property of the person whom he or she marries nor become incapable of doing any act in respect of his or her own property which he or she could have done 'if not married to that person."[16] In 1923, the Married Women's Property Act of

1874 was amended by Act XIII of 1923 so as to bring Hindu women and others within its jurisdiction. On 15 February 1923, the Select Committee's report on the Bill to amend further the Married Women's Property Act of 1874 was taken into consideration. The bill intended to provide a policy of insurance, which could be for the benefit of the wife, or the wife and the children of the insurer. The Bill was finally passed into law in March 1923.[17]

The year 1923 was indeed a landmark: this was the year when the Hindu woman's independent right to property was recognized for the first time, although to a limited extent. No doubt, Section 4 of the Widow Remarriage Act 1856 entitled the childless widow to a share of her husband's property, this right was very limited in scope. So the attempt made in 1923 may be regarded as the first move when women's economic rights began to be honoured.

The Married Women's Property Act of 1874 was further amended in 1927 by Act XVIII of that year. Its aim was to safeguard the interests of husbands—a part of limited their liability when his wife had obtained a probate or letter of administration and was a trustee, executive or administrative either before or after marriage.[18]

CONCLUSION

The above discussion shows that women did not enjoy a dignified and rightful place in society since time immortal. But in the modern times the situation changed. Many reformers came up and fought for the improvement of women's status in society. As a result, women's status became better, though many impediments still stood in the way of implementation of all the reforms.

NOTES

1. Kotovsky, G., *et al* (1979), "Ancient India" in *A History of India*, Progress Publisher, Moscow, pp. 38-39.

2. Sarkar, UC, *Epochs in Hindu Legal History*, *Vedic* Research Centre, Hoshiarpur, p. 207.

3. Thapar, Romila (2000), *Cultural Pasts-Essays in Early Indian History*, Oxford University Press, New Delhi, pp. 312-320.

4. Kant, Anjani (2003), "A Historical Study of Women in India", in *Women and Law*, APH Publishing Corporation, pp. 19-32.

5. Kumkum Roy *et at* (2005), "In Search Of Vedic Age" in *The Vedas, Hinduism, Hindutva*, Ebong Alap, pp. 14-14536-41.

6. Thapar, Romila (1978), *Ancient Indian Social History*, Orient Longman, New Delhi, 28-37, 43-47.

7. Kant Anjani, (2003), *Women and The Law*, APH Publication Corporation, pp. 37-39.

8. Sarkar, UC, *Epochs in Hindu Legal History*, *Vedic* Research Centre, Hoshiarpur, pp. 48, 201-205, 207, 402-407.

9. Gadkar, Gajendra (P.B.) (1951), *Hindu Code Bill- Karnataka University Lectures*, Karnataka University, Dharvad, pp. 35, 36.

10. Gadkar, Gajendra (P.B.) (1951), *Hindu Code Bill- Karnataka University Lectures*, Karnataka University, Dharvad, pp. 37-45.

11. Mukund, K (1992), "Turmeric Land", *Women's Property Rights in Tamil Society since Medieval Times, XXVII/17*, p. 2.

12. Agnes Flacia (2004), *Women and Law in India*, OUP, New Delhi, pp. 18-22.

13. Ghosh, Batakrishna, (1975), *Hindu Law and Custom*, Bhartiya Publication House, Varanasi, pp.132-136, 152-157, 161, 162, 190.

14. Nair, Janaki, (1996), *Women and Law in Colonial India*, Kali for women, New Delhi, pp. 197-203.

15. Desai, A.R (1948), *Social Background of Indian Nationalism,* Popular Prakashan, Mumbai, pp. 240-242274-276.

16. Act X of 1865, Section 4.

17. Mitra, N.N, ed., *The Indian Annual Register*, 1923, vol. II, pp. 265 and 296.

18. Agnes Flacia (2004), *Women and Law in India*, OUP, New Delhi, pp. 78, 79.

3
HINDU CODE BILL

GENDER IN HINDU CULTURE

Gender does not refer simply to the study of women. Rather it refers to the manner in which male and female differences are socially constructed. Invariably, culture plays an influential role in assigning gender roles. The construction of Indian women's identity is wholly defined by her relation to others. From late childhood itself there is a deliberate attempt to train and mould girls into 'good women'—docile, submissive and self-effacing. Marriage and removal from all childhood attachments confound the identity struggles of the adolescent girl. It is only motherhood that confers status, respect and identity to a female. But these problems and pictures are more complex in Hindu culture. In the name of '*sanskaras*', Hindu women are tied up with the bondage of superstitions, which they carry till their death. In the '*Manu Smriti*' the woman is born a sort of slave of her father when young, to her husband when she is middle aged and to her son when she is a mother.

The patriarchal Hindu structure is the product of this type of Gender formation, which resulted in over-emphasis on the male child, the preference for sons and neglect of daughters. Hindu Code Bill tries to change the laws of Manu, which were misogynistic and reduced a woman to a commodity. The Hindu Code Bill in a sense marks the end of the laws of Manu and brings forth a text that has possibilities for the liberation of women.[1]

Because of caste hierarchy and patriarchal structure women are second-class citizens in every day social life:

Before defining the above statement one has to look for what Hindu *dharma* is and how it works. In the Hindu *dharma* individual salvation (*moksha*) lies in coordinating in a balanced manner the three pursuits of human existence, which are *Dharma* (the laws of social order), *Artha* (prosperity) and *Kama* (pleasure). *Dharma* is the most important of these. How the Hindu understands the branch of *Dharma*? Briefly, *Dharma* refers to the norm of conduct and of duties on each man in accordance with his caste. It derives from both legal treatises of the past (often regarded as sacred texts) and from approved custom, particularly that which is not opposed to the sacred texts. The idea of *Dharma* is fully articulated in the theory of *Varna-asrama—Dharma*, where the definition of one's duty has reference not only to one's caste but also to the particular stage in every stage of life. Gradually, *Dharma* becomes the most significant concept in the Hindu tradition and the very basis of the status of the individual in Hindu society. Individual acts according to the rules of his *Dharma* meant that a man must accept his position and role in society on the basis of the caste into which he was born and the norms which had been set for that caste by the authors of the law books. Duties implied obligation and stress was far more on obligation than on rights. This tendency was further emphasized by the strongly patriarchal character of the family unity.

Dharma was essential because it promoted individual security and happiness as well as the stability of social order. Each individual has its own role in *Dharma*. The Hindu *Dharma* is, in comparison, far more complicated. This is the part to the fact that over-all framework of Hindu society where the emphasis is on duty and judging by the law books, access to rights is limited to the privileged class. The second prospective is that of the localize group or caste where the concept of rights did exist to some limited extent. Through Hindu *Dharma* is same for everyone, yet to some extent it dif-

fers from person to person, region to region, caste to caste
and creates confusion. The functioning of each small unit was
controlled by its own mechanism and within its own limits.

An important characteristic of caste is that an individual
is born into a particular caste and cannot acquire the status of
any other caste. This resulted in a check on individual's social
mobility. It also came to be associated with a basic religio-
philosophical concept of Hinduism—that of *Karma,* which
maintains that one's deeds and activities in one's present incarnation determine one's status and happiness in the life to
follow. Thus an individual's caste status was entirely of his
own making and he was in a position to improve it by conforming to *Dharma* and being reborn at a higher status in his
next incarnation. This, through a *Varna* system, became more
rigid.

The *Varna* system had watertight compartments—
Brahmins, Kshatriyas, Vaishyas, and Shudras. The Brahmins
who were known as the lawmakers formulated the rules of
Dharma. They naturally tried to maintain the superiority of
their caste. As a complement to this, it was necessary to formulate a system of social hierarchy. The Brahmins acted as
the custodian of the sacred lore and performing priestly functions, the Kshatriyas were responsible for the governance and
maintenance of peace, the Vaishya engaged in agriculture industry and trade and Shudra rendered general, including
menial services to the whole community. These four divisions
were recognized by the *Vedic* traditions as basic divisions.
And it is in this respect of them that rights, duties and privileges were enunciated both in regard to life and rituals. In the
ancient period caste is an essential requirement of marriage,
adoption and the status of an individual.[2]

In the orthodox view, caste was not a separate category.
It was a by-product of inter-*varnas* marriage, which was not
considered normal. However it was considered proper for

women to marry a person of a higher *Varna* (*anuloma*), but reverse (*pratiloma*) was strictly prohibited. Unlike in case of *Varna*, caste differentiation was based primarily on marriage and birth. The *Smritis* indicated the *Varna* status of each of the caste groups, howsoever, it originated. According to P.V. Kane, there are references to 172 of them. Caste proliferation and differentiation took place in a big way based on other considerations and circumstances too, and it was a custom that finally determined the status of each in the *Varna* hierarchy[3].

The rules of marriage were strictly enforced and marriage was primarily a social institution. The lower the status of women, the stronger was the legal tie of marriage. The patriarchal system tended to keep the status of women at a low level, and the emergence of the joint family system with special property rights for the male members, reinforced 'Patriarchy'.

According to the *Manusmriti*, women are not to be free under any circumstances. In the opinion of Manu:

- IX 2. Day and night women must be kept in dependence by the males (of) their (families), and if they attached themselves to sensual enjoyments, they must be kept under one's control.
- IX 3. Her father protects (her) in childhood, her husband protects (her) in youth, and her sons protect (her) in old age, a woman is never independent.
- IX 4. Considering that the highest duty of all castes, weak husbands (must) strive to guard their wives.
- IX 47. By a girl, by young women, or even by an aged one, nothing must be done independently, even in her own house. A woman does not have the right to divorce.
- IX 45. The husband is declared to be one with wife, which means that there could be no separation once a woman, is

married.

Manu does not prevent a man from giving up his wife. Indeed, he not only allows him to abandon his wife but he also permits him to sell her. But he prevents the wife becoming free. See this:

- IX 46. Neither by sale nor repudiation is a wife released from her husband. Manu reduced a wife to a level of slave in the matter of property.

He says:

- IX 416. A wife, a son and a slave, these three are declared to have no property: the wealth, which they earn, is (acquired) for him to whom they belong. When she becomes a widow, Manu allows her maintenance. Manu never allows her to have any domination over property.

In the context of the Hindu *Dharma* (religion), caste hierarchy and patriarchal system dominated the Hindu society. This ultimately led to the subordination of the woman status.

There were some reforms during the British period. Did these reforms help in improving the status and position of women or are there any loopholes? When British established their rule in India, the Privy Council contributed to the development of all branches of Indian law. The judges, the lawyers and the litigants of this country undoubtedly owe a debt of gratitude to the guidance, which they received, from the eminent judges of the Privy Council during this period.

To begin with, the law was based, even in that period, on social conscience of the Hindus. But later on British realized that there were cruel social customs practiced in Hindu society, for example sati system, child marriage etc. Similarly the conditions of widows were very bad which encouraged the replacement of Hindu law by their own laws. They passed Sati Abolition Act in 1829 and Hindu Widow Remarriage Act in 1856. Further the Child Marriage Restraint Act 1929 or Sharada Act was passed. Besides the Britishers, our own social reformers also played a great role in getting these acts passed.

One thing must be made clear here: Though the Britishers did some good work here, they played a double role. They allowed widows to remarry. But did not interfere in the matter of bad marriages and did nothing in the sphere of divorce law. [Chandra, 1998:186] Virdee [1972:36-37] thinks that the Native Courts Marriage Dissolution Act of 1866 provided an indirect way of divorce for converts to Christianity. When one of the Hindu Spouses adopted Christianity and the other refused to live with the spouse on that ground, a decree for restitution of conjugal rights or alternatively for divorce could be applied for. Divorce was made available under the Special Marriage Act of 1872, but this, too, applied to only few Hindus.[4] There was strong resistance from the orthodox elements in the Hindu society to such provisions.

In spite of giving us many social reforms against the evil customs, the Britishers did not place due emphasis on gender justice. Even in such a matter as adoption there is difference. In the Guardians and Wards Act, 1890 the father is the natural guardian of children born or adopted by the couple. In the Married Women Property Right Act, 1937, a widow and the widowed daughter-in-law were made heir along with the son but the property was to be treated as a limited ownership type. The second defect was that it did not recognize daughter as a simultaneous heir along with the son.

EVOLUTION OF HINDU CODE BILL

Dr. Ambedkar has given a history of the Bill. It had "its origin in the 1937 legislature and from that time·on the various provisions were enumerated from committee to committee". In 1941 the Rau Committee reported on the Women's Rights to Property Act of 1937. In 1942 two-draft bills, one on succession, one on marriage was presented. A Hindu succession bill was introduced in the Assembly in 1943 but it was referred to a Joint committee. (It should be noted that for the purpose of this Code, people who were not Muslims, Parsis or Christians were included in the Hindu category.)

The Parliament of India settled down to consider the Hindu Code Bill in 1950. As Law Minister, Ambedkar was in charge of presenting the facets of the bill, explaining the rationale of its various sections, answering questions, and especially defending the very idea of equality for women in marriage, divorce, adoption and property rights. He and his many supporters, including all women in the legislative body, were faced with the barrage of criticism. In the end the Hindu Code Bill was for the most part passed bit by bit in 1955 and 1956, but not the total bill. [5]

CODIFICATION OF HINDU CODE BILL

In his speech on the Hindu Code Bill, Dr. Ambedkar remarked at Siddharath College that

The title of the bill is "A bill to codify and modify certain branches of the Hindu law". The purpose is two-fold, they are:

- To codify and
- while codifying the bill to modify some of the existing principles of the Hindu law.

Every law must possess three attributes, namely:

- Certainty: the law must be certain; there must be no ambiguity. There should be no matters of doubt. One of the essentials of the law is certainty.

- Unity: so far as the society is concerned law must be uniform. It cannot be discriminatory as between one citizen and another. Secondly, the law cannot have territorial variation except within a very narrow margin. If you are about to commit murder you ought to know what the consequences are going to be whether you commit the murder in Mumbai or in Chennai. If you are dealing with property you ought to know that the law of property in Mumbai is the same as that in South India. The law cannot be varied from territory to territory.

- Accessibility: Every person interested in a particular matter, which affects him should be in a position to find out for himself, by pursuing an act of the State, what are his rights. It should not be necessary for the common man to have to go to a lawyer every time and depend upon his opinion. It might be in the interest of the lawyer that the law should not be known to the public and the public should be required by reason of their ignorance to have to go to them, waste their money to find out a sort of advice which would take them to court where they find not success but ridicule of the judges.

In modern, civilized and democratic countries the law must possess the above-mentioned three attributes which the Hindu law does not have. Therefore, there can be no objection to codify the Hindu law.

MODIFICATION IN THE HINDU LAW

The proposed modifications may be placed under five heads:

- Non-recognition of caste as an essential circumstance for the validity of marriage and adoption.

- Monogamy: There is a practice of men marrying any number of women. The principle of monogamy should be introduced.
- Divorce: There is a strong belief that a wife being *andhangini* (half the body), she cannot be separated from her husband. The husband and wife are like Siamese twins. To avoid living in misery and torture, divorce should be permissible.
- There are two systems of inheritance: one is *Dayabhaga* and the other is *Mitaksharas*. *Dayabhaga* system prevails in Bengal and certain neighbouring areas. In the rest of India we have *Mitakshara*. In the *Mitakshara* system if the father has inherited ancestral property then his sons have right in that property by birth. That is to say, father cannot sell the inherited property or transfer it or turn it into any use without the consent of his sons. Technically, it is called *Pratibandha*. In *Dayabhaga* system, the sons have no right. Father is the full owner of the property which he has inherited from the ancestor. Sons have no birthright to own it. Sons have to wait until the father dies to get the share of the father's property. It was proposed in the bill that the *Mitakshara* system should be substituted by the *Dayabhaga* system so that there was a uniform law throughout India.
- It is believed that the economic enterprise is of utmost importance for the prosperity of a nation. In order that the economic enterprises may be promoted there must be perfect liberty to the holder of the property to make use of it as he thinks best either in the interest of himself or in the interest of his progeny. Here, too, the *Dayabhaga* system is more suited than the *Mitakshara*.
- The last change in the bill relates to women's right to property. There are two proposals: every property, which goes to a woman by inheritance or by a gift shall be her

absolute property. In the old Hindu law, the property which went to a woman fell into three categories (1) property which she inherited from a male member of the family, (2) property which she got on her marriage and (3) property which was given to her by others. The bill proposed to abolish this distinction namely, ownership of property of limited nature. Under the bill all the property went to her.

The second reform proposed to give the daughter a share in the property of her father in the same manner as her son got. In other words, the daughter was made what is called simultaneous heir with the son. The position before the Act of 1937 was that no woman was a simultaneous heir with the male member of the family. Even the widow of the deceased or the daughter was not treated as absolute heirs. But this position was rectified under the Women's right to property in 1937 under which a widow and the widowed daughter-in-law were made heir along with the son. The property was, however, to be of a limited ownership type. They were not full owners. The second defect was that it did not recognize daughter as a simultaneous heir along with the son. The proposed bill removed both these defects. It made every woman a full owner. It also made the daughter an heir along with the son.

Did the above proposals conform to the Hindu tradition/*shastras*? Consider the monogamy. The rule in Kautilya's *Arthashastra* about monogamy is that a man shall not marry a second wife except under certain conditions. On the *Shashtra's* sanction of divorce under certain circumstances there could be no dispute at all. As for the widow's right to inherit property, the *Brihaspatismriti* discusses the right of widow to inherit property of husband. Then, the present Hindu law has nothing to do with the Hindu *Shastras*. There has been a com-

complete departure from there in countless cases. As far as orthodoxy is concerned it would be possible to find out some authority from some *Shastras* to thwart anything worthwhile for them. The proposals were, from every angle is in order.[5]

HINDU CODE BILL AND ITS TENETS

Dr. Ambedkar's views on various tenets of the Hindu Code Bill are worth noting: [7]

- LAND AND CUSTOMARY LAW

The bill confined only to property other than agricultural land. This codification was only a partial codification because a large part of the property which was the subject matter of inheritance was left untouched by the provisions of this Bill. Land is put in the Provincial List. As a result of the judicial interpretation given by the Federal Court it was held that word "land" or item "land", which is included in the Provincial List not merely covered tenancy land but also covered succession to land and consequently any provision with regard to the succession to land made by the central legislature would be *ultra vires*. The bill had not taken into consideration the customary law.

- ADOPTION

Ambedkar also dealt with the question of the right to adopted boy to divest the persons in whom the property was invested before the adoption took place. Under the Hindu law, "it was permissible to a boy who had been adopted, no matter at what stage he had been adopted—he may have been adopted forty years after the death of the father; time makes no change at all in his right to file a suit to set aside any alienation or transfer of property made by the widow who had adopted him."

The second thing that happened as a result of adoption under the Hindu law was that it "completely divested the widowed mother who made the adoption with the result that the entire corpus of the property passed into the hands of the adopted boy, who, in certain sense was a stranger, and notwithstanding the notional change that he entered into the family of the adopted father, he practically continued his affiliations with the members of the natural family. The result was that after the adoption had taken place, instead of the adopting mother getting any kind of security for herself as a result of adoption which a natural mother would get from a natural son, she found that this new adopted son ran away with the property and left the mother with nothing but the right of maintenance. We thought that was not a desirable state of affairs from the point of view of giving security to women, and consequently certain changes were made. The original distinction that was adopted by the Rau committee was deleted and a provision was made that the right of the adopted son shall accrue to him not from the date of his adoption, so that any alienation that may have been made prior to his adoption were beyond his reach, were unchallenged by him."

The second provision that was made was that the adopted son should not as a result of adoption deprive the adopting mother completely of her right of property. What the bill said in its altered form was that "only one and a half of the property of the widow will go beyond the adopted son. The other half, notwithstanding the fact that the widow has adopted will continue to be in the possession and enjoyment of the adopting mother. The result is that the committee has permitted adoption, which the Hindu community feels is a necessary thing for the purpose of perpetuating the family. But at the same time, we have taken care to see that the adoption does not beggar the mother altogether."

- MINORITY AND GUARDIANSHIP

Ambedkar dealt with the question of minority and guardianship. The Select Committee in this part of the bill made only
two changes. The first change was that the power of the
Hindu father as a natural guardian of his minor son was
taken away in case he "renounces the world or ceases to be a
Hindu". The original law was that the father was the natural
guardian and no matter what change took place in his condition either by his religion or in any other way, he still continued to be the guardian of his minor son. The Committee felt
that as this was a code intended to consolidate the Hindu society and their laws, it was desirable to impose this condition,
namely that the "father shall continues to be a natural guardian so long as he continues to be a Hindu. The code in its altered form also has introduced another change, namely, that
a Hindu widow has been given power to appoint a testamentary guardian if her husband has not appointed anyone. She
had not any such power and the Select Committee has given
this power to her."

- MARRIAGE – OLD AND NEW

According to Dr. Ambedkar, monogamy was not a new innovation. In our customary law and in our *Shastras* a Hindu
husband had at all times an unfettered, unqualified right to
polygamy. But this was never the case. In the *Kautilya's Arthashastra* the right to marry a second wife has been considerably limited: "In our own country various legislations have
been passed in various provinces and monogamy has been
prescribed. There is also a precedent of the whole world,
which recognizes monogamy as the most salutary principle
so far 'as marital relations are concerned."

- DIVORCE

This also is no way an innovation. Communities, "which are

called Shudras, have customary divorce. Shudras form practically 90 per cent of the total population of Hindus. Should the law of the 90 per cent of the people be the general law of this country or are you going to have the law of the 10 per cent of the people being imposed upon 90 per cent?"

The new principles, which have been introduced in the law of marriage or divorce, are both just and reasonable and supported by precedents not only of our *shastras* but the experience of the world as a whole.

INDIAN CIVIL CODE

The Indian Succession Act is a civil code. Unfortunately, this does not apply to Hindus. There are religions which have a legal system; and there are religions, which have no legal system at all, which are just pure matters of creed. The peculiarity about the Hindu religion, as I understand it, is this that it has got a legal framework integrally associated with it. Now, it is very necessary to bear this thing in mind because if one has a proper understanding of this, it would not be difficult to understand why Buddhists are brought under the Hindu religion. When Buddha differed from the *Vedic* Brahmins his difference was limited to matters of creed. Buddha did not propound a separate legal system for his own followers; he left the legal system as it was. The same is the case with the Sikhs.

It is true that elements of other cultures have been absorbed by Hinduism. It is, however, one of the great qualities of it that they have not changed their social structure as a result of the absorption of the doctrine of their opponents. Buddha preached equality; he was the greatest opponent of *Chatur Varna*. He was the greatest opponent of belief in the *Vedas* because he believed in reason and did not believe in infallibility of any book. He believed in *Ahimsa*. The Brahmanic society did not accept most of these things. Ambedkar was, thus, right when he said, "whatever else Hindu society may adopt, it will never give up its social structure for the enslavement of the Shudra and the enslavement of women. It is for this reason that law must now come to their rescue in order that society may move on."

The Preamble of the Constitution, Dr. Ambedkar further added, "speaks of liberty, equality and fraternity and therefore, bound to examine every social institution that exists in the country and see whether it satisfies the principles laid down in the constitution. No man who examines that institution in a fair and liberal spirit can come to find liberty or equality." What did the sacramental ideal of marriage mean? It meant polygamy for the man and perpetual slavery for woman.

SIGNIFICANCE OF HINDU CODE BILL

Highlighting the significance of the Hindu Code Bill, Dr. Ambedkar noted:

"No law passed by the Indian legislature in the past or likely to be passed in the future can be compared to it in point of its significance. To leave inequality between class and class, between sex and sex, which is the soul of Hindu society, untouched and to go on passing legislation relating to the economic problems is to make a farce of our constitution and to build a palace on a dung heap." This was the significance attached to the Hindu code bill. It was really a historical development as well as sociologic landmark in the country. The main objectives of the Hindu Code Bill were:[8]

- To help and encourage the entire family members to come together for mutual participation in matters affecting each and everyone.
- To give to the female member of the Hindu family full

rights in matters of property, marriage, inheritance, minority and guardianship.

- To provide all members of a Hindu family the individual freedom and social equality and also protection to womenfolk against the evils of dowry and deprivation, disease and hunger.
- To achieve the aim of making the widow, the daughter and the widow of a pre-deceased son eligible to inherit property.
- To give them the right to knowledge and the right to realize their spiritual potentialities along with men, and ultimately,
- To reform the basic structure of the Hindu social and legal systems in consonance with the spirit of the preamble and provisions of our noble constitution highlighting the principles of justice, liberty and equality, fraternity, the dignity of the individual and the unity of the nation.

It was the first step towards the gender equality in the Hindu society. See, for substantiation, the rights that Dr Ambedkar had given to women in the Hindu Code Bill:[9]

- The right of divorce.
- If a husband divorces, wife will get maintenance.
- The law permits only monogamy.
- Only one marriage is permitted and without any specific reason second marriages is not allowed and that is why women have got stability.
- The right of adoption is given to women.
- Girls could also be adopted unlike in the past where only boys were adopted.
- Women have right on their own property.
- Daughters have the same right as sons in their father's property.

- Daughters were given the right to be heir.
- Inter-caste marriage is allowed.
- The woman has got the right to appoint her heir.

The Hindu Code Bill was formulated to maintain justice, equality and security to women with a view to removing the atrocities prevailing in the caste system.

According to Justice Gajendra Gadakar, the relationship between ancient Hindu law and the Hindu Code Bill must begin with the emphasis that the Hindu code should be considered rationally and scientifically on its own merits. It is an illusion to entertain the belief that the Hindu law has never been changed from time to time, though the method adopted in introducing these changes was somewhat unusual. Attempts were made from time to time to meet crying needs for reform in some special parts of Hindu law but the time has come now when the problem must be attacked boldly and fearlessly and the whole of the Hindu law must be put on a rational basis. The first and the most obvious point on which there could be no difference is that the personal law which affects the lives of so many millions of Hindus should be made simple, clear and certain and this object can be achieved only by codifying the whole of the Hindu law. There should be no difference of opinion that the personal law affecting all the Hindus should now be made uniform. The most objectionable feature of the Hindu law is that the division of the Hindu law is the division of the Hindu community amongst four *Varnas.* No argument is necessary in support of the proposition that these *Varnas* have now become totally obsolete. It may be that historically speaking the origin of these *Varnas* may not have been so much religious as political and it may be assumed for the sake of the argument that these *Varnas* may perhaps have served some purpose in primitive times. But in the present age of India's freedom it is inconceivable that any

Hindu should stand up for the division of the Hindu community into four *Varnas* which are arranged on the basis of a hierarchical importance and superiority. We all take glory into the fact that we are living in the present historical times. Hindu code is based on absolute equality amongst all Hindus, irrespective of their caste, creed or sex. The position of women under the Hindu law as it is administered today calls for a similar change."[10]

CONTROVERSIES ABOUT HINDU CODE BILL

The objections against Hindu Code Bill were not directed against Ambedkar but against the idea of women's property rights, their right to divorce, the abolition of caste in the matters of marriage and adoption and the prescription of monogamy. Basically, controversies rested on these points:

- Abolition of *Mitakshara* law and implementation of *Dayabhaga*.
- To give rights to daughters in property inheritance
- To convert the rights into absolute rights.
- Monogamy
- The provision for divorce.

Pt. L.K. Mishra, for instance, said "I do not find anything Hindu about it. It can be more properly called an un-Hindu or anti-Hindu code. I do not breathe this spirit of Hinduism; it reeks of un-Hindu ideas; spirit of supreme contempt for anything Hindu permeates the whole bill from the beginning to the end."

He further added, "In the past generation, the late Pandit Vidyasagar was so much moved by widows' plight that he got passed the Hindu Widow Remarriage Act but the country was not prepared for it. And consequently the act virtually became a dead letter and has remained so till now. That is bound to be the fate of all social legislations which have originated not from a demand from within the society".

Mukut Biharilal Bhargav declared that "the Hindu marriage is sacramental and as such is indissoluble. It is a religious bond of unity between the couple. It is a contractual relationship that has got some spiritually about it. By no stretch of imagination it can be brought to add by a sweet whim and caprice of any of the parties. This is the conception of Hindu Marriage. He challenges many *Smriti* or citation of Hindu scripture. So far as Hindu scripture is concerned *Smriti* understands which would negate this idea of sacramental marriage and will prepare any sort of marriage Act." He further added, "that Hindu code bill aims at the utter demolition of the structure of Hindu society." Therefore his submission was "that the provision of civil marriage and divorce in Hindu code bill is absolutely foreign to Hindu law and thus it should not be incorporated in Hindu law." He submitted that "adoption in Hindu law rest upon the religious belief, which says of departed man that he should have a son who would be able to give him ablutions so as to make him attain *Moksha*. Thus it is important to understand the essence of adoption in Hinduism. Caste is one of the most important factors in adoption. Adoption in the same caste is viable under Hindu law." He mentioned that he was not happy with the three conditions laid down in the adoption. The three conditions were that the age of boy must be below 15; he must not be married; and must be a Hindu. In Hindu customs marriage is neither a disqualification nor an age a bar, as such there was no problem related to boy being married before adoption. The Hindu law only allowed sons to be adopted and not the daughters.

Bhargav also questioned the property rights given to an adopted person. He said, the succession laws relegated brother to a very inferior position and gave importance to the daughter and that was irrelevant to the Hindu customs. Ch. Ranbir Singh pointed out that according to Hindu customs a person could not establish matrimonial connections with the same Gotras. None has courage, he observed, to go against the same. But the present bill was providing for marriage in the same Gotra which was against Hindu custom.[11]

On 24 March 1943, the Hindu Code Bill relating to intestate succession came up before the Assembly for discussion. Bhai Parmananda, opposing the Bill, criticized the government for taking upon itself the task of framing a code for Hindu society, particularly when there was no demand for change among the people. Under the circumstances, [12] the Bill was likely to interfere with Hindu religion, destroy the family structure and lead to fragmentation of property. Babu Baij Nath Bajoria, opposed the Bill and moved an amendment for its postponement.[13] He argued that if simultaneous heirship of the daughter was recognized as in the Bill, the moral obligation felt by the brother to maintain and marry off his sisters would vanish.

K.C. Neogy of Bengal pointed out that the measure had evoked a great deal of controversy in the province of Bengal at least.[14] Insofar as it had made a departure in essential particulars form the laws of inheritance prevailing in other parts of India. *Dayabhaga* was itself the result of a reformative movement. He argued that people who were governed by the *Dayabhaga* school should be the last persons to take exception to the process of reform going on according to modern ideas to suit modern conditions. Unfortunately, however, the opinion in Bengal was mostly opposed to the Bill.

Lalchand Navalri warned women and the association of women that "more or less we are plunged into the ocean of western ways and we should not allow ourselves to be drowned". He raised an objection regarding the right of a married daughter, who would get a share on her husband's side, and also a share in her parental house. Therefore, she would get two shares whereas the son would get only one. He, however, overlooked the fact that the sons enjoyed shares brought by their wives from their parental homes.[15] Amarendra Nath Chattopadhyaya of Bengal welcomed the Bill and said that men and women should have equal rights.[16] He fully appreciated the idea of codification of Hindu Law by which Hindu society would be brought into harmony all over the country. Govind V. Deshmukh supported the Bill and refuted the argument that it would led to the breaking up of Hindu society, contending that the society was a living organism which could exist and did exist by adopting to the circumstances that cropped up from time to time.[17] P.N. Bannerjee pointed out a number of defects in the Bill and supported its reference to select committee because he felt that "it would provoke Hindus throughout India. He demanded that adequate steps be taken to secure the fullest possible publicity and discussion."[18]

In response to these questions, Dr. Ambedkar challenged that this bill was not violating the spirit of *Smritis* and *Shastras*. This was not as revolutionary as the provision of monogamy. Polygamy did not exist earlier. With monogamy existing in the Southern areas such as Nattukottai Chettiyar where monogamy was practiced. This has been reported in a Privy Council Report. Among the Nattukottai Chettiyar caste second marriage could not be done without the permission of the first wife. And if this was not done then the husband had to give certain property to the first wife so that she could live a secure life.

Later, giving example from Kautilya's *Arthashastra* where the right to get married second time was limited. Plainly, the second marriage could not be conducted within 10-12 years of the first marriage. This was binding, so that women could have an opportunity to have a child. During the time of second marriage the *Stridhana* of the first wife should be rightly returned to the first wife.

In different regions in our country law has permitted the right for monogamous marriage. For example, in the laws in the region of Marumakkathayam and Aliyasthanam where the right to have a monogamous marriage is considered to be a way of life. During that time even in Mumbai, Chennai and Baroda the laws for monogamous marriage was implemented. [19]

All that the bill said was this: the law shall protect those who are reformers and want to marry outside the caste. Those who want to adopt children outside the caste are free to do so. By this legislation an orthodox is not prevented from adopting a child of his own estate. In case of a daughter's share in the inherited property even the orthodoxy may not raise their voice against it, as the bill permits every Hindu to make a will of his property. He may in his will, if he so wishes, that my property may be taken away by anybody else except my daughter.

THE EMPOWERMENT OF WOMEN

Many scholars believed that the Hindu Code Bill was a catalyst for the liberation of women. According to them Dr. Ambedkar had, through it, sought to change the Laws of Manu, which, were misogynistic as they were, reduced a woman to a commodity. As an architect of the Indian Constitution, he granted the basic rights to justice, equality and security to the woman.[20]

- He saw the caste system and the class system being responsible for the subordination of women.
- This subordination, he believed, would not end until the caste system and patriarchy were not attacked.
- He took a stand that "Personal is political". He exposed

how the women suffered as private within the confines of the home. Issues of bigamy, maintenance etc. were all brought into the public gaze.

* He preferred the Buddhist, non-Brahmanical tradition because it granted freedom to women and gave them access to knowledge. In short, he believed that any social transformation was incomplete till gender discrimination in that society did not come to an end.

CONCLUSION

The Hindu Code Bill is a landmark in Hindu legal history. Although it was not passed as drafted by Dr. Ambedkar it, nevertheless, empowered Hindu women.

NOTES

1. Pardeshi, Pratima (2003), The Hindu Code Bill for the Liberation of Women, in Anupama Rao (ed), *Gender and Caste*, Kali for Women, Delhi, 2003, pp. 346.

2. Thapar, Romila (1978*), Ancient Indian Social History : Some interpretation's,* Orient Longman Ltd, New Delhi, pp. 30, 31.

3. Char, Desika S V (1993*), Caste, Religion and Country : A view of Ancient and Medieval India,* Orient Longman Limited, New Delhi, pp. 16.

4. Menesky, F. Werner (2003), *Beyond the tradition and modernity,* Oxford Press University, New Delhi.

5. Zelliot, Eleanor (2003), Dr. Ambedkar and the Empowerment of women, in Anupama Rao (ed), *Gender and Caste,* Kali for Women, New Delhi, p. 212.

6. Speech delivered by Dr. B.R. Ambedkar to the Siddharath College Parliament on 11th June 1950 in Annual Magazine published by Prof. D'Souza, J.F.D., Siddharath College, Mumbai pp. 23-31.

7. Jatava, R.D. (2001), *Sociological thoughts of B.R. Ambedkar,* A.B.D. publishers, Jaipur, p. 180-190.

8. *Ibid.* 213.

9. Moon, Meenakshi, and Pawar, Urmila, *Amhi Ghadawala Itihaas,*

Mumbai.

10. Gadkar, Justice Gajendra (1951), *Hindu Code Bill—Karnataka University Lectures*, Karnataka University, Karnataka, pp. 46.

11. Ambedkar Dr. Babasaheb (1979), *Writing and Speeches*, volume 14, part 1, 2, complied by Vasant Moon, Education Department Government of Maharashtra, Mumbai.

12. *Amrit Bazar Patrika*, 25th March 1943, pp. 1414-18.

13. *Ibid.*

14. *Legislative Assembly Debates*, 30 March 1943, vol. II, pp. 1599-1602.

15. *Ibid.*, pp. 1605-11.

16. *Ibid.*, 29 March 1943, p. 1555.

17. *Ibid.*, 30 March 1943, p. 1621, *Amrit Bazar Patrika*, 31 March 1943.

18. Agnes, Flavia (2004), "Hindu Women And Marriage Law-Right to Property" in *Women and Law in India*, Oxford University, New Delhi, pp. 136.

19. Ambedkar, B.R. (1982), *Hindu Code Billsambhandi*, ed. Vimal Keerti, Pragativadi Prakashan, Nagpur, pp. 24, 25.

20. Pardeshi, Pratima (2003), The Hindu Code Bill for the Liberation of Women, in Anupama Rao (ed), *Gender and Caste*, Kali for Women, New Delhi, pp. 346, 360.

4
LEGAL REFORMS IN POST-INDEPENDENCE PERIOD

GENDER IN HINDU CULTURE

The provisions in Hindu Code Bill took the shape of independent Hindu Personal Laws, viz. Hindu Marriage Act, Hindu Divorce Act, Hindu Succession Act, etc. This was the first major legal step in the direction of providing gender equality in Hindu society.

MARRIAGE

For the formal validity of a Hindu marriage, two alternative ceremonies are available to the parties:

1. *Shastric* ceremonies and rites, as laid down by *shastric* Hindu law;
2. Customary ceremonies and rites.

More often, than not, Hindu couples solemnize their marriage under *shastric* rites and ceremonies. It is not possible to enumerate the essential and non-essential ceremonies in two separate lists, as there is a lot of judicial disagreement in this regard. However, there is no confusion as far as *saptapadi*, an absolutely indispensable measure, is concerned. It validates Hindu marriage. It is the most material of all the *shastric* rites, and the marriage becomes complete and irrevocable on the completion of the seventh step. This is recognized in the provisions of Section 7(2) of the Hindu Marriage

Act, 1955. If this ceremony is not performed, the marriage is null and void. Children borne of such a marriage are not granted legitimacy under the provisions of Section 16 of the Hindu Marriage Act 1955.

Inter sub-caste marriages had been validated under the Hindu Marriage (Removal of Disabilities) Act, 1946. The Hindu Marriage Act 1955 widened the space by allowing "any two Hindus, without requiring them to be of the same caste or sub-caste" to tie the marital knot. In other words, to get married to someone under Hindu law today, both parties do not have to belong to the same caste but have to necessarily profess the Hindu Religion (which includes Sikhs, Buddhists, Jains or any other person domiciled in the territories to which the Hindu Marriage Act applies) and who is not a Christian, Parsi, Jew or Muslim.

The Hindu Marriage Act gave the Hindu women the following matrimonial reliefs:[1]

1. Judicial separation,
2. Declaration of nullity and annulment, and
3. Divorce.

In order to get their marriage registered, the parties to the marriage must submit 'FORM A' to the registrar in whose jurisdiction either party to the marriage has been residing for at least six months (immediately preceding the date of marriage). This form, along with age proofs, and marriage photo, should be submitted within one month from the date of solemnization of marriage. Both the parties to the marriage and the guardian, if any, must appear before the marriage Registrar personally. If, for some reason, there was delay of above one month but up to 5 years in filing the above form, the same could be condoned by the Sub-Registrar. Where the delay was above 5 years, that would be condoned by the District Registrar.

DIVORCE

Divorce under the Hindu Marriage Act, 1955 can be obtained by both the spouses on the basis of any of the following grounds:

- Adultery;
- Cruelty;
- Desertion for two years;
- Conversion of religion;
- Unsound mind;
- Suffering from venereal disease and/or Leprosy;
- Has renounced the world;
- Not heard of for 7 years;
- No resumption of co-habitation for one year after the decree of judicial separation, no restitution of conjugal rights for one year after decree for restitution of conjugal rights;
- Husband guilty of rape, sodomy or bestiality;
- If after an order of maintenance is passed under the Hindu Maintenance and Adoptions Act or the Criminal Procedure Code, there has been no cohabitation for one year.

In addition to the grounds, stated above, a wife may also present a petition for the dissolution of her marriage on the following grounds:

- Where the marriage was solemnized before the commencement of the Hindu Marriage Act, 1955:
    1. The husband had married again before such commencement;
    2. That any other wife of the husband whom he had married before such commencement was alive at the time of the marriage;

- Where the husband has, after the marriage, been guilty of rape, sodomy or bestiality;
- Where her marriage, whether consummated or not, was solemnized before she attained the age of 15 years and she has repudiated the marriage after attaining that age but before attaining the age of 18 years.

Under the Hindu Marriage Act, 1955 the spouses, who desire a divorce by mutual consent, have to present a joint petition in the Court with an appropriate jurisdiction. The parties, presenting such a petition, must claim with proof that:

(i)   They have been living separately for a period of one year;

(ii) They have not been able to live together;

(iii) They have mutually agreed that marriages should be dissolved.

Once the petition for Divorce by mutual consent is filed, the Court gives the parties 6 months' times to reconsider. The Court may pass a decree of divorce after a period of 6 months from the date of presentation of the petition and not later than 18 months after the date of presentation, in case the petition is not withdrawn.

Also, a wife can file an application under Section 125 of the Criminal Procedure Code for maintenance. ('wife' here includes a woman who has been divorced by, or has obtained a divorce from her husband and has not remarried).

If any person, who has sufficient means, neglects or refuses to maintain his wife (who is unable to maintain herself) then the wife can file an application before a Magistrate, 1st class, for maintenance. The Magistrate, upon proof of such neglect or refusal, will order such person to make a monthly allowance for the maintenance of his wife.

Also, one can claim maintenance from her ex-husband under law provided that she did not get remarried after divorce. If one remarries, she has to forego maintenance.

SUCCESSION

A person, who owns property in any form, is definitely concerned about his property after his demise. The disposal or distribution of property by a person during his lifetime is generally not favoured. This is mainly because it results in loss of control over one's assets as well as one's family members. Moreover, this will also incur Stamp Duties.

There is often a reluctance to make a will. This could be owing to ignorance about the making of a will; or, it could be the wish to avoid the unpleasantness of facing up the possibility of death. However, the fact remains that many people avoid making a will until it is too late. Some people execute will, prepared by themselves or with the help and advice of well-meaning friends or relatives. Often, these turn out to be ineffectual in law during implementation after the death of the person. The absence of a will (or the invalidity of a will, or parts of a will) creates problems for the legal heirs and successors. This can result in unintended injustice. The Indian Succession Act, 1925, is the main Statute that governs wills in India. It may be noted, however, that Muslims are generally governed by their personal law, which differs from the law that is laid down in the Act.

A will is an important document whereby any living person can bequeath (leave behind) his property to other persons after his death. The person who makes the will is known as the testator. A will is enforceable only after the death of the testator. In India, the Indian Succession Act, 1925 is applicable to Hindus, Sikhs, Jains or Buddhists. However, most of it doesn't apply to Muslims as Muslims are largely covered by Muslim Personal Law. In any case, some important features of a will are as follows:

- Legal declaration: Will is a legal declaration. Certain formalities must be complied with in order to make a valid will. It must be signed and attested as required by law.
- Disposition of property: There must be some property which is being given to others after the death of the testator.
- Operation after death: A will becomes enforceable only after the death of the testator. It gives absolutely no rights to the legatee (the person who inherits) until the death of the testator. It has no effect during the lifetime of the testator. The testator can change his will, at any time prior to his death, in any manner he deems fit.

A codicil has been defined as an instrument, made in relation to a will that explains alterations and additions to its disposition. It shall be deemed to form part of the will. For instance, after a will has been made, the testator may still want to make some changes. By means of a codicil, he may cancel the entire earlier will and make a fresh will, incorporating the desired changes, or he may alter only the relevant parts of the will suitably. Such a codicil will form part and parcel of the existing will. A codicil is valid only if it is executed and attested in the same manner as a will. It is a supplementary document to the will and, cannot stand independently.

According to Section 59 of the Indian Succession Act, any person of sound mind, who has reached the age of majority, can make a will. However, the following persons cannot make a will:

1. Lunatics, insane persons.
2. Minors, i.e. below 18 years of age. In case a guardian is appointed to a minor, such minor reaches age of maturity

only at the age of 21 years.

A Hindu woman cannot alienate the property that she receives from her deceased husband, who is a member of Hindu Undivided Family (HUF). However, she can dispose of by will any property which is part of her own earnings or which she has received by way of gift during her life time.

Persons who are deaf or dumb or blind are not, thereby, incapacitated in making a will, if they are able to know what they do by it.

A person, who is ordinarily insane, may make a will during an interval while he is of sound mind.

No person can make a will while he is in such a state of mind, whether arising from intoxication or, from illness or, from any other cause, so that he does not know what he is doing.

A privileged or oral will can be made or executed only by a soldier employed in an outing or engaged in actual war, or, by an airman, so employed or engaged, or, by a sailor at sea, if he has completed the age of 18 years, to dispose of his property by a will.

Such wills may be in writing or may be by word of mouth. The rules governing privileged wills are as follows:

- Such wills may be written wholly by the testator with his own hand. In such a case, it need not be signed or attested.
- It may be written wholly or, in part, by another person and signed by the testator. In such a case, it need not be attested.
- In case the instrument is written wholly or, partly, by another person and, is not signed by the testator, it shall be deemed to be the testator's will only if it is shown that it was written under the testator's directions or, that he rec-

ognized it as his will.

- If it appears on the face of the instrument that its execution was not completed in the manner intended by the testator, the instrument shall not be invalid just for that cause. However, non-execution must, reasonably, be ascribed to some cause other than the abandonment of the testaments

- If the soldier, airman or mariner has written instructions for the preparation of his will, but has died before it could be prepared and executed, such instructions shall be considered to be a valid will.

- If the soldier, airman or mariner has, in the presence of two witnesses, given verbal instructions for the preparation of his will and, they have been put to writing in his life time, but he has died before the instrument could be prepared and executed, such instructions shall be considered to be a valid will.

- The soldier, airman or mariner may make a will by word of mouth, by declaring his intentions before 2 witnesses present at the same time.

- A will made by word of mouth shall be null and void at the expiration of one month after the testator, being still alive, has ceased to be entitled to make a privileged will.

- Conditional or contingent wills become enforceable only on the happening of a particular event. E.g. 'A' will be entitled to a flat at Mumbai after my death (death of testator), only if he marries 'C.'

Joint wills: A common example is a single will, made jointly by a husband and wife, where each may make a disposition of his or her respective properties in favour of their child/children.

Reciprocal wills: When two or more persons make a will, whereby they bequeath their properties to each other, it is known as a reciprocal will. Such wills may be revoked by any of the testators, during their joint lives. However, it is necessary for that person to give previous notice to the other testators so as to enable them to make changes in their wills.

The rules for making a valid will are as follows:

(1) The testator shall sign or shall affix his mark to the will or, it shall be signed by some other person in his presence and by his direction.

(2) The signature or mark of the testator or the signature of the person signing for him, shall be so placed that it shall appear that it was intended, thereby, to give effect to the writing as a will.

(3) The will must be attested by two or more witnesses, each of whom has seen the testator sign or, affix his mark to the will or, has seen some other person sign the will, in the presence of and, by the direction of the testator. Or he may have received from the testator, a personal acknowledgment of his signature or mark or, of the signature of such other person, and each of the witnesses shall sign the will in the presence of the testator. However, it is not necessary that more than one witness is present at the same time, and no particular form of attestation is necessary.

(4) The testator shall sign or shall affix his mark to the will; or, some other person shall sign it in his presence and, by his direction.

(5) The signature or mark of the testator or the signature of the person signing for him, shall be so placed that it shall appear that it was intended, thereby, to give effect to the writing as a will.

(6) The will must be attested by two or more witnesses, each of whom has seen the testator sign or, affix his mark to the will or, has seen some other person sign the will, in the presence and by the direction of the testator. Or, he may

have received from the testator, a personal acknowledgment of his signature or mark or of the signature of such other person, and each of the witnesses shall sign the Will in the presence of the testator. However, it is not necessary that more than one witness is present at the same time, and no particular form of attestation is necessary.

A will or codicil may be revoked or cancelled by the testator, only in writing. He must declare his intention to revoke the will or codicil and, execute it in the same manner as the will or codicil. A will or codicil may also be revoked by the burning, tearing or destroying of the same by the testator or, by some other person in his presence and, by his directions, with the intention of revoking the same.

A joint will by two testators, in respect of their common properties may be revoked by either of them during the lifetime of both or, by the survivor, on the death of one of them.

An executor is the person appointed ordinarily by the testator's by his will or codicil to administer testator's property and to carry into effect the provision of the will. A testator is entitled to deposit his will in a sealed cover, super-subscribed with the name of the testator, either personally or by his duly authorized agent. On receiving the cover, the Registrar, if satisfied that the person presenting the same for deposit is either the testator or his agent, must keep the sealed cover in his custody.

If a testator, who has deposited such cover, wishes to withdraw it, he may apply either personally or by a duly authorized agent, to the Registrar who holds it in deposit. The Registrar, if satisfied that the applicant is actually the testator, or his agent, shall deliver the cover to him.

After the death of the testator, any person may apply to the Registrar to open the cover and if the Registrar is satisfied that the testator is dead, he must open the cover in the presence of the applicant and cause a copy of the will to be made in his prescribed book at the applicant's expense. He must hold the original in his custody, till ordered by a competent court to produce the will before it. In such a case, the Registrar will open it and send it to the court, after making a copy in the appropriate register.

The Hindu Succession Act, 1956 abolished limited ownership and made a Hindu woman the absolute owner of the property acquired from a male Hindu dying intestate.[2]

REFORMS: AN ONGOING PROCESS

HINDU SUCCESSION AMENDMENT BILL, 2004

Five decades after the Hindu Succession Act, 1956 was passed, the Union Government sought to reform the law relating to reducing the gender inequalities in it. The said Bill was introduced on December 2004. Indira Jaisingh has analysed how this amendment was flawed and has emphasised the need for a uniform material property law and equality of succession rights for women of all communities.

The proposed amendment has once again raised the question; do we need reform for Hindu women or for women generally regardless of the religion to which they belong?

In Muslim personal law only one-third of the man's property can be willed. In Christian law, the Indian Succession Act, 1925 determines intestate succession to all property. A man's widow and children, male and female, inherit equally.

However, a man may, by will bequeath his property to anyone, totally disinheriting his own children and widow.

THE COPARCENARY : A COMPLEX INSTITUTION

Hindu law recognizes a difference between ancestral property and self-acquired property. It also recognizes a coparcenary. A coparcenary is a legal institution consisting of four generations of male heirs in the family. Every male member, on birth within four generations, becomes a member of the coparcenary.

This meant that no person's share in ancestral property could be determined with certainty. It diminished on the birth of a male member and enlarged on the death of a male member. One of the coparceners, generally the senior most was the *Karta*, that is the manager. Women could never become the members of the coparcenary. Any coparcenary had a right to demand partition of the joint family. Once a partition took place, a new coparcener would come into existence, namely the partitioned member, and the next three-generation of males would form the new coparcenary. As the member who sought a partition got his property from his ancestors, the property became ancestral property and hence capable of being coparcenary property.

In the 1950's, in an attempt to reform Hindu law and make it more gender just, the Hindu Succession Act was amended and it was clarified that the death of a man would result in a deemed partition of his share in the joint property. This partitioned share would then be distributed equally among his children and widow. His self-acquired property would be divided equally among his sons and daughters and widow.

WHO WILL BENEFIT?

The proposed amendment now attempts to make a daughter a coparcener at birth in ancestral property. In the present context most property is self acquired and that property must follow principles of succession under the different succession laws. It will actually disadvantage widows, as the share of the daughter will increase in comparison to the widow.

MOTHER AND WIDOW'S RIGHTS

The proposed amendment will, in no way, improve the position of the female members of the joint family. Hindu law not only recognized the coparcenary but also the Hindu joint family, which was a more inclusive institution. It will actually disadvantage widows as the share of the daughter will increase in comparison to widow. With a daughter along with the sons acquiring a birthright, which she can presumably partition at any time, the rights of other members of the joint family get correspondingly diminished. While the reforms of the 1950's disadvantaged a divorced wife, the reforms of the later days disadvantage married women as well. The married women, who lived in a joint Hindu family, had the protection of the family home. This protection will now stand eroded.

Something similar will happen to Hindu widows. While daughters will acquire a birthright in Hindu joint family property, mothers stand to lose a portion of the cake as an inheritance. Since Hindu law does not grant any rights to wives in marital property, their only chance of getting anything was on an inheritance in equal share with the sons and daughters in case the marriage subsisted on the death of a husband. On divorce, of course, even the right to inheritance disappears.

The birthright in Hindu law is the root of many problems. Birthright by definition is a conservative institution, belonging to the era of feudalism, coupled as it was with the rule of primogeniture and the inalienability of land. When property becomes disposable and self-acquired, different rules of succession have to apply. It is in the making of those rules that gender justice has to be located. The proposed amendment reinforces the birthright without working out its consequences for all women.

Justice cannot be secured for one category of women at the expense of another. It is impossible to deal with succession laws in isolation. One has to simultaneously look at laws of matrimonial property, divorce and succession to ensure a gender just regime of laws.

Uniform law on marital property is needed on certain grounds:

* Reform must be sought in the commonly agreed areas that will benefit women. There is no law concerning the family which does not have a negative impact on women of all communities.
* The major gap in our laws is the absence of rights for women within a marriage in all-personal laws.
* This gap needs to be filled by law reform. A uniform law on marital property will go a long way in securing the rights of women.
* In any event, reform of marital property law and succession laws must be discussed simultaneously. Otherwise we will be left with an uncertain inheritance.

To attempt reform without considering the status of women of all communities is an exercise doomed to failure. What is needed is a national debate on the rights of all women and the movement towards a common gender justice for all women.[3]

The inequitable provisions in the Hindu Succession Act (HSA) have been discussed in the 174th Report of the Law Commission of India on "Property Rights of women". In 2000 Commission *suo moto* undertook the study of the Act to reduce ambiguities and inequalities in the inheritance/ succession processes. This was followed by recommendations to modify certain provisions.

The states of Andhra Pradesh, Tamil Nadu, Maharashtra and Karnataka have since then amended the provisions of HSA declaring the daughter to be a coparcener. Kerala has abolished the Joint Hindu family system. As a result, members of the family who are governed by *Miatakshara* law, irrespective of their sex, become tenets in common. In the remaining States daughters are excluded from ancestral property.

Eventually, the Law Commission recommended that daughters should be included as coparceners under section 6 of the HSA, 1956. They must have the same rights and liabilities as sons in a joint Hindu family governed by the *Mitakshara* law. Courts should not proceed against a son, grandson, or great grandson for the recovery of any debt due from on the ground of the pious obligation. When a male Hindu dies, devolution of property should be testamentary or interstate succession and not by survivorship.

PROJECTED BENEFITS AND PITFALLS

A share in the property will make the women's role in the family important. Admission into the coparcenary might even lead to her becoming the head of the family. Women's right to property will also help to diminish social evils like dowry.

Property rights for women must be for real and not notional. Passing the law is only the first step; compliance and enforcement will be the major challenges ahead. The main conflicts will emerge from reluctant male members of the parental family who will be unwilling to break the patriarchal monopoly.[4]

Bina Agarwal highlights three sources of gender inequality. For gender equality we need to bring all agricultural land on par with other property, abolish joint family property and partially restrict testamentary rights as elaborated below.

The Bill of 2004 will leave intact especially three major sources of gender inequalities in the HSA, stemming from

* Agricultural land;
* *Mitakshara* joint family property;

- Unrestricted rights to testation (i.e. to will away property).

THE AGRICULTURAL LAND

The HSA in Section 4(2) exempts significant interests in agricultural land. Broadly, states fall into three sections:

- In the southern and most of the central and eastern states the tenurial laws are silent on devolution so inheritance can be assumed to follow the 'personal law' which for Hindus is the HSA.
- In a few states the tenurial laws explicitly note that the HSA or the personal law will apply, but in the North-Western states of Haryana, Punjab, Himachal Pradesh, Delhi, Uttar Pradesh and Jammu and Kashmir, the tenurial laws not only specify the order of the devolution but they specify an order that is highly gender unequal.

Agricultural land is the most important form of rural property in India, and ensuring gender equal rights in it is important not only for gender justice but also for economic and social advancement. Gender equality in agricultural land can reduce not just a women's but her whole family's risk of poverty, increase her livelihood options, enhance prospects of child survival, education and health, reduce domestic violence and empower women.

The proposed 2004 Bill will enhance the share of daughters by making daughters coparceners on the same basis as sons in the *Mitakshara* coparcenary. But in doing so it will alter the shares of other class I female heirs of the deceased such as the deceased's mother and widow. The effect on the share of the widow will vary according to whether the state allows the wife to take a share on partition of joint family property.

The proposed Bill leaves untouched a person's unrestricted testamentary rights over his/her property. In principle this right is gender-neutral since both men and women enjoy it, but in practice (given male bias in Indian society) the provision can be used to disinherit female heirs.

Restricting testamentary rights say half or two-thirds of the property as found, in some other rural systems in India and elsewhere would be a step in the right direction. For instance, Islamic law limits testation to 1/3 of the property, and European countries, which follow the 'civil law' legal system, such as Germany, France, Spain and Italy, also partly restrict testamentary freedom.

The 2004 Bill is based on the recommendations of the Law Commission's 174th Report, 2000 and reproduces its shortcomings.[5]

SHOULD FAMILY LAW BE OR NOT TO BE WITHIN THE PURVIEW OF THE INDIAN CONSTITUTION

Article 44 of the Constitution, which directs the state to enact a uniform civil code for all citizens, has been both a perennial as well as a source of permanent embarrassment ever since the Constitution was adopted. Some are annoyed because the article is still in storage. Others are embarrassed because the article continues to exist. The individuals in the first category give supreme consideration to fundamental rights guaranteed to all citizens, particularly the right to equality before law and the right to life. The second group feels equally strong that the family law is or should be outside the purview of the Constitution. Somehow, the debate has contrived to hide a basic truth. A uniform civil code may, however, not solve all problems unless the UCC is made free of dependence upon religion and custom. There is a lobby of individuals who would like to please both sides. They want an optional UCC. By that some of them mean right to choose personal law or be automatically bound by UCC. This confusion inbuilt into the choice, particularly for nightmarish.[6]

FAMILY LAW AND ROLE OF CUSTOM

Religion and custom are not always distinguishable. Custom is even more amorphous and vague than religion. It is more localized; it is determined by small and local social groups and depends on memory for its formulation. The high tradition of religion is vitalized by little traditions of rituals, fasts, feasts and an intricate code of conduct. It includes rules for what to wear, eat or do, even who can greet whom and in what manner. The great and the little traditions together determine who can marry whom and by what rituals. This, the great tradition, lays down certain broad principles while the minutiae are generally determined by the little tradition. For example, the great tradition has banned marriage within the 'gotra' or 'sapinda', that is, between close relatives. But surely it is the little tradition in Punjab and Haryana that prescribes that a widow must marry her husband's younger brother or male cousin. It is the little tradition that forbids a marriage within the same village. Taken together the little and the great tradition dedicate the life of the community. They decide what acts shall be termed transgressions; what shall constitute evidence or proof and also decide punishments.

The great tradition throughout India specifies funeral rites including a community meal within certain days of a death. It is only a little tradition in Rajasthan which encourages marriages to be celebrated along with the funeral dinner, in order to save time, money and trouble. But the influence of non-formal legal system does not stop with the family law or social conduct. Neither religion nor custom has made or observed a clear distinction between civil or criminal law. They have determined the hold of the caste over India.

The British policy was to leave family law severely alone.

They only interfered in a limited and somewhat unplanned way with regard to Hindu personal law. Generally, this intervention was at the demand of the Hindu social reformers. The first intervention was the Sati regulation in 1829. Moreover, this intervention was extremely selective: for example, the Hindu widow remarriage act was introduced in 1858 but there was no provision for divorce. Here it must be said that the lower castes had always permitted divorce as well as remarriage for widows and divorcees. The Widow Remarriage Act was meaningful for upper caste Hindus. The Hindu Marriage Act introduced divorce for upper castes in 1955. If under the legal system the state interfered but little with Hindus personal law, after independence the situation was reversed. Between 1954 and 1958, Hindu family law was extensively codified and virtually replaced the *Shastras*, but not the custom. Even codified family law leaves enough space for intervention by the non-government actors in the shape of religion and custom.

It must be admitted that the Hindu Marriage Act 1955 (HMA) has revolutionized the law of marriage for Hindus. It has introduced monogamy. It has legalized inter-caste marriage. It has removed the bar on some *gotra* marriage — according to Hindu law a couple belonging to the same *gotra* could not marry. Most important of all, the Hindu Marriage Act has introduced divorce (for the upper castes, the lower castes already permitted it). By this single step, it has converted the sacrament of Hindu religion into a contract.

The HMA contains rules on whatever the lawmakers considered to be of vital importance. It lays down who can marry, and with whom. It prescribes the manner by which one can enter into a valid marriage and the conditions for a valid marriage. It provides that the groom must be over 21 years of age and the bride must have completed 18 years. Both must be of sound mind. They must not be prohibited degrees of relationship. They must be both Hindus. As to prohibited degrees of relationship the HMA specifies which relationships are taboo for persons aspiring to marry. The grounds for divorce are specified in detail. So too are situations in which a marriage may be void and others on which it is avoidable.

Paradoxically, on all these points the HMA leaves much to custom. It enumerates the conditions and then it allows them to be violated if there is an unbroken caste custom to the contrary. In this context, one may ask questions about the performing of marriage. How is it to be performed? The HMA does not make registration of marriage compulsory. There is no need to undergo a civil ceremony. The validity of marriage rests upon performing the necessary rites of marriage. But these rites are also not prescribed. Presumably, to escape imposing the Brahmin rites on non-Brahmins, of '*La-jahom*' and '*Saptapadi*' or the rituals according to their own unbroken caste custom. Similarly, divorce can be through law or it can be by caste custom. But caste custom is not always easy to explain. Indeed, it can often create problems. [7]

Certain kinds of prohibited relationships have been left to the caste custom. For example, in Tamil Nadu custom permits a man to marry his sister's daughter. In Karnataka cross-cousin marriages are permitted. In the Punjab and Haryana a widow is not to remarry anybody other than her dead husband's younger brother.

All these marriages are recognized by the HMA on the grounds of there being an unbroken caste custom to support them. As with marriage, HMA allows the divorce through caste panchayats as well as through courts. This is natural as prior to the HMA divorce was regulated only by custom. It dealt with procedure and also the essential substantive law, namely the grounds of divorce.

WOMEN'S RIGHTS: LACK OF AWARENESS

The Hindu code Bill of 1955-1956 gave the Hindu girls the right to inherit the paternal property even after they got married. However, despite this, numerous women, all over India, willingly sign away this right after they get married in order to appear in their brother's eyes as good loving sisters. The act happens by choice, though there are no doubt cultural pressures that promote this particular decision. This is a peculiar anomaly that marks the lives of many women in India—women who in every other way are politically conscious, socially active citizens of the nation. Women's decision to give up their property rights implied that they are locked in a patriarchal system where they "maximized their short-term priorities at the cost of undermining their long term material interests and feelings of love and loyalty towards parents and the natal family were enacted in ways that bolstered male privilege."[8]

CONCLUSION

In Hindu society there are many personal laws. Therefore, what is required is not only the formulation of these laws but also creation of awareness on their utility and usefulness for one and all.

NOTES

1. Agnes, Flavia (2003) "Hindu Women And Marriage Law-Severing the Sacred Tie", *Women and Law In India*, Oxford University, New Delhi, p. 99.
2. www.familylaw.htm.
3. Jaisingh, Indira (February 2005), "An Uncertain Inheritance –A critique of the Hindu Succession (Amendment) Bill" in *Lawyers Collective*, vol. 20, No. 2. All India Reporter Private Ltd, Nagpur, pp. 8-10.

4. Sharma, Betwa (February 2005), "Hindu Women's rights (or the lack of them) in ancestral property", in *Lawyers Collective*, vol. 20, No. 2, All India Reporter Private Ltd, Nagpur, pp. 14, 15.

5. Agarwal, Beena (February 2005), "Far From Gender Equality "in *Lawyers Collective*, vol. 20, No. 2, All India Reporter Private Ltd, Nagpur, pp. 16-18.

6. Dhagamwar, Vasudha, (April 2003), "Invasion of Criminal Law by Religion, Custom and Family Law", *Economic and Political Weekly*, Sameeksha Trust Publication, Mumbai, pp. 1483.

7. Dhagamwar, Vasudha, (April 2003), "Invasion of Criminal Law by Religion, Custom and Family Law", *Economic and Political Weekly*, Mumbai, pp. 1484-1486.

8. Mujumdar, Rochona (May 2003), "History of Women's Rights: A Non-Historicist Reading" in *Economic and Political Weekly*, pp. 2130-32.

5

HINDUTVA IDEOLOGY AND UNIFORM CIVIL CODE (UCC)

I

MISINTERPRETATION OF HINDUISM

Hinduism is a distinct philosophy rather than a religion. As such, it has its own distinct set of values and culture. Today, with rising communal conflicts, the philosophic and religious doctrines of Hindu *Dharma* have been communalized and taken over, in a big way, by the Hindutva ideology which, in many ways, has distorted Hinduism as a whole. This has led to the debasement of even certain dynamic aspects of Hindu tradition, values and the whole way of life and living of people affecting their everyday lived reality.

Essentially, Hindu *Dharma* with its spiritual dynamism preaches love, compassion, *ahimsa*, peace and tolerance. However, the Hindutva forces politicised Hindu *Dharma*. It has communalized the mainstream politics in the country. This has led to the emergence of various Hindu revivalist and supremacist forces proclaiming the hegemony of Hinduism over other religions and belief systems. They are trying to frame a monolithic structure or blueprint upon India in the name of cultural nationalism.

Communal political parties like the BJP adhering to the Hindutva ideology are influencing and directing the mode and content of human relationships as in the case of family or personal laws. Their ideological interference has and continues to have immense impact on the issue of Uniform Civil Code (UCC). Shah Bano case is an illustration of this controversy — the product of Hindutva ideological politics as well as the interference of Muslim fundamentalism. Basically, Shah Bano case was the struggle of a Muslim woman to achieve her rights. In this incident, UCC got various dimensions like the emergence of identity politics.

Hindu and Muslim fundamentalists are misusing religion as a weapon against women. In the nineteen-nineties, the Sangh parivar or BJP misused various religious symbols like *Mandir* and *Trishul,* etc to provoke communal conflict in the name of nationalism. In the name of religion, vile propaganda was made slowly across the country, which helped creation of communal atmosphere. After the demolition of Babri Masjid, this feeling became stronger. This incident also gave rise to the question of Muslim identity in India. The Muslim community underwent the feelings of anxiety and insecurity. In this political atmosphere the Hindutva forces presented UCC from its own blinkered position distorting an objective understanding of the issue.

II

HINDUTVA AS RELIGIOUS FANATICISM

Hinduism has been horribly degraded in recent years by the so-called Ram Bhaktas. For their vested interests they grossly misused and abused Hindu religious sentiments. Hindutva is an anti-Hinduism concept, which is regarded by Swami Agnivesh as 'pseudo-Hinduism'.[1] Hindutva is Hinduism's internal enemy because Hindu fundamentalists use this term and do nothing but spread virus that can infect and harm.

The Hindutva forces hijacked the eternal values/spirit of Hindu *Dharma.* Romila Thaper in her analysis posits "the new Hinduism which is propagated by the RSS is an attempt to restructure the indigenous religions as a monolithic uniform religion, rather paralleling some of the features of Semitic religions. This seems to be a fundamental departure from the essentials of what may be called the indigenous 'Hindu' religions. Its form is not only in many ways alien to the earlier culture of India but equally disturbing is the uniformity which it seeks to impose on the diversity of 'Hindu' religions." Thaper calls the Hinduism, currently being propagated by Sangh Parivar as 'Syndicated Hinduism'. This projection is made by the social base of the Sangh Parivar, a powerful urban middle class with a reach towards the rural rich who find it useful to bring into politics, a uniform, monolithic Hinduism created to serve its new requirements.[2]

EMERGENCE OF 'HINDUTVA'

The origin of the expression 'Hindutva' is to be traced to the political ideas and concepts of Vinayak Damodar Savarkar. It was Savarkar who first introduced and defined 'Hindutva'.

'Hindutva' rests on three pillars: 'geographical unity, racial features and common culture'. The concept of Hindutva comes in succession on the construction of Brahmanism as Hinduism. This Brahmanical Hinduism forms the base of Hindutva politics. Savarkar began to articulate the ideology of Hindu elite (Zamindars, Brahmins, Kings). By integrating Brahmanical Hinduism with nationalism, calling it Hindutva, which further showed the way for building the Hindu Rashtra. His key sentence was "Hinduise all politics and militarise all Hindudom".[3]

Hindutva also has the merit at another level. It excludes the 'others' – all who are not Hindus. The Hindus are projected to be a homogenous Hindu mass, in which it has an 'assigned' *Dharma* to which it has to stick for the harmonious society to flower. The concept of homogenous and harmonious is propagated by the upholders of the status quo, and by those who are beneficiaries in the present power equations. It is proclaimed, ours is a casteless society, the caste politics is divisive, we should overcome (the lower castes) psychology. The woman is given the 'respectable' place—she is 'mother, 'sister', 'wife' and 'daughter'. These relations, which are patriarchs order, exploit women to the hilt.[4]

HINDUTVA IDEOLOGY AND POLITICS

Hindutva ideology is a highly organised and institutionalised political formation rather than a concept. It operates all over India by different names. The RSS is its origin. Its ideology begins with Savarkar's definition of 'Hindu'. Savarkar's book *Who is a Hindu?* is the foundational text for the Hindutva ideology. He asserted that India is a land of Hindu culture; it belongs only to those who see her as Holy Land of our ancestors and lands of our action. It was *punyabhoomi* which signified that one's sacred sites must be located within the territorial boundaries of India. By that definition, Muslims and Christians get excluded from belonging to it since their sacred sites also lay outside these confines. They were now defined as exiles in their own country, as non-Indians and as anti-nationals.[5] M. S. Golwalkar, the second major ideologue of the RSS, would say in the late thirties that "Hindus should treat the Indian minorities the way Hitler treated the Jews." Savarkar's concepts were further redefined and given parallel projection by Golwalkar with ideology based on Brahmanical Hinduism. He aspired for the formation of Hindu Rashtra. (Pannikar) Hindutva ideology is propagating hatred against other faiths. This ideological view strands in their message that India is the land of Hindus, and Hindu culture is the essential core of Indian civilization and second whatever lies outside the Hindu community is, therefore, not authentically Indian. All other non-Hindu cultural and religious traditions are either extraneous or they are dangerous and alien. So the violent and aggressive propagation of otherness is the essential hallmark of Hindutva.[6]

The Hindutvavadi presents nationalism as to replace the definition of India from a secular, multicultural nation state to a Hindu one—that is, Hindu Rashtra. That is the intention and self-image of the brigade. In order to attain such a nation, they rely on systematic aggression against people of other faiths to drive home the message that as non-Hindus they have neither secure place nor any claim within this country. They also claim that religious identity is the only one that matters. This denotes hatred of all other religious identities.[7]

As a result, we see religious identity used in the form of communalism almost everywhere these days. Political parties organised around communal ideologies and their programmes around communal goals. For instance, the Muslim League during the pre-independence period had an Islamic State as its goal. The Hindu Mahasabha during the same period worked for a Hindu Rashtra. On the basis of these religiously defined goals they mobilised their supporters. In contemporary India, the best example of this political formation is the BJP whose main plank is Hindu nationalism— 'Hindutva'.

During the freedom struggle the RSS's slogans '*Hindu-Hindi-Hindustan*' and '*Hindu Raj amar rahe*' resounded on the streets even before the Muslim League accepted the slogan of Pakistan. Many of the inflammatory slogans adopted by the Sangh Parivar (a unit of RSS) during the Ayodhya mobilisation ('*Agar Hindustan mein rehna hoga to...*' "*Mussalman ke bus do Sthan....*") show the direct influence of

that ideology. They explicitly make their political programme around a communal goal geared to the creation of
Hindu identity and Hindu consolidation. This aim is expressed in all that they do, beginning with the choice of the
colour of their flag to the distribution of trishul to Ramshila
puja, to Advani's Rathyatra and to instigation of riots.
Otherness factor constantly stands in their ideology and
they use this weapon very sharply.

HINDUTVA AND HATE-PROPAGANDA

Hindutva ideology has been shaped through a campaign of
propaganda and indoctrination with the Hindutvavadis
mobilising Hindus on the basis of religious sentiments and
emotions. The Shah Bano Case and the Babri Masjid controversy gave these forces the pretext to destroy secular and
democratic set up of India. During the period of Ratha Yatra
the use of slogans like '*Garva se Kaho Hum Hindu Hain*'
and the one of Lord Rama with an aggressive posture were
used with effect not only to mobilize Hindus but also to in-
timidate the minorities. So these communal forces have been
cleverly using the symbols and imageries to polarize the
communities and one recalls its culmination in the post-Rath
Yatra communal violence and demolition of Babri Masjid
and horrific riots in Mumbai and various parts in India.
(RAM).

After that, Gujarat carnage is a very important example
of the creation of this type of communally charged atmosphere. Initially, RSS declared its primary agenda to create
Hindu-Hindutva-Hindustan (Hindu-Hinduism-Hindustan)
in real sense of the terms. This agenda nurtured by their
various wings like Bhartiya Janata Party (BJP), the political
wing; Vishwa Hindu Parishad (VHP), an outfit for popular-
ising and guarding Hinduism; Bajrang Dal, a militant youth
organisation; and Durga Vahini, an all women militant out-

fit. The anti-Muslim (vile) propaganda was always spread by them. They openly say, 'Gujarat is the laboratory for a Hindu Rashtra (Hindu nation)'. This was the main reason why Gujarat faced such a terrible situation.[8]

The Hindutva forces' major points for propaganda against Muslims have been:

- They (the Muslims) are responsible for dividing India.
- They tend to be loyal to Pakistan rather than to India and also harbour an anti–India feeling. As such their patriotism is highly questionable.
- They, as a people, have invaded India and destroyed our culture.
- They want to increase their population and can do so because they keep four wives. They also resort to conversion to achieve this.
- Major political party of India, Congress, appeases them.
- They are involved in smuggling, bootlegging and other illegal activities.
- Islam is a highly militant religion. It has been spread at the point of sword.
- They are violent by nature because they slaughter animals and eat meat.

This propaganda has given the backdrop to enhanced communal mindset in Gujarat. Much time has elapsed but the agenda of spreading hatred is not stopped. The coming to power of BJP in 2003 Madhya Pradesh has introduced Hindutva in its full aggressive mode. They tried to introduce another laboratory of Hindutva and Bajarang Dal organised the function of Trishul Diksha under the leadership of Pravin Togadia of Vishwa Hindu Parishad. In the function, it was stated that all efforts would be made to make the Hindu Rashtra. Trishul Diksha has been devised by VHP as a mechanism to use religious and cultural symbols for political mobilisation of people.

The intense violence in Gujarat was preceded by the period of BJP rule in the state where the VHP and the Vanvasi Kalyan Aashram had a free run and the manipulation of the issue of conversion and terrorism and the culmination of this into the violence and latter ghettoisation, has become a 'model' pattern of Hindutva politics. BJP had tried to apply this phenomenon in Madhya Pradesh. They had provided certain strategies. First the government went on to ensure that 'Vande Mataram' was brought in, in offices and at schools. The activities of Vanvasi Kalyan Ashram were stepped up in the Adivasi areas. With the Trishul Diksha, the intensity of communal polarisation went up tremendously.

The issue is not just of the insecurity of minority; the issue is of violation of basic democratic norms of society. Under the name of Hindu religion, they make violent propaganda and intensify the polarisation of the communities. This shows that even when there is a secular government at the centre, such type of activities in the name of Hindutva are openly carried on in the BJP ruled states like Madhya Pradesh.[9]

III

HINDU-MUSLIM CONFLICT : ORIGIN AND CONSEQUENCES

During the colonial period various questions were raised like share in power, share in jobs, etc. In the monarchical pattern, the rules made by the king were important. Caste and religion were important before British came. But after the advent of the British rule there arose an umbrella identity. In 1881 census, the British created religious identity. In the later 19th century, linguistic communalism also emerged in some parts of the country—in North India, for instance—

for separate identities. The difference between the Devnagari script and the Urdu script was deliberately used by communal forces for this purpose. The Nagari Pracharani Sabha began to Sanskritize modern Hindi while Urdu was heavily Persianized to break up a shared use of a common language. This communal separation of language use was an indication of the larger communal ambition that religious difference must encompass all aspects of life. The message was clear: nothing is to be held in common territory—not even a common nation state.[10]

There were linguistic conflicts even after partition for a few years. Religious identity came in the forefront in a big way in 1960's. Indira Gandhi talked about secularism in the religious identity background. It was in communally surcharged atmosphere that the then Jana Sangh passed a resolution, in its Patna session of December 1969, on 'Indianisation of Muslim' which further stated the otherness attitude towards Muslims. In 1970's confrontation between the two communities arose and the emergency was declared. The BJP adopted the mask of secularism about this time to get votes but in 1984 they lost the Parliamentary elections. With this setback they started espousing the strategy of the so-called appeasement of the Muslims.

After the nineteen-eighties the country was engulfed in communal fore. Varanasi, Jamshedpur, and Moradabad, Bihar Sharif were affected, followed by anti-Sikh riots. The Muslim community were under a sort siege about this time and it dropped out of the mainstream. The Khalistan movement asserted itself and caused a lot of chaos and confusion. BJP gave their slogan that Hindu was being overshadowed by Muslims. Entire atmosphere was communalised. The Bofors issue also arose about this time. The Muslim middle-class got weakened and many unpleasant things, like politicization of the Shah Bano case happened. As Judge

Kuldip Singh gave the verdict that Islam oppressed women and did not treat them with dignity, Muslim fundamentalists felt outraged and declared that Islam was in danger and they would lose their identity. After sometime, the Babri Masjid demolition took place, increasing their feelings of fear and insecurity.

The Shah Bano controversy was exploited by the Hindu right wing parties and pressed their claims on the disputed Babri Masjid in Ayodhya. They launched their attack on India's cultural pluralistic ethos and the secular view embodied in the Constitution. They asked for UCC, giving a new dimension to national integration and launched the Hindutva ideology of one language, one law and one country. these communal forces held that because of separate Muslim identity national integration was under threat. They singled out Muslims, especially women, against oppression of Muslim fundamentalists.

POLITICS AND UCC IN THE 1980S

The BJP, the RSS, the VHP, commonly known as the Sangh Parivar, began agitating for a Hindu Rashtra, in opposition to India's secular ethos. According to their Hindutva ideology, Hindu values and customs would reign supreme in national politics and minorities would only be respected if they conform to the norms of the Hindu majority.

Since nineteen-eighties the Sangh Parivar has constantly kept in view one symbol or the other to ensure that Ayodhya remained in focus and the Hindus remained mobilised. The state helped them by permitting to worship at Ayodhya.

The same was the case with the fundamentalist Muslims. They, too, kept their Muslim followers mobilised. Take the Shah Bano case. The court gave maintenance allowances to Shah Bano. The Muslim fundamentalists expressed outrage at the Court's decision and it's disparaging comments about Muslim law. Prime Minister Rajiv Gandhi succumbed to their pressure and overturned the Supreme Court decision through an Act passed by the Parliament which greatly restricted the rights of Muslim Women.

Thus the State strengthened both Muslim and Hindu identity. In the 1950s the State strengthened community identities by refusing to pass a Uniform Civil Code. In the 1980s it strengthened Muslim fundamentalism and Hindu Communalism by making concessions to Muslim groups around the Shah Bano issue and to Hindu groups by permitting them to worship at Ayodhya.

Let us examine the issues at hand a little carefully. Take the Shah Bano Case. The court verdict was criticized and was resented by the 'ulemas' who observed that the judgement as an attempt to undermine the Shariat. Their reaction was most pronounced in opposing the reference to Article 44 of the Constitution, which provides that "The State shall endeavour to secure for citizens a Uniform civil code". Indeed, by bringing this in the judgement broadened the scope of the debate from an interpretation of a precise point of law to a general consideration of the validity of Muslim Personal law. This was, they said, an infringement of the 'covenant' of composite nationalism and secularism that bound different communities together in India. The Jamiat al-ulema made the whole thing crystal-clear: "the demand for UCC tantamounts to a fundamental departure from the position that in the present day situation where the Muslim community is deeply entangled in a struggle for the search and safeguard of its self-identity, it is only the personal law that can be a paramount grantee for its preservation.

Thus, the controversy moved out of the law courts into public arena where the much larger issue of minority identity was raised for rallying Muslims on a united platform.

There was no dearth of people opposing them. In consequence, the issue of women rights turned into a major confrontation between the majority and minority communities. Opposition to the judgment was abetted by the strident support the judgment got from Hindu organisations. They signalled a new positioning of reform vis-à-vis the State and the Muslim community. Singling out Muslim women as the group most oppressed by religion contributed to a powerful critique of Muslims as backward and obscurantist, and of the State as one that not only countenanced this but also perpetuated it through protection and 'appeasement'.

All in all, the Shah Bano judgment created a communal controversy and an opportunity for the Hindu Right organisations to press their claims on the disputed Babri Mosque site in Ayodhya and launch their attack on cultural pluralism and the secular view embodied in the protection of minority rights, arguing that such pluralism and cultural distinctiveness was harmful for national integrity. (Communalism, State policy, and the Question of women's rights in contemporary India, by Zoya Hasan)

Many of the movements following from this phenomenon impinge not just on the areas of marriage, divorce, inheritance, sexuality and reproductive rights, but also define the place of women and assign them a certain status within the community. These roles cannot be understood without recognizing the link between gender relations and State policy (which has a major role to play at different levels of society), the ways in which the State accords to women an unequal status in relation to men, and the contradictory notions of equality and citizenship practiced by the State and by communal and fundamentalists groups. But after the Babri Masjid demolition the renewed growth of communal politics and the sharpening of religious identities have instead of clearing things, confused them badly. As a result, we find not only noticeable subordination of gender loyalties but a rise in the politics of religious self-assertion, claiming to speak in the name of majority and minority rights and seeking to negate and suppress divergent interests and rights of individuals and social groups. The vested interest play a key part in legitimising gender differences embodied in traditional attitudes and perspective of family and gender relations.[12]

POLITICS OF THE BJP

In their manifesto of 2004 elections the BJP has demanded UCC on the ground of gender equality. It stands for consensus over uniform civil code stating forcefully that all laws, including personal laws, must be in accordance with the guarantees available to all citizens under the Indian Constitution. The Constitution, the party observed, calls for enactment of a Uniform Civil Code. The Supreme Court has reiterated this need. Therefore, this couldn't be seen as an issue of any single party. It should be implemented with social and political consensus.

Other point BJP reaffirms is its commitment to the construction of a Ram temple in Ayodhya. That is what they profess. But what they do is totally opposite to it. To find more political space, they play Hindu card. They promote Hindutva ideology. They have their strategy of otherness against minority community.[13]

Their Ram Temple movement is a case in point. It gives lie to their claim that they stand for national consensus and national unity. Also it exposes them.

The BJP's earlier manifestoes always included the issue of the review of the Indian Constitution. Later they took it on the national agenda in alliance with other parties. This agenda betrayed the intolerance of Hindutva forces. They took many such other measures. One fine morning Prime

Minister Vajpayee asserted that 'the reconstruction of the Ram Mandir was an expression of national sentiments'. The debate on this dubious statement brought out the hypocritical commitment of the BJP to keep Hindutva agenda out of the government's ambit! Also the 'liberal' mask of Vajpayee was exposed. The Ayodhya issue also showed his Government's designs when it offered legitimacy to the *Shiladaan* program sponsored by the VHP and the Ramjanmabhoomi Nyas even as the matter was pending before the Supreme Court. Along with this the Bajrang Dal also took up various activities like Pravin Togadia's major campaign to distribute trishuls along with his hate speeches on the political necessity of exterminating Muslims. During this period non-stop persecution of Muslims in Gujarat took place.[14]

BJP'S GENDER PERSPECTIVE?

The BJP's philosophy of working for their religion is understandable but not their programme of hatred of the 'Other' and 'pandering to minorities'. Also their programme to reassert the traditional role of women in the family, and thus seeking to turn the clock back on much of progress that women in India have made in last two decades is not intelligible.

They do it cunningly. They speak the language of equality. What sort of equality? Giving them opportunities to go to the position they once enjoyed in the so-called glorious-ancient period. "Men and women are equal", they say, but they are not the same and in this logic then in fact talking that the reinforced sexiest stereotypes. For example the BJP support policies that emphasise women's roles as mothers and wives (maternal health care), while rejecting policies that go too far beyond these traditional roles for women (compensation for housework). (WAF articles on women and Hindutva—*Journal*, no. 5, pp. 42-43)

The approach of BJP towards most of the things is based on the Hindutva ideology. Community and gender, or more specifically, religion, and equality are often seen as conflicting and oppositional. The cases of Shah Bano and Roop Kanwar are good examples to prove the point. It is only through the deconstruction of oppositions—between religion and equality, between community and gender—that we can begin to understand the impact of the discursive struggles on women. We will attempt to illustrate the ways in which the discourses of religion and equality, and of community and gender are mutually constituting in the Hindutva discursive strategy, i.e., women are constituted in and through communal identity, and conversely, community is constituted in and through women's gender identity.

In the context of gender equality, the protectionist approach has been and continues to be dominant. The approach reflects patriarchal and familial discourses, in which women have traditionally been constituted as different and weak. As wives and mothers, they are inferior and subordinate. Sometime we hear liberal discourses here and there which show women as equal to men. But, despite that, the patriarchal discourse remains powerful, and continues to influence the political and legal claims of women to equality.

Very clearly, the BJP supports women in their traditional family roles. As such, their approach to women's equality remains elusive. They seem to appeal to a formal approach to equality, coupled with a protectionist approach to difference, infused with religious and patriarchal discourses that ensure that women do not have to be treated the same as men.

Seen from a closer point, the power to define gender difference is crucial in both the approaches. This definitional power, while relying on a multiplicity of non-legal discourses, also resides in law, that is, law has the power to decide which gender differences are relevant in which context. Legal discourses both reflect and reconstitute particular understandings of gender difference. Within the framework of Hindu communal discourse the aim is to deploy this definitional power to reconstitute a traditional and patriarchal understanding of gender difference, and of identity for women.

Also, when the BJP argues that all women must be treated equally, they mean that Muslim women should be treated the same as Hindu women. In this respect, their approach to equality corresponds to their approach to secularism. Any recognition of difference between the women in different religious communities is seen by them to constitute a violation of secularism and the constitutional guarantees of equality. We can thus begin to see a second paradox in the way in which the concept of equality is used in Hindu communalist discourse. Their discourse of equality in the context of all women is deployed to undermine the identity of minority religious communities. Treating the Muslim community equally means treating them like the Hindu community, which means, in effect, subordinating Muslims to Hindu norms and practices.

These facts came to distinct light during the Shah Bano controversy. In the BJP's view, the Muslim Women's Protection Act violated both secularism and equality—secularism because the Muslim community was being treated differently and equality because Muslim women were being treated differently from Hindu women. The Shah Bano case and Muslim Women Protection Act are used to reinforce the image of the Muslim community as 'other'. And in doing so, the discourse of equality is, in effect, being used to undermine substantive equality, that is, real equality between women and men, and substantive secularism, as also respect and accommodation for minority communities.[15]

In Gujarat carnage Muslim women were used as a weapon against minorities. Human Right Watch report shows how the rise of the BJP in Gujarat has paralleled and even been attributed to the increasing activity of Hindu nationalist groups in this direction.

At various times, the BJP and after that their alliance partner leaders made statements that promote gender discrimination against women. For instance, Mridula Sinha, ex-president of BJP Mahila Morcha, in an interview in *Savy Magazine*, April 1994 said this[16]

- A woman should not work outside the home unless her family is economically deprived.
- I gave and received dowry.
- I oppose women's liberation, as it is another name for loose morals.
- We oppose equal 'rights' for both sexes.
- There is nothing wrong with domestic violence against women—very often it is the women's fault. We advise women to try and adjust, as her non-adjustability creates problem.
- Women's future lies in perpetuating the present because nowhere else are women 'worshipped' as they are in India.

Next, Vijayraje Scindia, one of the BJP's tall leaders at the time of Roop Kanwar Sati incident referred supported the event. She did not stop there. She also lent the support of religious scriptures to the obnoxious practice. She drew a highly questionable distinction between voluntary sati, to which she attributed a glorious tradition, and the coerced sati of recent times, which she considered immoral. She was evasive when asked how she would describe Roop Kanwar sati. It must have been wrong if in fact it had been coerced.

In other respects, too, she questioned the equality of sexes, women's primary duties as wives and mothers. Thus Hindutva forces use sati as a powerful national symbol, and even though it is banned in India, BJP leader Vijay Raje Sindia openly supported the sati of Roop Kanwar in Rajasthan.

The RSS approach towards the rights and dignity of women victims of violence, etc., is to fight a social attitude which victimizes the victim, blaming her, and not the perpetrators for the crime committed against her. Usha Tai Chati, the Pramukh Sanchalika of the women's wing of the RSS, when asked about the shocking increase in sexual crimes against women said, "The girls in the university are also responsible... They dress provocatively which invites teasing.... They deliberately don dresses to attract the boys... Mothers fail to educate their daughters."[17]

After the Gujarat carnage one Kausar Banu, was brutally raped and killed by the fanatic mobs. When the media highlighted the incident, Uma Bharti, the woman Minister of the NDA government asked in feigned disbelief, "Who is she whose stomach was slit and foetus taken out? No one has heard of this woman. She is a fiction created by media".[18] This stance throws light on insensitive communal mindset of these Hindutvavadis. Shockingly, George Fernandes, the then Defence Minister of India, had in a way justified Gujarat sexual assault against Muslim women in a debate in Parliament saying "This is nothing new, it has been happening in India for ages". This is enough to show how the Hindutvavadis treat the minorities both at the religious level as well as at the gender level.

CONCLUSION

After reviewing all the aspects of Hindutva ideology and its functional aspect, one thing is clear that its believers always demand UCC on their own ground which is communal in nature. They always strive to break the secular fabric of this country. In the name of ideology and nationalism they always play partisan politics. Even when they talk about the gender equality, they do not look into the issue of UCC in a proper perspective. Instead they try to widen the gap between the minority and majority communities. Their intense propaganda of Hindutva ideology worsens the situation still further. As if this was not enough, they misinterpret history and use women as a weapon to increase their social (communal) base. Their such short sighted, selfish endeavours create many problems for Muslim women. Worse, by making the UCC a majority and minority issue, they have turned the whole thing to an untiable knot, although the need of the hour is that it should be seen under the constitutional framework, that is by focusing on citizenship rights.

NOTES

1. Agnivesh, Swami (2005), *Hinduism In The New Age,* Hope India Publication, New Delhi, p. 105.
2. Ram, R P (1998), "Hindutva Offensive—Social Roots and Characterisation" in *Secular Challenge to Communal Politics,* Vikas Adyayan Kendra, Mumbai, pp. 92, 93.
3. *Ibid,* p. 96.
4. *Ibid,* p. 112.
5. Sarkar, Tanika et. al. (2005), *The Vedas, Hinduism, Hindutva,* Elbong Alap, Kolkata, p. 117.
6. *Ibid,* p. 107.
7. *Ibid,* p. 109.
8. Khan, Sophia (2003), "Gujarat : India's Laboratory Fascism" in Pendse Sandeep, ed., *Lessons from Gujarat,* Vikas Adyayan Kendra, pp. 47, 48.
9. Punyani, Ram, "Trident Shadows", *Indian Currents,* 25 September 2005, pp. 11-13.
10. Sarkar, Tanika et. al. (2005), *The Vedas, Hinduism, Hindutva,* Elbong Alap, Kolkata, pp. 112, 113.

11. Basu, Amrita, "Women and religious Nationalism in India- An Introduction", *The Bulletin of Concerned Asian Scholars*, vol. 25, No. 4, Oct –Dec. 1993, p. 4.

12. Hasan Zoya, "Communalism, State Policy, and the Question of Women's Rights in Contemporary India", *The Bulletin of Concerned Asian Scholars*, vol. 25, No. 4, Oct –Dec. 1993, p. 7-11.

13. Bhartiya Janata Party – Vision Document 2004, Press Release, March 31, 2004.

14. Basu, Nilopat, "Subversive Sangh", *Communal Combat*, September 2002, pp. 16-18.

15. Ratna Kapoor and Brenda Crossman, "Communalising gender" in Tanika Sarkar and Urvashi Butalia, ed, (1995), *Women and Hindu Rights,* Kali of Women, New Delhi, pp. 84-102.

16. Punyani, Ram (2003), "*Communal Politics : Facts Verses Myths"*, Sage Publication, pp. 222.

17. Karat, Brinda, (2005) "*Survival and Emancipation Notes From Indian Women's Struggle*", Three Essays Collective, New Delhi, p. 176.

18. Agnes, Flavia, "Gender and Community", *Communal Combat*, September 2002, p. 27.

6
WOMEN'S MOVEMENT AND UNIFORM CIVIL CODE

The issue of Uniform Civil Code and question of gender justice has been an important part of the agenda of the women's movement in the last century. The French revolution gave principle of liberty, equality and fraternity to the people. At the same time, the consciousness about women rights also began to arise. Naturally, women in India were also affected by these developments. As a result several women's organizations like the Women's Indian Association (WIA), the National Council for Women in India (NCWI) and the All India Women's Conference (AIWC) came up. These organizations, specially the AIWC, played a major role in articulating women's issues of which the following three issues were important:

(1) Participation of women in electoral politics,
(2) The Hindu Code Bill,
(3) Women's Subcommittee of the National Planning Committee.

The All-India Women Conference passed a resolution advocating the establishment of an unofficial committee in 1934 to investigate and reform Hindu law. The committee did a lot of useful work by collecting information on various problems and issues. Three years later, in 1937, the demand for Uniform Civil Code was raised for the first time in the All India Women's Conference with the objective to give equality and justice to women. The committee recommended a rationalisation of Hindu law to the Constituent Assembly established in 1945. In the Constituent Assembly the Uniform Civil Code became especially contentious as an instrument of national unity.

In 1947, the idea was seriously debated in the Assembly and a Committee formed for drafting fundamental rights held that the proposal for a UCC should be a part of the Directive Principles of the State Policy. Thus there came the Article 44 saying the objective of this law is to ensure that all human relationship and needs are not differentiated on the basis of religion. The framers of the Constitution adopted an insensitive stance and by leaving the nice thing there only. They included it in the Directive Principles of State Policy to be implemented, if the State desired, at a later date. Women were thus subjected to a grave injustice. Personal laws prevalent at the time of the British continued to remain in vogue— unchanged. In other words, this allowed personal laws to increase their hold upon communities.

Its some impact can be seen even in the women's movement demanding Uniform Civil Code. There are marks of cleavage reflecting divisions of caste, class and community within the movement. Even the appellation 'Indian' in the movement has come to be questioned, for it implies political and cultural singularity that obscures the movement's diversity, differences and conflicts. The problem is not simply one of disunities but rather has to do with intractable conflicts involving the word 'women' that derive from the central position of gender in postcolonial Indian culture and politics, indeed process of gender construction of identities, role in the historical formation of the Indian nation-state. But gender cannot be separated from other, conflicting political identities, all of which play a crucial role in the life of the nation.

Since 1930's the major agenda of the women's movement

had always been the discrimination against women in personal law. The women's movement had challenged discrimination at all levels be it in family, society or law. In 1990s when the Hindutva forces raised their heads high, issue was badly communalised. In the aftermath of the demolition of the Babri Masjid, when anti-minority (Muslim) hysteria became stronger, things got worsened. After that, when BJP government was formed in 1995, the whole issue was hijacked by Hindu fundamentalists in a big way. In the changed circumstances, the women's organisations did not talk about Uniform Civil Code on the basis of uniformity in all-personal laws but reframed the issue on the basis of gender justice. They argued that every personal law is discriminatory in some way or the other towards women and that problem has to be solved through reforms in personal laws.

Recently, the law Commission, India, has, mercifully, come to the help of the women organizations. The Commission has supported their viewpoint that the UCC should be based on gender justice. The DVCM Memorandum suggested that women of all communities should have equal property rights in inherited property and in the marital property acquired by spouses after marriage. It also urges that all marriages be registered and the gifts given on the occasion to the parties be recorded. It demands legal relief for those women who become victims of dowry harassment and other kinds of violence for being economically dependent and not having an option but to stay in the matrimonial home and suffer.

These are various provisions, recommendations and amenities recommended by pro-women organisations for gender equality. This is indeed a big leap from the struggles for women's suffrage in its early decades to the participation and leadership of women in freedom movements to end colonial rule to the struggle for social, economic and political equality in the present times.[1]

While the issue at hand has been well analysed by feminist scholars, it has been difficult to translate their insights into strategies on the ground. The class, caste and religious status of feminist leaders and their organizations caused confusion at various levels. The politics of difference could not be successfully negotiated and many groups retreated as the fundamentalists appropriated and distorted the very issues they had been raising. By early 1990s, Hindu fundamentalist groups became so powerful that they re-positioned this issue as one between the states and the religious and cultural exclusivity, and disloyalty of specific groups, posing a threat to the integrity of the nation. They reconstructed the Uniform Civil Code around a Hindu norm, chiefly based on the practices of a few upper caste and upper class Hindus, ignoring the great diversity of customary laws among them. They disregarded the fact that the Hindu Code itself had been reformed in a very reactionary fashion, in some instances restricting the advantages that women actually enjoyed under customary law in some instances.

The feminist groups did not know how to reconcile the notion of individual rights and equality of women with the notion of the rights of specific communities. An important lesson learnt from this experience, however, was that in a highly diverse society like India level of polarization along religious and ethnic lines, the concept of 'uniformity' was deeply problematic, specially if one did not want to contribute to the fundamentalists' agenda of creating a theocratic state. This realization led to the emergence of far more complex frameworks of positions among women groups where there was a high ranging from a common gender-just code to reforms from within communities to rejection of formal court procedures in favour of community-based arbitration forums.[2]

LEGAL STATUS OF WOMEN AND THE CONSTITUTION

Women have equality of status under the Indian Constitution. Still, there are anomalies in different laws. During the 25 years of the women's movement the government has amended several laws to benefit women — e.g. laws related to dowry, rape, cruelty, maintenance, prostitution and obscenity. India has ratified international conventions such as the Convention on the Elimination of Discrimination against Women (CEDAW) 1993. Family courts have been set up in some states and the judiciary has issued a series of progressive judgments in favour of women, including a recent judgment on sexual harassment at the workplace and on child custody.[3] The registration of marriage, some people believed, was "not practical in a vast country like India with its variety of customs, religions and level of literacy". The CEDAW has shown hollowness of this claim. Although not legally required, the CEDAW says marriage is registered under different procedures in different religions. For example, Hindu and Muslim couples are registered under the Hindu Marriage Act and Kazi Act, respectively (Marriage Registration, December 8, 2002).

Influenced by the work of the CEDAW and other organizations, the Government of India has declared that it would make an effort to regulate gender-biased customary practices "in conformity and with its policy of non-interference in the personal affairs of any community without its initiative and consent"[4]

This non-interference policy strengthens the personal laws of different communities which control matters such as inheritance, property rights, and adoption. For example, according to Hindu personal law, daughters are denied most of the important coparcenary property rights that are granted to sons; women's guardianship of their children is subordinate to that of men's; and wives cannot initiate adoption. These measures are opposed to the CEDAW proposals—equality before the law and equal access to administer property (Article 15), and requires steps to ensure equality in marriage and family relations (Article 16). Though the principal of women's equality has been recognised and respected in many of our laws affecting public life, the private life is thoroughly regulated according to patriarchal principles. Because of this contradiction it is not possible for women to exercise their public rights in a meaningful way.[5]

Also, the governmental efforts when made to reach the domain of Uniform Civil Code are many a time flawed in so much as to show that the Hindu law was being imposed in the name of a Uniform Code ignoring even the positive aspects of Personal Laws of other communities. Since 1980s, when the BJP began to demand a Uniform Civil Code, even the most progressive feminist groups have begun to suspect that the Hindu Code Bill could come in through the backdoor, passed off as a Uniform Civil Code the feminist politics seeks to eliminate discrimination.

COMMITTEE ON STATUS OF WOMEN IN INDIA ON INHERITANCE (1975)

The well wishers of the Indian women have come to the conclusion, after studying the women problems in all seriousness, and found that the question of inheritance of women is of paramount importance. The above mentioned committee also came to the same conclusion and it made many important recommendations on the subject in 1975 like: In order that a widow is not left completely destitute, the Indian Succession Act should incorporate restrictions on the right of testation, similar to that prevailing under Muslim Law; Legislative measures be taken to bring Christian women of Kerala under the Indian Succession Act; Indian Succession Act should be extended to Goa and Pondicherry respectively to undo the relegation of widows to fourth position in matters of succession and to undo the inferior position to which Christian women are relegated by not being considered as full owners of property; the right of succession to property by by birth should be abolished and the *Mitakshara* coparcenary should be converted into *Dayabhaga* (the retention of *Mitakshara* coparcenary perpetuates inequality between sons and daughters as only males can be coparceners, and inheritance is only through the male line); the exception provided in Section 4 (2) of the Hindu Succession Act relating to devolution of tenancies should be abolished (because it excluded devolution of tenancy rights under State Laws from the scope of the Act); the discrimination between married and unmarried daughters regarding right of inheritance of dwelling houses caused under Section 23 of the Hindu Succession Act should be removed; and the right of testation should be limited under the Hindu Succession Act, so that female heirs are not deprived of their inheritance; legal recognition should be given to the economic value of the contribution made by the wife through household work for purpose of determining ownership of matrimonial property; on divorce or separation, the wife should be entitled to at least one-third of the assets acquired at the time of and during the marriage.

AMENDMENTS RECOMMENDED BY THE NCW

The National Commission for Women has also made elaborate recommendations in this regard. Some important ones in this catalogue are as follows:

The Indian Succession Act 1925 Sections 15 and 16 should be amended, removing mandatory linkage of wife's domicile with that of the husband. Appointment of testamentary guardian should be the right of both the parents acting concurrently. Widow should be granted letter of administration to deal with the Estate of the deceased husband unless excluded by the Court for sufficient reasons (Section 219 (a)). Application made by the widow disposed of within a year (Section 218 (2).

HINDU SUCCESSION ACT, 1956 AND RECOMMENDATIONS BY NGOS FOR ITS AMENDMENTS

The Hindu Succession Act, 1956 provides for equal distribution of not only separate or self-acquired properties of the deceased male, but also of undivided interests in coparcenary property. Daughter of a coparcener in a Hindu joint family is governed by *Mitakshara* Law. She can be coparcener by birth in her own right in the same manner as a son; she has right of claim by survivorship as a son.

Right of any heir to claim partition of a dwelling house after settlement of widowed mother's rights.

Coparcenary is, clearly, a primary entitlement of males. The law, no doubt provides for equal division of the male coparcener's share between all heirs, male and female, on his death; but, the law puts the male heirs on a higher footing by providing that they shall inherit an additional independent share in coparcenary property over and above what they inherit equally with female heirs. Then, despite their entitlement to have a share, there is practice that female heirs are asked to relinquish their share by making relinquishment deeds under their signatures in the courts. If the intestate property includes a dwelling house, the female heirs have no right to partition until the male heirs choose to divide their respective shares. If a Hindu female dies intestate, her property belongs first to husband's heirs, then to husband's father's heirs and finally only to mother's heirs. Thus the intestates Hindu female property is kept within the husband's lien.

THE GOVERNMENT'S DECLARATIONS

While ratifying CEDAW (1993), The Government of India

made the following declarations and reservations:

On Articles 5(a) and 16(1) of the CEDAW, the Government of India declared that it shall abide by the provisions that eliminate all forms of discrimination against women in matters relating to UCC but in conformity with its policy of non-interference in the personal affairs of any community without its initiative and consent.

With regard to article 16(2) of the CEDAW, the Government declared that though in principle it fully supported the principle of compulsory registration of marriages, it was not practical in a vast country like India with its variety of customs, religions and level of literacy to have any uniform method of doing it.[6]

The declarations may sound innocently pious but they make no improvement in the matters relating to the UCC. They also, stand opposed to the constitution of provisions granting equality to males and females in life and telling the Government in clear terms that there was nothing which could "prevent the state from making any special provision for women and children."[7] In this regard, the following provisions are worth noticing:

- Equality before law (Article 14).
- Non-discrimination, *inter alia* on grounds of sex – specifically in the matter of gaining free access to places of public resort.
- They have authority to make special provisions for women (Article 15).
- Equality of opportunity in public employment (Article 16).
- Equal rights for men and women to adequate means of livelihood (Article 39(a)).
- State directing its public policy towards securing the health and strength of workers, men and women (Article39 (e) &(f)).

- Humane conditions of work and maternity relief for women (Article42).
- State endeavouring to establish a Uniform Civil Code (44).
- Fundamental duty of every citizen to renounce practices derogatory to the dignity of women (Article 51A (e)).[8]

TRANSFORMATION OF WOMEN'S MOVEMENT

An urge to remove gender inequality and 'empower' women have constituted the motive force for the 'feminist' movement.[9] The ideology is clearly reflected in their stand on the UCC issue. Unfortunately, however, the issue has been, as indicated above, communalised over the years by communal parties. The women's movement has not been able to check the rot. In the present confused state, the Indian feminists have got formed several different schools of which three are prominent. First, the Liberal school, which demands reforms in those aspects of the polity which affect women. The Second school, primarily of leftists, situates oppression of women within a holistic analysis of the general structures of oppression and calls for coming together of specific movements for social change in order to effect the revolutionary transformation of society. The Third school comprising radical feminists concentrates on defining the development of femininity and masculinity in society as fundamental polarities, and experiments with reclaiming traditional sources of women's strength, creativity, etc.

The Liberal school holds that the rights of individuals as traditionally understood in a liberal society should transcend gender differences. The law must be persuaded to apply these standards more rigorously in case of women. The liberal values must be revised to recognise gender as a source of social justice. Their main objective is to give women equal rights in real sense or special rights where the social situation so demanded. The radicals argue that liberal jurisprudence can make no impact on law's treatment of women so long as categories, such as crime or family law, and legal concepts such as provocation or marriage, embody male norms and fail to address women's experiences. Such legal categories and concepts must be transformed, they say, to address women's social position and experiences. They attack the liberal principles as neutrality of law, equality and individual autonomy for their 'patriarchal' roots.[10]

Other schools, though differ from one another, all advocate gender justice. Women should get, they say, freedom and justice to live a meaningful life. They all believe that the continuance of various personal laws that accept discrimination between men and women violate the fundamental rights. Interestingly, the Committee on the Status of the women, 1974 also thought in the same vein.[11]

SHAH BANO CASE AND ROLE OF WOMEN'S MOVEMENT

Some Supreme Court judgements have also played a very significant role in giving due space to the women. Initially the judgements were favourable to the women's causes. Later it took a communal tone. The Supreme Court called for Uniform Civil Code in 1985. Shah Bano, a divorced Muslim woman got maintenance from her husband as a right under Section 125, Cr. P.C. against the Muslim personal law. There was much noise on this count as a result of which the issue got communalised. The violation of Muslim personal law became a rallying point for different Muslim interests. They made a huge protest against interference in their lives. The Hindu Communalists and even some feminists denounced the Muslim reaction and argued, by implication, that Muslim law was especially harsh on women. They, the courts and the state, should protect the oppressed Muslim women. They supported Uniform Civil Code which, they thought was necessary to promote unity and uniformity among the essary to promote unity and uniformity among the people. Others have argued that the way to rescue the agenda for women's rights is to focus on gender equality, rather than personal laws as such (Indira Jaisingh, *The Lawyers*, 1986). Many people have argued in favour of a common code provided that its framing involves human rights and women's groups and it is kept away from the 'vortex of patriarchal and communal formulation of the issue' (Mukhopadyay 1998:11)[12]

After Shah Bano Case, the women's movement was constrained to address, for the first time, the complexities of the demand for UCC. The political sub-text beneath the apparent gender concerns, the activists believed, warranted a more complex framework. While gender equality continued to be the desired goal, the demand had to be reformulated within the context of cultural diversity and rights of marginalize sections.

In 1993, for instance, at the Northern Region Nari Mukti Sangharsh Sammelan (Women's the Liberation Struggle Conference) held in Kanpur, two resolutions were raised one calling for UCC and the other for a rethinking of the notion of uniformity, keeping in mind the use of the demand for a UCC by the right-wing forces of the majority community. At the Fifth National Conference of Women's Studies held in Jaipur in1995, what emerged was a broad range of positions, from the reassertion of the demand for UCC to outright rejection of such a move and calling instead for reforms within personal law.[13]

Meantime, the Supreme Court once again suggested going to the UCC in the Sarla Mudgal Case, 1995. The Case related to Hindu men converting themselves to Islam to commit polygamy. The Judgement invalidated such polygamous marriages and invoked the need for a Uniform Civil Code to plug such loopholes, contributing the belief that the provision for polygamy in Muslim Personal law constituted a male

privilege and victimised Muslim women. The decision, intriguingly, obscured loopholes in Hindu law and courtroom
practices that systematically condoned Hindu Polygamy. (4.3
percent; Agnes, 1995)[14]

The BJP's approach to the problem, however, ruined the
chances, as indicated above, of going in favour of Uniform
Civil Code. Muslims feared, and not for nothing, that the
vested interest wanted to impose a Hindu Code I the guise of
a Uniform Civil Code. The women's movement, as noted
above, is too divided to adopt any forceful agenda for reform
of family laws. That is why, of late, the movement's focus has
shifted from demanding legislation on the present issue to increasing women participation in the processes of the state, to
legislative and political decision making outfits.[15]

UCC AND POLITICS

Because of political muddle, many a people have begun to
look suspiciously on the UCC. According to Flavia Agnes,
"Gender is not a neutral terrain. Issues of gender are deeply
entrenched within politics: be it the discourse on sati in the
last century or the debate about the rights of Muslim women
in post-independent India. Whether in colonial times or now,
the cultural practices of the subordinate race/community are
often subject to criticism and ridicule. And the question of reforms usually gets articulated as a kind of civilising mission.
One notices, this trend has been clearly visible in the post-
Shah Bano phase where an aggressive Hindu right wing political party has begun to defend the rights of minority
women. Clearly, such a concern never gets in the context of
communal violence, for instance, where sexual violation of
minority women is routinely ignored". Agnes opposes UCC.
And so do many others in the women's movement. They
rather work on the question of safeguarding women's rights
within diverse magic wand laws. But that is a pretty complex

issue which has to be constantly negotiated.[16]

Brinda Karat of the All India Democratic Women's Association believes that the uniformity should not be viewed narrowly—'from a single perspective'. Those who purpose, uniformity of personal laws, she says, speak from the perspective of uniformity "between communities, not within communities." This is because "they ignore the equality aspect, and look at the issue from the position of men in different communities rather than as an issue of equality between men and women." The issue of personal law is an issue of unequal laws within communities, and between men and women, she notes.

According to Indira Jaisingh, there exists what can be called a "gender plus" formula, which is repeatedly applied to subvert the Constitutional guarantee of equality. In almost all domains, public and private, women are subjected to injustice and inequality on the basis of their gender. But insofar as personal law is concerned, it is gender plus religion and culture. Further, she says, there is no use talking about a common civil code or a uniform civil code with no understanding of equality or gender justice. "Unless we get things sorted out there is no point in talking about uniform civil code or personal law reform, these are only routes to equality, and which route you adopt depends on the needs of the community". The state and its institutions lack a vision of equality or of gender justice, and there is no political will to address the problems of women, she asserts. There is only one common civil code in operation, "common code of inequality", she adds.

Jurist Fali S. Nariman's prognosis is equally bleak. He says it is our 'thinking' that needs re-orientation. "Men in India still treat women as chattel like they did 200 years ago. They do not think of them as individual human beings who are entitled to consideration separate from their husbands."

Nariman sees no way out of this except women fighting and building a consensus "within their own communities, especially in the atmosphere of intolerance; any other way would super-charge the atmosphere. The imposition of a common code would be oppressive, for the majority may want to have its own view." The best thing is, says feminist academic Kumkum Sangari, "to leave personal laws as they are, let them reform or change at their own pace, but make a provision for women to opt for a common civil code. There are issues such as dowry and domestic violence, which not long ago were accepted as traditional or customary practice, but which are today governed by secular law", she adds.[17]

CONCLUSION

To sum up, the purpose of UCC is very clear. Article 44 enjoins the state to endeavour to secure for its citizens a uniform civil code throughout the territory of India. But the issue having religious background the communal forces not only confuse things but create serious problems of various types whenever any attempt is made to do something about it. The foregoing discussion says this clearly. Initially, the demand of UCC was aired by the women's movement. But the movement always fought for women rights rather than the uniformity in personal laws of different communities. But as time went by even the women's movement got divided on ideological bases but mercifully, their goal remained the same, that is to protect women rights on the basis of equality. The feminist element that got hold of the movement after some time gave a clear-cut dimension to the problem that it will not be discussed on the communal grounds, but since all women are equal, they must be provided equal rights.Now almost every right thinking person has begun to appreciate that the issue of UCC must be based primarily on justice for and security to women.

NOTES

1. Singh, Kirti, *Violence against Women and Indian Law*, pp. 146.
2. Dhanraj, Deepa, Geeta Misra and Sarilatha Batliwala, A South Asian Perspective, Occasional paper no. 2, October 2002. ﹀
3. See http://www.wcd.nic.in for CEDAW report.
4. *Ibid.*
5. www.indiacasestudy.com.
6. Women's Entitlement to property, Times Foundation, india-times.htm, Dr. Sarla Gopalan.
7. Jaisingh, Indira, "The Indian Women's Movement", source world-wide web.
8. Gopalan, Sarala (2000), "Empowerment of Women" in M. K. Santhanam, *Fifty Years of Indian Republic*, Government of India. p. 334.
9. *Ibid*, p. 329.
10. European Academy of Legal Theory.htm
11. http://www.wcd.nic.in.
12. http://www.worldbank.org/gender/prr, p. 36.
13. Menon Nivedita, *Gender And Politics In India.*
14. http://www.worldbank.org/gender/prr, p. 42.
15. *Ibid.*, p. 43.
16. Flavia Agnes, interviewed by Tanu Thomas K., Indiatimes.com, September 21, 2004.
17. http://www.hinduonnet.com.

7

CONCLUSION

Personal laws have been discriminatory. The discrimination can, however, be resolved through reforms in these laws. But, one important aspect, which needs to be noted, is that while interfering with personal laws one should take care not to interfere in religious affairs. This can be done easily because personal laws as they exist today have hardly anything to do with religion, especially the Hindu personal laws have virtually no connection with religious texts.

Even prior to the reform of 1950's, Hindu law as practiced had hardly anything to do with Hindu scriptures. In fact, it was essentially custom based and it varied widely from region to region. What *Smritis* and *Dharmashastras* provided and what was actually practiced was vastly different. Each locality followed its own custom of marriage, custom of succession, etc. Obviously this has nothing to do with Hinduism. When these laws were reformed sometime ago, what was reformed was not Hindu law as such but diverse customary laws and practices. To believe—as some people did—that there was interference with Hindu religion is contrary to the facts. The Hindu Marriage Act/Succession Act is a very secularized version of traditional Hindu scriptures. It is 'Hindu' in its concept. To interpret these texts in a progressive manner is difficult, because in the Hindu law Hindu women were not treated equally. But various reforms took place and after the formation of Constitution the Hindu women's position improved.

Women got the right of Divorce, principle of monogamy

and daughter's property rights but the security of women is always questionable. In spite of the dowry prohibition Act, a pretty large number of people still go for dowry in various regions. Polygamy is in vogue in many places. Married women do not get HUF (Hindu Undivided Family) Property Right under the Hindu Succession Act. A large number of families still refuse to accept the divorced women in their homes. Divorce in the context of economic matters is also a challenge. So the UCC alone is not the answer to the solution of the problem of gender justice.

Unfortunately, in the recent times the question of UCC has been debated in a communal atmosphere. In consequence, no satisfactory answer has come out. Nevertheless the discussion has led us to some happy conclusions like that reforms in personal laws are necessary to empower the position of women in our society. Secondly, 'uniformity' in civil laws does not mean uniformity between communities but uniformity or equality between men and women. Thirdly, reforms in personal law do not mean to destroy the tradition and culture of different communities but to destroy the wrong practices and customs prevailing there. This means reforms have to be progressive measures which dilute inequalities concerning gender.

I have examined the whole issue in a historical perspective. My findings show that in the *Vedic* period women had rights but only a few women were benefited fully by these rights. Nor did the women in general enjoyed equal status everywhere, as is ordinarily made out. But broadly, the position was not bad. Unfortunately, even this situation did not last long. We witness a decline in the status of women in the post *Vedic* period. And unfortunately there was further fall during the *dharmashastra* period when women were brought at par with Shudras. The reasons for this deterioration in the position of women was basically for two main reasons: (1) patriarchal structure and (2) caste stratification.

There was, unfortunately, no improvement in the hopeless situation during the medieval period. Rather, for obvious reasons, things slided down to still Power depths in those confusing days. During the British period there was some improvement. There were several reforms in Hindu law which attack wrong customs and bettered the status of women. But not to the extent it was required. The influence of patriarchy and casteism in the Hindu society were again the villains.

Lately, the women's movement has done a god job in improving the situation. Some enlightened elements are also working in the right direction. But there are road-blocks too. The Hindutva forces are prominent there. Of late, they have communalised the issue to such an extent that the UCC has become a suspect in the eyes of many. They are trying to impose Hindu Civil Code, they say, in the garb of a Uniform Civil Code.

The saner element in our society has, fortunately, not given up its hope and programme of reform for gender justice, equality and empowerment. Thanks to it, the whole question of UCC is being debated in a proper historical perspective. What is required today is that the debate should not be restricted to only the intellectual sphere but it should also reach the public arena.

SECTION TWO

MUSLIM PERSONAL LAW AND UNIFORM CIVIL CODE

1

EVOLUTION OF ISLAMIC LAW

It is intended here to emphasize on the social and political conditions during the Prophet's time and formation, by and by, of an Islamic State and a society based on equality and justice, proper administration and protection of the rights and freedoms of weaker sections. An endeavour is also made here to understand the evolution of *Shari'ah* and developments of different juristic systems created by different Caliphs after the death of the Prophet (PBUH).

After the advent of Islam Mecca became an important centre of international commerce and complex financial operations. According to some historians it was no more a mere trading centre. The leading men of Mecca during the Prophet's time were, mostly financiers, always eager and interested in exploring potentialities to expand their trade with lucrative investment from Aden to Gaza or Damascus. In the financial net that they had woven were caught not merely the inhabitants of Mecca, but also many notables of the surrounding places. So The Qur'an appeared not in the atmosphere of the desert, but in that of high finance.

Geographically, Mecca was surrounded by a vast desert called al-Rub'a al-Khali. It was sparsely populated by the Bedouin Arabs who were nomads. They lived in the shadow of tribal morality and traditions before the rise of Islam. Although commercial operations were taking place on ever-growing scale in this mercantile town situated on an important international trade route, the new morality, and the new mercantile culture had not struck deep roots. Prophet

Mohammad (PBUH) sensed the social malaise and spent long years in the cave of Hira in meditation. After the revelation of God's message to him, he came back from the cave of Hira not only to preach but also to transform the old social structure. He was, it must be remembered, not, unlike many other preachers, interested in teaching individual morality within the old structure of society. For him the moral problem was at the same time a social problem and hence his new morality could take shape only by transforming the old social structure.[1]

There was, at that time, neither an elected head nor the elected senators to run the administration of the city. No taxes were collected. There was no army. No police. The question then arises, in the absence of any governmental control, how social stability was ensured in the Meccan society? A decision-making body called *Mala'a* (senate) looked after these functions. *Mala'a*, in fact, comprised tribal chiefs called Sheikhs. These Sheikhs sat on the *Mala'a* in Mecca and took unanimous decisions. Since the responsibility of enforcing the decision was on respective tribal chiefs, any tribal chief who did not like the decision could go for non-implementation of decision within his tribe. *Mala'a*'s decisions had, thus no universal validity. Hence all the *Mala'a* decisions had to be unanimous. *Mala'a* was a powerful outfit. After transformation of nomadic economy into mercantile economy, it became still stronger when the Sheikhs who composed it became wealthy merchants.

In Mecca of those days there was economic prosperity but not everywhere. It was only at the top. Rest of the people were poor and weak. They were not cared for. One saw there the familiar evils of a wealthy commercial society, extremes of wealth and poverty and under world of slaves and hirelings, and social injustice. Prophet Mohammad (PBUH) denounced social injustice and exploitation. He worked towards emancipation of the poor, the weak and the fallen.

Maulana Shibli, an eminent Indian biographer of the Prophet (PBUH), says that the Prophet (PBUH) was a spiritual and a moral teacher; he created new political institutions; his main work was to have established security system for the whole of Arabia. The police and the army were, as indicated above, not there. There were no laws except the tribal traditions. The tribal chief ran the affairs of the society. The chief was, at best, first among the equals. The chieftainship was not hereditary. After the death of the chief, his successor used to be elected by the tribal assembly. The tribal chief could be subjected to severe criticism for his failures although he normally held the office till his death.[3]

However, as discussed earlier, the socio-economic scene at Mecca had radically changed after the advent of Islam. The new conditions created pressure for the establishment of a state authority. But it could not get translated into practical shape due to strong influence of tribal traditions and the rich merchants' resistance to be subordinate to any authority.

The Prophet (PBUH), however, drew up a tactful document to shift the centre of power from the tribal units to the newly created confederation called *Ummah*. But, very wisely, he allowed various groups to follow their traditional laws and enforce order within their locales by observing these traditional laws.

The verses revealed to the Prophet (PBUH) in the earlier Meccan period[4] were very important. They were mostly of juristic nature, which could lay foundation of a theocratic state. Even the concept of *zakat*, during this period, was of purificatory nature, rather than a levy. It was much later in Medina that *zakat* became a compulsory state-levy. The verses prescribing various laws like those of marriage, divorce, inheritance, certain commercial transactions as well as those prescribing punishments for various crimes like theft, adultery, fornication, murder, etc. were all revealed in Medina over a period of time.

Initially, when the Prophet (PBUH) drew up the agreement to set-up the confederation in Medina, he had allowed, as noted above, the various constituents to follow their respective traditions for maintaining law and order. It was only when the number of Muslims gradually swelled and complicated problems were faced, he looked for the divine guidance and the relevant verses were revealed.[5]

Qamaruddin Khan, Professor of Islamic history, Karachi University, is of the opinion that "the Qur'an does not aim to create a state but a society."[6] There was no radical break with the tribal ethos, even when socio-economic transformation was taking place in Mecca and Medina. Many Bedouin tribes had embraced Islam as it symbolized a new emerging power but they did not undergo any social transformation. There was dialectical interaction between these desert tribes and those who had taken to the sedentary way of life in the urban conglomerations at Mecca and Medina.

Abu Bakr, the first successor of Prophet Mohammad (PBUH), thus had assumed power as a result of some sort of consensus among the important people of Medina. It was, of course, not an election on the basis of adult franchise as it happens in the parliamentary form of government in our own time. What Abu Bakr said on assuming charge as caliph exhibits some sort of responsibility to the people. Note his these words: "O people! Behold me, charged with cares of government, I am not the best among you; I need all your advice and all your help. If I do well, support me; if I mistake, counsel me."[7] The words are full of democratic spirit. Despite this, the Islamic State had not developed the repressive machinery by this time. There was no paid army, police or bureaucracy to carry out the repressive functions of the state. It is for this reason that during the reign of first four caliphs we find many instances of fearless criticism of the government voice in public. The tribal in Mecca often opposed any law enforcing system because that would mean curtailment of their much-valued freedom they enjoyed in the desert.

Islam also had made *Zakat* (poll tax) obligatory on every Muslim. After the establishment of state it had to be paid to the state treasury every year. Abu Bakr, on being elected as caliph, took measures to collect *Zakat* from all the Muslims including the nomadic tribes. This move was resisted by the Bedouin tribes who, on the death of the Prophet (PBUH), had again shown the signs of turbulence.[8]

According to Suyuti, "when the news about the death of Prophet (PBUH) spread around Medina, many Arab tribes renounced Islam and refused to pay *Zakat.* Abu Bakr ordered troops to march against the rebel tribes. It was first rebellion against the Islamic state in Medina and it was crushed by Islamic troops. This is known as the war of *Ridda* (apostasy) in the history of Islam.[9]

While choosing successor to the Prophet (PBUH), everyone present was unanimous on the question—electing caliph either from amongst the Immigrants (from Mecca) or from Ansars (i.e. the helpers from Medina), although theoretically all Muslims were equal. The tribal factor kept the Islamic state democratic in spirit as the caliphs were subjected to the frank criticism in the Arab tradition.

Suyuti narrates an interesting episode in this respect. "Umar", he says, "one day said by God I do not know whether I am a king or a caliph, if I am a king it is better. Someone from the audience said, O Commander of the Faithfuls, there is great difference between a king and a caliph. There upon Umar inquired of the difference. The man said the caliph is who does not extract (money) unjustly nor does he spend it unjustly and you are like that. A king, on the other hand, oppresses (his subjects) to pay and spends whimsically. Hearing this Umar became silent."[10]

The incident shows that the Arabs were not tempera-
mentally prepared to accept the institution of kinship easily
and, like the head of their tribe, wanted their caliph to be ac-
countable to his people. At the time of Abu Bakr's death, the
question of succession again became important. Abu Bakr
nominated Umar his close associate and trusted lieutenant, as
his successor, a practice which even the Prophet (PBUH) had
not followed. But, it must be said to the credit of Abu Bakr
that in that difficult situation he made a very appropriate
choice. Umar's period as a head of Islamic state is extremely
important in its history. Abu Bakr had to devote his energies
in crushing the rebellion of the Bedouin tribes and setting
things right after the death of Prophet (PBUH). He hardly had
time to resolve other problems. It was during Umar's time
that the Muslim armies conquered vast territories and
brought back home, along with them, fortunes the Arabs had
not seen before. The wars of conquest were good diversion
for the turbulent Bedouin tribes who lived in harsh desert
conditions.

There were no well-built institutions when 'Umar took
over from Abu Bakr. The state had recent origin and everything had to be learnt from the experience in the fast changing situation. The conquered provinces had to be utilized to
cope with the situation. He summoned his colleagues for advice. 'Ali, in keeping with the old tribal tradition, advised him
to distribute the booty to the last penny among the deserving
people. This advice was not in keeping with changed situation. 'Uthman opined that if proper system was not established, the multiplying wealth might aggravate the situation.
At last it was decided to establish registers, fix daily allowances for the people, and the surplus was reserved for the
welfare schemes for the Muslims.[11] We are also told that
whenever he appointed any governor he strictly warned him

not to ride (expensive) Turkish horse, not to eat delicious food, not to wear fine clothes and not to close his doors over the complainants and if he did not conform to these instructions, he had to face severe punishments.[12] But 'Umar did not succeed in building up a just and equitable social order. The march of events overtook him. Umar, the strong man of Islam with all his strict enforcement of Islamic teachings and ruthless measures for prevention of corruption, could not check the growth of concentration of wealth and concomitant imbalances in the socio-economic structure of the early Islamic society. Under the impact of the new forces generated as a result of conquests, the peninsular Arabian community with its primitive tribal structure, was shaken and began to assimilate the new mores.[13] Moreover, Islam with its universal teaching and no less emphasis on this worldly aspect of life (renunciation and asceticism, in fact, has been disapproved by the Prophet (PBUH)) paved the way fir this developments.

In the Islamic system, right from the beginning, there was total absence of the feudal institutions as in a desert there was no question of landed estates to grow. In the oases the land was owned collectively by the tribes. Umar in the conquered provinces ordered such a system to be abolished and the cultivators were left in possession of the lands they cultivated. 'Umar issued instructions to confiscate all the lands left behind by the Roman rulers to be given to the native cultivators. This was a revolutionary step, which widened the base for the Muslim invaders among the natives. Umar prohibited all the Muslim officers from acquiring landed property in the conquered lands even through purchases from the natives.[14]

Umar's was great contribution in establishing the just land revenue system and restoring ownership of land to the cultivators. Umar, who consolidated the Islamic revolution and state, was guided in his state policies, apart from the Islamic teachings, by practical considerations.

Until Abu Bakr's time, there was, as noted above, no paid army or paid bureaucracy or the regular police force. But after the large-scale wars, etc., these services could no longer be efficiently maintained purely on voluntary basis. And during the Umar's reign the situation became much more complex and it became necessary to organize regular army, police and state treasury. A pucca structure was constructed to house the state treasury, which was kept adjacent to a mosque to avoid theft.[15] Similarly, there were no regular judicial services. Most of the cases were brought to the Caliph who decided them on the basis of the Qur'an, *hadith, sunna* or, if there were no precedents, by *qiyas* (analogy) and *ijtihad* (interpretation). If the Caliph found it difficult he would consult the other senior companions of the Prophet (PBUH) like 'Ali or 'Abd-allah bin 'Abbas. Of course the Caliph's decision was final. The Caliph was also installed in office by *bay'ah* (oath of allegiance) not for any fixed term, but for life. There was no regular police force either to keep watch against crimes. The case was voluntarily reported. Until the rise of Islam and the state based on it, the tribal assemblies used to perform these functions according to the age-old traditions. In view of the fast changing situation after the conquests of the former Byzantine and Sassanid provinces which had well established administrative structure, the pressure was felt for a thorough organization of similar administrative apparatus for the new state. 'Umar made a beginning in this direction. He established a separate police service under Sahib-al-Ahdath (the chief of police). The function of Ahdath included maintaining watch over weights and measures, preventing people from constructing houses on the public roads or erecting other obstructions, stopping over loading of animals, enforcing prohibition, etc. There were no prisons.[16] The punishments prescribed by the Qur'an (called Hudud) were in keeping with the social ethos of the tribal Arabia life for life, tooth for tooth, eye for eye, etc. as prescribed by God in Torah also. Here I would like to clarify that such Hudud were very much contextual in nature and in keeping with the social circumstances existed at that particular time. For theft Qur'an prescribed amputation of hand and for illegitimate sexual intercourse hundred lashes. To come to prison houses. In the new situation, these were needed. Umar' established prison houses.

Umar also organized the judicial service. He appointed a chief Qadi and number of qadis under him. It would be interesting to quote here from the letter "Umar wrote to governor of Kufa, Abu Musa Ash'ari on the principles of justice. He wrote: "Administration of justice is necessary duty. Treat people equally be it private audience or public sitting in matters of justice so that the weak should not despair of your justice and the strong should not hope for favour. It is for the plaintiff to produce proof and it is for the defendant to deny on oath. Compromise is permissible provided it does not violate what has been permitted or prohibited [by *Shari'ah*]. If you have passed any judgement yesterday there would be nothing wrong in reversing it today on second thought in the interest of justice. If it is not there in the Qur'an or Hadith contemplate over it deeply taking into account examples, similar cases and drawing analogies. Fix a time limit for the plaintiff to produce proof. Justice be done to him if he produces proof or else, his case be dismissed."[17]

While the above letter of 'Umar shows his deep concern for justice without discriminating between the weak and the strong, it also throws light on the primitive state at which the administration of justice was in the Islamic state at that time. 'Umar took pains for organizing the department of justice and fixed high salaries for the judges to insulate them from temptation of corruption. He was also careful in the choice of qadis, his main criteria being Islamic learning and personal integrity. Umar's was essentially a religious vision and he left behind him laws, inspired by his vision, many of which had universal solidarity while some were product of local milieu. His, successors, however had to confront very complex problem after the conquered provinces of Byzantine and Sassanid empires were integrated into the Islamic state. It was then that a complex structure of a Islamic state began to built up by assimilating, integrating or devising institutions unknown before in the simple and unsophisticated milieu of tribal Arabia.[18]

About this time, the class composition of the society was changing so fast that it was becoming increasingly difficult to reconcile the different interests. During the reign of the third Caliph 'Uthaman, the conflict began to surface. 'Umar was a strong man and ruled with an iron hand. Things changed after him. It was no easy task to keep the Bedouins in checks that were basically passionate lovers of personal freedom. Then there were many new groups like the townsmen who were fast becoming rich due to the new opportunities opened up by the conquest of new provinces. They had to be cared for. According to Dr. Taha Hussein there developed four groups namely, (1) the Quraysh of Mecca, (2) the Helpers (Ansar), (3) the nomadic Arabs, and (4) the subjects of the conquered countries. These groups contended against each other for more power and control over material resources. The most dominant group was that of Qurayshites. The Qurayshites had been rich businessmen and skilled diplomats. The Qurayshites now considered it as their monopoly to rule over others and control all the resources.[19]

The second group was of the Ansars. They fought along with the Prophet (PBUH) against the Qurayshites of Mecca and made sacrifices in the cause of Islam. Although some important leaders of this group were consulted in all important state matters, the new generation of Ansars, which came of age when, Uthman took over as Caliph strongly resented their secondary role and nursed grievance against the Qurayshites. The third group was that of the nomadic Arabs to whom the new state was like a fetter to their freedom inflicted on them by the townspeople. They had rebelled soon after the death of the Prophet (PBUH) but their rebellion was crushed. The fourth group was that of non-Arab peoples from the conquered provinces, which was worst of all as it had no say in the state affairs monopolized only by the Arabs. Kufa, a huge military camp in Iraq, became centre of non-Arab mawalis captured in various wars. They were highly discontented. Moreover, new pressures developed when the children born of the female slaves in various expeditions came of age. Kufa thus became a great centre of turmoil.

Uthman took another decision of far reaching economic consequence. In order to induce the Hejazis settled in Kufa to go back to the Hejaz to ease pressure of population on Kufa, he permitted them to exchange their lands held in Iraq with those holding in Hejaz. 'Umar had wisely disallowed this. Many shrewd people took advantage of this opportunity and exchanged their barren lands in Hejaz for the most fertile lands in the provinces and in no time became big landholders. Some of them made most of it in Hejaz also by acquiring huge chunks of lands and importing slaves from outside to work. The slaves captured in the wars were easily available to work on the fields. The slave labour converted even the barren land of Hejaz into a fertile land. Thus came into existence in the Islamic society a class of big landowners. This was the beginning of feudalism in Islam.[20]

IN MEDIEVAL PERIOD

The Islamic 'republic' lasted for about thirty years after the death of the Prophet (PBUH). As we have seen with new conquests and the land exchange policy followed by the third caliph 'Uthman', there emerged a wealthy and powerful class to change the course of history when the tide of historical forces were against him. The flow of wealth and the formation of the powerful groups of big landlords had brought forever an end of the classless tribal structure of the Arabian society.[21]

The concept and form of the Islamic state was now completely transformed with the growth of new classes, productive forces and property relations. Although the ruler was still called Amir-al-Mu'minin (commander of the faithful), he was no more than a monarch. In the metamorphosed state set-up there was nothing more Islamic than the fact that the ruler professed Islam and enforced certain provisions of the *Shari'ah* in personal and criminal matters.

The state was otherwise getting increasingly feudalized inasmuch as more and more landed properties came into existence. The rulers were no longer inspired by the Islamic vision; nor did they show much concern about it. They adopted all the feudal customs prevalent in imperial court. The early Islamic Caliphate, as we have seen, had not known kingly court and differences of ranks. The Arab tradition was strongly influenced by the nomadic environment around and was totally against all this. So the first four caliphs heading the Islamic state strictly observed these traditions. But later, things changed. Now not only the rulers or the members of the dynasty who took to the luxury and courtly ways but also the ruling class. "With this increased flow of wealth the two holy cities became less holy. They developed into a centre of worldly pleasure and gaiety and a home of secular Arab music and song. In Makkah was established a kind of clubhouse patronized by guests who, we are told, had facilities for hanging their outer garments on pegs—apparently an innovation for al-Hijaz—before indulging in chess, backgammon, dice or reading. To al-Medinah Persian and Byzantine slave song stresses flocked in increasing numbers. Amorous poetry kept pace with other new developments. Houses of ill repute (*bu-yut-al-qiyan*) flourished in al-Medina and were patronized by no less a poet than al- Farazdaq of national fame."[22]

Despite many attempts by the Kharjites and other puritanics '*Ulama* to restore early conditions and strengthen the moral foundations of the state, nothing much could be achieved. The Abbasid period outdid the Ummayyad period in wealth and splendour.

In short, we can say that the Ummayad or Abbasid rule, in substance as well as in form, was no different from the Byzantine and Sassanid rule, which it had overthrown with revolutionary zeal. The earlier simplicity and Puritanism could not be restored as the material conditions had totally changed and new classes had emerged with powerful interest in maintaining the system. *Kharaj* (land tax) was the main form of revenue although trading activities also supplemented it. It means the system was based on exploitation of the peasantry. The area where Islam originated was not agricultural; in fact there was no production of any sort except date palms in a few scattered oases. The Meccan economy mainly depended on profits made by exchange of goods and not their production and hence trade was highly encouraged by Islam.[23]

Now the whole basis of economy had changed; and so did the composition of the ruling class. As it was not possible to change the new productive forces and hence the structure of the state, the political theory of Islam was made to conform to suit the new conditions. When the Ummayads usurped power and confined it to their dynasty against the Islamic tradition, the '*ulama* at first strongly resented this move and kept themselves aloof from the rulers. Some '*ulama*, who had high character, continued to boycott the rulers and could not be swayed by temptation or fear for their lives.[24]

We have seen above, what kind of socio-economic and political scenes were prevailing in Mecca in those days. The period of glorious caliphate lasted only for 30 years. Later, the reigns of government passed into the hands of Mu'awiyah, a dynastic rule, under which the Islamic polity underwent fundamental transformation. Further the composition of ruling classes also changed with mercantile losing influence and bureaucracy, landed aristocracy and military officers gaining upper hand. There were hardly any positive developments during the Umayyad period. Islam lost its true essence which caused unrest among the *ulama*. Some of them considered the Umayyad and Abbasid regimes as un-Islamic.[25]

After disintegration of the Abbasid Empire various independent Muslim states came into existence. The rulers in these states were secular monarchs. There was nothing Islamic about these rulers except the selective enforcement of *Shari'ah*.

EVOLUTION OF *SHARI'AH*

The term *Shari'ah* refers to the general normative system of Islam, which wass developed by Muslim jurists during the first three centuries of Islam. The term Islamic law is generally referred to legal aspects of *Shari'ah*. It evolved in course of time to cope with different social challenges and circumstances. *Shari'ah*'s principle is a legal binding for enactment of law by the state and enforcement of the same by the court. Interestingly, Islamic Family Law is also a part of *Shari'ah*. It governs family relations such as marriage, divorce, inheritance and custody of children. It is also called Muslim Personal Status Law--*Shari'at al- ahwal al-shakhsiyah* in Arabic.

It is important to know that the *Shari'ah* did not come into being all of a sudden; it went through a tortuous process of evolution over the centuries; and, secondly, it never remained static, and hence immutable as commonly assumed.

The *Shari'ah* is based on Quran, Sunnah, Qiyas and Ijma. And a little more — *Ijtihad*, i.e. creative interpretation and application of Islamic *fiqh* (jurisprudence) in the face of new circumstances. The principle of *Ijtihad*, so long as it was applied, constituted a dynamic element in Islamic law. Unfortunately, the gates of *Ijtihad* were closed soon after the decline of the Abbassid Empire in A.D. 12th century. *Shari'ah*, unlike Qur'an, is not devoid of human opinion. It is for this reason that the schools of jurisprudence differ from each other on many questions. There is nothing wrong there. The principle of *Ijtihad* referred to above was incorporated in the *Shari'ah* methodology for this reason only. The objective conditions in the world vary so much that it is almost impossible to develop one uniform view of all problems. Moreover, geographical, racial and cultural traditions also influence our judgement in one way or another.[26]

Contextually, it is necessary to highlight here some aspects of argument related to the nature and development of *Shari'ah* particularly the aspects dealing with the family law. Much of confusion that we come across at places about the role of *Shari'ah* in modern context is caused by two factors, one is lack of appreciation to critically examine the conception and development of Islamic Law, and two, the popular notion among the community that it is divine and hence immutable. However, the reality is that it has been developed in different periods of time and within various schools of Islamic jurisprudence (*Madhahib*). These schools of thoughts themselves have extreme diversity of opinions.

Let me elaborate it. The evolution of *Shari'ah* started, in a major way, with the emergence of different school of though based on different political, social and demographic factors.[27] The Hanafi and Maliki schools became the most geographically widespread. The Hanafi school had originated in Iraq, the centre of power of the Abbasid dynasty. The Hanafi school got support in Afghanistan and later in the Indian subcontinent, while emigrants from India took it to East Africa. The connection with the ruling authority of the Hanafi school went down to the period of Ottoman Empire. Currently, the Hanafi law is followed in Turkey, Iraq, Syria, the Balkan states, Cyprus, Jordan, Sudan, Israel and Palestine (together with Shafi school), Egypt and Indian sub-continent.

The Maliki school grew out of the city of Medina, and spread to Sudan, Libya, Tunisia, Algeria, Morocco, Gambia, Ghana, Nigeria and Senegal and to the eastern coastal territories of Arabia on the Gulf.

The Shafi'i school started in Cairo, where its founder lived for the last five years of his life, spread to Yemen and Indian coastline, and to East Africa. Currently, Shafi'i views predominate in Malaysia, Indonesia, Singapore, the Philippines, Sri Lanka and the Maldives.[28]

The timing of the emergence and the early dynamics of each school also seem to have influenced the content of their views on Shari'a. Like the Hanafi and Maliki schools drew more on pre-existing practice than did the Shafi'i and Hanbali schools, which elaborated their views from the theory of Shari'a. These differences reflect the influence of the timing and intellectual context in which each school emerged and developed.[29]

The principle of consensus (*ijma*) apparently acted as a unifying force that tended to draw the substantive content of all these four Sunni schools together through the use of independent juristic reasoning, i.e. (*ijtihad*). Moreover, the consensus among the main schools has always been that, if there are two or more variant opinions on an issue, they should all be accepted as equally legitimate attempts to express the particular rule *(hukm)*.[30]

On the negative side we find that possibilities of *ijtihad* somehow came to an end by the tenth century because

Shari'ah had been fully and exhaustively elaborated by that time. However, there were subsequent developments in the world in social, political and economic spheres which required changes as per the principle of *ijtihad*. As a result, it went out of touch with the realities of the modern context.[31]

The Abbasid rulers inherited the legacy of Umayyad, mainly in the areas of government administration and judicial decisions that were founded on judge's personal opinions of the relevance and meaning of principle of Quran and Arabic or local customary practices.[32] It is also said that Abbassid rulers also actively encouraged the application of *Shari'ah* by state appointed judges. A chief judge, *qadi-ul-quda* coul appoint and dismiss the other judges like Abu Yusuf (d 798), the leading Hanafi jurist of the time. The Abbasid state transformed *Shari'ah* into positive law through the judiciary. But these *Shari'ah* judges did not have complete monopoly over the judicial process. A variety of openly Secular (*Mazalim)* courts had jurisdictions in a wide variety of fields of the administration.[33]

In the legal history of Islamic societies associated with the religious nature of *Shari'ah* we come across the development of private legal consultation (*ifta*) and independent states issuing legal opinions at the request of provincial governors and state judges.[34]

SHARI'AH'S TRANSITION INTO THE MODERN ERA

The *Shari'ah* that has come to us in modern era has influence of Ottomon Empire. During the Mamluk period (1250-1516) in Egypt and Syria, *Ifta*, that is advice by independent scholars, was still a private activity that was independent of state control or regulation. In other words, the authority of those independent scholars was derived from the confidence of the general public in their competence and piety. This was the same process from which the main Sunni schools evolved.

The religious and legal opinion was issued from different establish schools of *Shari'ah* from tenth century onwards. The Mamluks did appoint small number of *Muftis* to advise them on matters of policy.[35]

The independence of *Muftis* continued into the early Ottoman period, but as the state expanded and developed into an empire, they were gradually incorporated into an increasingly centralized judicial administration. *Shaykh-ul-Islam* (the wise and the learned scholars of Islam) came to be known as ultimate source of authority in matters relating to *Shari'ah*.[36]

A related significant development during that period was the patronage of the Hanafi school by the Ottomon dynasty. From the earliest day of their rule, the Ottoman sultans appear to have given official status to this school. The need for systematic reasoning and citation of sources in the expanding field of *Ifta* gave rise to a form of legal literature that consisted almost entirely of quotations. The majority of *fatwas* survive in the collections of devoted to the opinion of either a single or several *Shaykh al-Islam*. The compilers of these volumes organized the *fatwas* under legal headings and sub-headings such as marriage, lease, trust or lawsuits which became a practical source of reference for students, judges, *Muftis* and others with interest in law. But the basic legal concepts and methodology, as they had been established by the eleventh century, remained unchanged as jurist continues to follow the doctrines and techniques of their *madhabs* or school of thoughts.[37]

Similar developments can also be observed in the Safavid school of Iran from 1501 to 1722, where Twelver Shi'ism (Ja'fari school) became the state religion, and *Shari'ah* scholars occupied a range of positions. Also in Timurid Central Asia and the Indian subcontinent an official bearing the title *Shaykh al-Islam* or its equivalent was in charge of all religious matters, including the issuing of *fatwas* (Masud et al.1996: 13-15 ref. Abdullahi An Naim). Throughout these areas, earlier efforts to reconcile and negotiate the relationship between *Shari'ah* and secular administration of justice continued, subject to regional context and theological variations between Sunni and Shi'a approaches.[38]

In Ottomon Empire *Shari'ah* was the law of religious community, while *qanun* was the law of the state. The two systems had grown independently of one another, *Shari'ah* as the outcome of juristic speculation that reached its maturation before the emergence of the Ottomon imperial state, while *qanun* was a sytematization of specifically Ottoman feudal practice in many essential areas, such as land tenure and taxation.

With the rise of European imperial power since the sixteenth century, a new dimension was added to the dynamics of transition. It took the form of Consular courts of European cases involving their nationals and also Ottoman nationals belonging to the religious communities taken under the protection of these foreign states. This system developed into a powerful political structure that combined with military and economic pressure form European imperial power. This further led to *tanzimat* reforms of the Ottoman law and the legal system in the second half of the nineteenth century. This process began after the Egyptian occupation of Palestine and Syria between 1831 and 1840, when criminal and administrative matters began to be transferred to local councils, set up in districts, leaving *Shari'ah* court to deal with personal status/family law and property matters.[39]

In addition to justifying these changes in the name of strengthening the state and preserving Islam, also there was a need to ensure equality among Ottoman subjects, thereby laying the foundation for a major reconstruction of the legal system regarding the rights of non-Muslims. This edict provided a secular or *nizamiyah* mixed court composed of Muslims and non-Muslims judges to hear commercial and criminal cases between people of all religions. It also stipulated that non-Muslims of recognized communities could take inheritance issues to their own religious courts, as had been the practice.

The formulation of *Majallah*, which came to be known as the Civil Code, 1876, took ten years to codify the rules of contract according to the Hanafi school combining European form with *Shari'ah* content. This major codification of *Shari'ah* simplified a huge part of Islamic law and made it more easily accessible to litigants and jurists/lawyers alike, especially as the latter group became increasingly less familiar with *Shari'ah* principles and methodology.[40]

Important reforms of family law matters in particular began with an imperial edict in 1915 that granted wives a limited right to petition for divorce (*faskh*), contrary to the doctrine of the Hanafi school. These reforms were extended for application as law in *Shari'ah* courts, as promulgated in the Ottoman Law of Family Rights of 1917, and includes rules and procedures that did not exist in the Hanafi school. This had an impact on the laws applicable throughout the domains of the Ottoman Empire in the Middle East and North Africa, but in its establishment of a reform methodology beyond the confines of any particular school (*madhab*).[41]

One significant consequence of these developments, owing to openness and accessibility of *Shari'ah*, is inconsistency of its application in the modern context. This is the result of exposing major theoretical problems and differences within and between different schools and traditions of Islamic societies. Besides obvious difficulties of agreement between Sunni and Shi'a communities that co-exist within the same country, as in Iraq, Lebanon, Saudi Arabia, Syria and Pakistan, different *madhab* followed by the majority of the Muslim population in the country, as in North African countries that inherited official Ottoman preference for the Hanafi *madhab,* while popular religious practice is according to the Maliki *madhab.*

The *Shari'ah* in course of time exposed to various social transformations and the true nature of *Shari'ah* has been trying to keep alive the intellectual and normative character. The study of Islamic jurisprudence (*fiqh*) was removed to pure Islamic institutions or to specialized law schools, where it competes with offerings in secular law. After independence from the colonial rule, Islamic societies have freely chosen to be bound by a minimum set of national and international obligations of membership in a world community of nation-states. While there are clear differences in the level of their social development and political stability, all Islamic societies today live under national constitutional regimes. And also if these countries were to live in accordance with *Shari'ah,* they would have to transform themselves according to the social, economic and political nature of the country.

As indicated above, the Islamic thinkers of the earlier time had also recognized the necessity of the change in the view of the changing circumstances and it is for this reason that Imam ibn Taymiyya came out with the doctrine that religious edicts change according to changing times. Even an orthodox thinker like him thought it necessary that *Ahkam* (edicts) should change in accordance with circumstances is very important. And, it was in keeping with the spirit of this doctrine that the *'ulama* agreed to the abolition of slavery when the time came for it, though the Qur'an had permitted it and the Prophet (PBUH) had not prohibited it altogether.[42]

As we have seen above the *Shari'ah* has, apart from others, two important sources of formulation: the Qur'an and the Sunna and both, as pointed out above, have two ingredients: the normative and the contextual. The Qur'an was undoubtedly revealed for the whole of mankind, but the people to whom it has been revealed must have immediate relevance and use. The scripture may draw from their history, culture and traditions. This is what I prefer to call contextual.

The Prophetic *Sunna* too has both these ingredients: the contextual and the normative. If the Prophet's behaviour had to have any relevance for his people, it had to draw from their history, culture and traditions. Also, he had to set out exemplary behaviour before them. For the he drew from what was normative in the Qur'an and thus he exemplified the Quranic teachings *par excellence*. This is why the Qur'an also describes the Prophet's behaviour as the best and most exemplary. For the Arabs of his time, and specially those who lived in the peninsular area, his whole conduct was of great relevance because it exemplified not only the best in Quran but also the best from their history, traditions ('*adat*) and culture.[43]

It was for this reason that when the *fuqaha* (the jurist) formulated the *Shari'ah,* they drew immensely from both the Qur'an and the traditions of the Prophet (PBUH). Sometimes the normative in the Qur'an, which imbibed principles, did not appeal to them as much as certain traditions which were closer to their *'adat* (practices) and hence they went to the extent of giving precedence to the *Sunna* over the Qur'an. As the *Shari'ah* is based on Qur'an and the *Sunna* pointed out before, there is much in it, which is contextual and hence needs to be reassessed in the changed context.

As far as women's question is concerned, cultural and traditional influences tend to be quite strong. The Qur'an undoubtedly gave a great many rights to women and spelled them out in detail. The Qur'an was the first scripture to have conceded so many rights to women and that too in a period when women were very oppressed in the major civilizations, namely the Byzantine, Sassanid, etc. And yet we see that the later *Fuqaha* (Islamic jurists) drew much from the Arab '*adat* (pre-Islamic traditions) and resorted to formulations which curtailed, if not trampled upon, women's rights.[44]

On the venturing out of home alone Imam Shafai's view seems to be more reasonable. Justice Aftab Hussein observes: "The view of Imam Shafai is clearly based upon the principle that the idea underlying the command [*Shari'ah* not Quranic] to travel with *mahram* [i.e., a man with whom marriage is prohibited] is to provide security for her person and property. A *mahram* is the best possible security *inter alia* for preservation of her chastity. If her safety is otherwise vouchsafed there is no harm in her travelling with stranger men or women."[45]

Unfortunately, many *Shari'ah* formulations are based on such traditions and thus many of the rules reflect the cultural prejudices of the Arabs and the Persians rather than the greatness of the Qur'an and its just liberal outlook.

The *Shari'ah* should be seen both in its cultural context as well as in its normative transcendental spirit. Unfortunately, at present it is viewed more in its cultural context. A diligent search, both in the Quranic text and in the *hadith* literature and exegetic works is required to reconstruct Islamic Law in its true, liberal, humanistic and progressive spirit.[46]

PERSONAL LAWS DURING MUSLIM RULE

Islamic law from the very beginning had a well–defined line of demarcation between (1) public law (*huququllah*) and (2) private law (huquq-ul-ibad). Under this classification, criminal law and public administration were placed in category (1), but marriage, family relations, succession, etc., were regarded as private law. Whenever in history the Muslim found themselves in the ruling position in places having a mixed population, they applied the Islamic public law to all their subjects, but the Islamic private law was always applied to Muslims only. In matters falling in the domain of private law all non-Muslims were left free, always and everywhere, to follow their own religious laws and customs. From the very beginning, this rule was adhered to as a matter of state policy (*Siyasa Shari'ah*).

In actual practice Muslim rulers did not strictly enforce, in many places, Islamic private law even for the Muslims, leave alone non-Muslims. This explains the continued prevalence of numerous local customs in the Muslim dominated lands like Morocco and Indonesia. And this is precisely the reason how in India the British found many Muslim communities (converts from Hinduism) continuing with their indigenous customs of the non-Muslims relating to marriage, family relations and succession, etc. even though they were extremely different from Islamic laws. They did not prohibit even practices relating to *sati* and *devdasi* customs, despite their conflict with Islamic public law. Eminent Arab travellers to medieval India, including Ibn-e-Batuta of the Tughlaq period, have affirmed the undisturbed prevalence of the Budhdhist and Hindu religious laws under the Muslim rule.[47]

Hindu religious law and custom were, indeed, placed by the Muslim rulers of India on par with their personal law. It is an indisputable historical fact that Hindu law in fact reached the heights of scholarly development during the Muslim rule in the country. According to Dr. Tahir Mahmood, "before what is commonly called Muslims rule in the country, all law was derived from what is now known as Hindu religion and its injunctions and precepts as found in the *Srutis* and *Smritis* including the Holy *Vedas, Dharmashastras* and *Dharmasutras*. Legal treatises like the *Manusmruti, Yagyavalkya-smriti* and Kautilya's *Arthashastra*, were legal codes of their respective times based on *Vedic* and *Dharmic* foundations. The law given by these ancient Indian codes is now called Hindu law. Muslim rulers of the country did not interfere with it and left the process wholly free from State intervention. Vigyaneshwara's *Mitaksharas* (11th c. AD) and Jimutavahan's *Dayabhaga* (12th c. AD) both were produced after the advent of Islam and were accepted and acted upon as veritable codes of Hindu law [the latter in eastern India and the former in rest of the country] during the reign of the succeeding Muslim rulers. Devanna's *Smriti Chandrika*, the Dravid code of Hindu law, was also produced in South India towards the end of 12th century AD. In North India Vachaspati Mishra's *Vivada Chintamani* and Mitramishra's *Viramitrodaya* appeared in the 15th and 17th centuries respectively during the Mughal rule. At the peak of Mughal authority in the country western India witnessed emergence of Nilkantha's *Vyavahara Mayukha* (17th c AD). All these were legal codes of their ages based on Hindu religious sources but taking into account the exigencies of the time. They eventually gave birth to the four sub-schools of the *Mitaksharas* [Madras, Mithila, Benaras and Bombay schools]. This massive development of Hindu law during the so-called 'Muslim rule' in India confirms the historical facts of an absolute non-interference by the state at that time in the juristic evolution of indigenous law."[48]

Thus each religious community had its own personal law in the country when the British came here in the 17th century and no ruler ever interfered there. Most certainly it was not a gift from Warren Hastings, who arrived here over 150 years later as governor of the Bengal Presidency. When his judicial plan of 1772 Warren Hastings provided for the application of "law of the Koran with respect to Mohammedans and those of Shasters with regards to the Gentoos" (section 23), he was simply guaranteeing that the legacy of the Muslim rule under which the Hindu law was to apply to the Hindus and Muslim law to the Muslims would not be changed.

NOTES

1. Dr. Asghar Ali Engineer, *The Islamic State*, New Delhi, 1996, p. 11.
2. *Ibid.,* p. 11.
3. Maulana Shibli's view *ibid.,* p. 17.
4. *Ibid.,* p. 28.
5. *Ibid.*
6. Qamaruddin Khan, Al-Mawardi's Theory of State, *Bazm-e-Iqbal,* Lahore, p. 4, *vide* Dr. Asghar Ali Engineer, *op. cit.,* p. 35.
7. Sayed Athar Hussain, *The Glorious Caliphate,* Academy of Islamic Research and Publication, Lucknow, 1974, p. 19. *vide* Dr. Asghar Ali Engineer, *op. cit.,* p. 37.
8. *Ibid.,* p. 37.
9. Suyuti, *Tarikh al-Khulafa,* Urdu tr. Maulavi Hakim Shabbir Ahmed, Kitab Khana Ashrafiyah, Delhi, p. 73.
10. *Ibid.,* p. 37.
11. Dr. Asghar Ali Engineer, *op. cit.,* p. 40.
12. Suyuti, *op. cit.,* p. 131.
13. Dr. Asghar Ali Engineer, *op. cit.,* p. 43.
14. Maulana Shibli Nu'mani, Al- Farooque, Kutubkhana Hamidiyah, Delhi, 1968, p. 301 cited by Dr. Asghar Ali Engineer, *op. cit.,* p. 44.
15. *Ibid.,* p. 50.
16. *Ibid.,* p. 52.
17. *Ibid.,* p. 53.
18. *Ibid.,* p. 53.
19. *Ibid.,* p. 55.
20. *Ibid.,* p. 55.
21. *Ibid.,* p. 58.
22. Philip K. Hitti, *History of the Arabs,* Macmillan and Co., London, 1958, p. 215 cited by Dr. Asghar Ali Engineer, *op .cit.,* p. 60.
23. *Ibid.,* p. 62.
24. Dr. Asghar Ali Engineer, *op. cit.,* p. 62.
25. *Ibid.,* p. 63.
26. Dr. Asghar Ali Engineer, *The Rights of Women in Islam,* Malaysia 1992, p. 8.
27. Abdullahi A An-Na'im, *Islamic Family Law in a Changing World,* New York, 2002, p. 5.
28. *Ibid.,* p. 6.
29. *Ibid.,* p. 7.
30. Weiss B., *The Spirit of Islamic Law,* Athens, 1998 cited by Abdul-

lahi A An-Na'im, p. 7.

31. Abdullahi A An-Na'im, *op. cit.*, p. 7.

32. Esposito, J. L., *Women in Muslim Family Law*, New York, 1982, pp. 122-7, cited by Abdullahi A An-Na'im, *op. cit.*, p. 7.

33. Weiss, B.G. and Green, A.H., *A Survey of Arab History*, revised edition, Cairo (1978), p. 120.

34. Masud, M.K, B. Messick and D.S. Powers, *Muftis, Fatwas and Islamic Legal Interpretation*, in M.K. Masud, B. Messick and D.S. Powers (eds.), *Islamic Legal Interpretation: Muftis and Their Fatwas*, Cambridge, 1996 pp. 226-42.

35. *Ibid.*, p. 10.

36. *Ibid.*

37. Imber C., Ebu's Su'ud, *The Islamic Legal Tradition*, Stanford, 1997, cited by Abdullahi A An- Na'im, *op. cit.*, p. 10.

38. Masud et al. 1996, pp. 13-15 cited by Abdullahi A An- Na'im, *op. cit.*, p. 12.

39. *Ibid.*, p. 12.

40. *Ibid.*, p. 13.

41. *Ibid.*, p. 14.

42. Dr. Asghar Ali Engineer, *The Rights of Women In Islam*, p. 11.

43. *Ibid.*, p. 12.

44. *Ibid.*, p. 13.

45. Justice Aftab Hussian, *Status of Women in Islam*, Lahore, 1987, Dr. Asghar Ali Engineer, *The Rights of Women*, p. 13.

46. *Ibid.*, p. 13.

47. Tahir Mahmood, *Statute—Law Relating to Muslim in India : A Study in Islamic and Constitutional Perspectives*, 1995, p. 8.

48. *Ibid.*, p. 9.

2

MUSLIM PERSONAL LAW IN THE COLONIAL TIMES

The *Shari'ah,* as the law of Islam, is a complete legal system. Regrettably, a pretty large number of Muslims naively practise an awfully distorted version of it. The Personal Law (*ahwal al shaksiya*), one of its important disciplines, is the worst sufferer at the hands of the ignorant. As a result, there are many wrong notions of the Muslim personal Law prevailing around us. A Muslim husband can have four wives. He can unilaterally divorce his wife; Muslim women remain in their homes and never come out except under thick black veil are some of the examples to substantiate the point.

The British were the first to present to the world a distorted image of Muslim Personal Law in India. Though they, fearing opposition, professed non-interference therein, slanderous campaign against the Muslim Personal Laws. These laws are 'inhuman and uncivilized', they said. And to prove their point, they distorted them—systematically, cunningly. They took hold of Muslim educational institutions and played their game there. Take this case of the Muslim College, Kolkata. W.W. Hunter tells us as to what happened in this institution in 1871:

At this time the head of the college is an English gentlemen, ignorant of a single word of Arabic or Persian, who draws Pound 1000 a year from a Mohammedan religious endowment for teaching things hateful to every Mohammedan.[2]

They did this everywhere. And having done that they entered the judicial arena.

MISINTERPRETING CASE LAW AND MISREPRESENTING LAW BOOKS

For the sake of their judicial administration they took to their game of distorting the Islamic law. The *qadis'* courts were abolished in 1864 and their jurisdiction was transferred to the English-educated judges, the so-called muftis. They were attached to the civil courts. They misinterpret the Islamic law, partly due to their own bigotry and partly under pressure from the court that they had to serve.

The English judges could thus comfortably distort the Islamic law without initially, taking the blame on themselves. Later, not satisfied with the performance of the so-called 'native law officers', the British assumed the job of directly applying and interpreting the personal law of Islam. They prepared their own English versions of the treatises on Islamic laws. Most of these versions were faulty. Hamilton's translation of the celebrated *Hanafi* legal treatise, the Hidaya, was full of mistakes. Maulvi Muhammad Rashid of Burdwan quickly detected the mistakes and notified to the then Chief Justice, T.H. Harrington who however chose to keep mum.[3]

Rashid Saheb's strong objections to the faulty translation of the *Hidaya* though did not move the Chief Justice, it did one good thing. It made the British abandon their plan to translate other treatises on the Muslim laws. Translation of the great Indian authority on Islamic law, the *Fatwa-e-Alamgiri,* which was then in progress, was abruptly stopped. But this did not check their designs. What judges did in respect of the *Shari'at* law was, however, much worse than a 'marginal distortion'.[4] They changed the very nature of the Islamic legal principles by ignoring their true rationale and spirit.

A question may arise here: Did the British do this to the Muslim law alone? No, they did it to Hindu law too. But their policies and attitudes to the *Shari'at* were much harsher than to Hindu law. The reasons behind this difference lay in the age-old rivalry between Christianity and Islam. Ever since the emergence of Islam in the seventh century A.D., the Christian world regarded the new creed as a big menace. It felt gravely challenged by a great faith, which did acknowledge one God as a creator of the universe but denied the doctrine of the Trinity, and which accepted Christ as a Prophet (PBUH) and the Bible as a revealed book but gave supreme and final authority to a new scripture, the Holy Qur'an. Not only that, the Christian world also felt politically threatened by the success of the growing Muslim power, which probed the depths of Asia, Africa and Europe.[5]

To come to the point. Bound by their declared imperialist strategy of non-interference with native law, the British though hostile to Islam, could not outlaw the *Shari'ah* in India. The reason was its superiority. The system was triumphantly competing, on an international level, with their own laws, both ecclesiastical and common, for its theories and principles were distinctly more progressive. In India, too, it did the same and it was precisely because of this fact that while they played the role of silent spectators insofar as the misinterpretation of the Hindu Law by the vested interests, in regard to the *Shari'ah* they actively participated in the game of gradual distortion. And having done that they encouraged the compilation of these distorted things. [6]

In textbooks like W.H. McNaughten's *Principles and Precedents of Muhammadan Law,*[7] N.E. Baillie's two-volume *Digest of Muhammadan Law,*[8] V. Fitgerald's *Muhammadan Law: An Abridgement* and R.K. Wilson's *Anglo-Mohammedan Law.*[9] In 1906 a prolific Parsi lawyer, Sir Dinshaw Faridunji Mulla artificially codified the British-Indian judicial precedents in the area of Muslim law in his book erroneously titled *Principles of Mohammedan Law.*[10] Faridunji Mulla had never read even the most elementary of the original treatises on Islamic law; nor did he ever claim to have done so. He only honestly codified that law as understood and interpreted by the British-Indian judges with their prejudiced brains and sinister designs.

By 1933 Mulla had published the 10th edition of his book, adding to each new edition scores of fresh cases decided by the British Indian courts. This book though presenting a very mistaken and distorted version of most of the principles of Muslim personal law, ironically became a classic and the courts accepted it as the most authoritative work on the subject. Intriguingly, even the two learned Muslim judges, who later edited the book, namely, Sir Sultan Ahmed[11] and Mohammed Hidayatullah,[12] also failed to apprehend the extensive misreading of Islamic legal principles underlying its provisions. So whom the best of law brains among the Muslims like Sir Sultan Ahmed and Muhammad Hidayatullah could allow Mullah's faulty work to pass for authentic Muslim law, how could the not so enlightened ones do any better? Therefore, Mullah's book – with all its unnoticed distortions – is regarded as the greatest authority on Muslim law in the courts even today in independent India.

Thus in the colonial times, the misinterpreters and ill informed non-Muslim exponents of Muslim law like McNaughten, Fitzgerald, Wilson, Baillie played havoc with the Muslim Personal Law. But that was not all. Even *mullahs* of the mosques added their own ignorance to the finest things in it. Further, the *Qadis'* courts, which were once presided over by real specialists in the *Shari'at* law were replaced by *muftis* who were in fact ordinary theologians having a superficial knowledge of Islamic law. Under the patronage of the British, these ill-educated *maulavis* thoughtlessly and unconsciously put their seal of approval on many distorted versions of many *Shari'at* laws which actually suited the interests and objectives of the rulers.[13]

After independence, a change in this situation was visualised by enlightened people. But the civil courts in the country, exercising jurisdiction and authority of the personal law of the Muslims, did not do anything different from their predecessors. Worse, the naïve *maulavis* of the mosques worked as the principal carriers of a distorted and misunderstood *Shari'at* law. Standards of Islamic jurisprudential learning having deteriorated considerably, the petty *maulavis* are generally ignorant of the true postulates of the *Shari'at*. Of late, unfortunately, India has ceased to produce Muslim scholars of the stature of 'Allamah Shibli Nu'Mani, Mufti Kafiyatullah, Maulana Ashraf 'Ali Thanavi and Shaikh al-Islam Maulana Hussain Ahmad Madani. They were profound thinkers, fully conversant with the true *Shari'at* laws and they did a lot for the protection of Muslim law in this country.[14] Maulana Thanvi and other religious leaders, alarmed by the growing distortion of the Islamic law in the British Indian courts made strenuous effort to revive Muslim religious court but failed. As a result the masses remained under the influence of the mediocre *maulavis* who, being lawfully ignorant of the true postulates of the *Shari'at*, kept on transmitting their wrong notions and misconceptions to the common man through their *fatwas* and counseling.[15]

It is need of the moment that a system be developed under which true information and provisions of the noble jurisprudence could be easily located in authentic sources. The Muslim scholars of eminence from Deoband's Dar-ul-'Uloom and the Nadwatul-ul-'Ulama of Lucknow must come forward and remove the distortions and work for creating awareness about how the principles of Islamic law are misunderstood and misused in this country.

SELECTED CONCEPTS AND INSTITUTIONS OF ISLAMIC PERSONAL LAW

Let us see the selected institutions of Islamic laws and how other communities have misunderstood them. There is a popular misconception that no sanctity or religious sanction is attached to a Muslim marrying four wives. He can do it as per his whims. I would like to give some examples of *Shari'ah* laws on marriage, divorce, polygamy, dowry, etc. which have been projected in such a way that they show that Muslim laws are not for the betterment of the community and need be changed. Dinshaw Faridunji Mulla distorted the Islamic concept of marriage and defined Islamic marriage as "A contract, which has for its object the procreation and the legalising of children.[16] However the original Islamic idea of marriage being a sacred partnership between the man and wife. The Qur'an describes marriage as a sacred covenant (mithaq-e-ghaliz). In one verse the Holy Book ordains that men and women are joined in marriage so that they can live with each other in love and solace. In a third verse it says that by marriage the man and wife pas into each other's protection. It repeatedly declares that men and women are *muhsan* and *muhsanat* who entered the protective fortress of marriage.[17] No doubt, Islam does not regard marriage as a *sanskara* (sacrament) in the Hindu religion sense of the term. In the formative stage the marriage in Islam is contractual. But once the marriage is solemnized it is much more than a civil contract. Islam does not require a ceremonial solemnisation of marriage. Marriage is to be proposed by or on behalf of one of the parties. This is *Ijab*, the proposal. It is, then, accepted by or on behalf of the other party. This is *qubul*, acceptance. Thus it is sacred partnership between the husband and the wife, which the Qur'an calls a 'sacred covenant' and a protective fortress.[18]

Besides this, marriage in Islam is much more than a "contract for production of children". The contractual element in marriage is, in fact, introduced by Islam exclusively for the benefit of the parties. They enter into a life partnership, permissible by the *Shari'at*, on their own mutually agreed terms and conditions.

THE *MAHER*

The right of the Muslim wife to receive and the liability of the husband to give her what is known as *maher*, 'dower' is a salient feature of Muslim marriage. Interestingly, no other aspect of the marriage law has been given by the doctors of Islamic law so much importance as *maher*. But this concept is widely misunderstood. Some people take it as an ordinary civil contract, while some others confuse it with the local Indian concept of dowry. The fact is that the *maher* is neither a contract nor dowry; it has a unique position of its own. It is the absolute and exclusive property of the wife which her husband gives her, but on which neither he nor his parents or guardians have any rights whatsoever.

INDEPENDENCE OF MUSLIM WIFE

The spouses are regarded, under the Qur'anic law, as each other's *libas*.[19] A Muslim wife is neither the 'half part' nor the 'better half' of her husband. In Islam the husband and wife are equal partners in a sacred relationship of trust and confidence. The Muslim wife legally retains her maiden name, her property, her independent legal status and even her school of law, if different from the husband's. The latter, by marrying her, does not acquire any rights to tamper with any of these things.[20]

THE MYTH ABOUT POLYGAMY

Polygamy is one of the main points of criticism on the part of non-Muslims and some others claim to be Muslims. However, polygamy is not something special that has appeared with the advent of Islam. It was practiced in many parts of the world much before the coming of Islam. Men used to marry several women at a time. Even the Prophets (upon whom be peace) were not immune from it. Sayyiduna Ibrahim (peace be upon him) had two wives, Sayyiduna Ishaq and Sayyiduna Musa (peace be upon them both) had many wives, Sayyiduna Sulayman (peace be upon him) had several wives whilst Sayyiduna Dawud (peace be upon him) had hundred wives. In fact, there are only two prophets who never married, one being Sayyiduna Isa and the other Sayyiduna Yahya (peace be upon them both). Historically, the Jews and Christians were polygamous. The ban on polygamy in Christianity is a man-made prohibition, not a divine law. Polygamy was practiced among the Persians, Greeks, Arabs and Hindus. Unrestricted polygamy was permissible in all the religions before the advent of Islam. It was practiced without any restriction or limitation. A man would marry many women. In most of the cases, the women who were in his marriage were oppressed and treated unjustly.

Islam came and banned the ill treatment of women. It limited unrestricted polygamy. It laid certain conditions for polygamy. The following verse of the Qur'an is very relevant:

If you fear that you shall not be able to deal justly with the orphans, marry women of your choice, two, three, or four, but if you fear that you shall not be able to deal justly (with them), then only one...(*Surah al-Nisa*, 3).

The circumstances in which this verse was revealed illustrate the element of great sincerity in the teachings of Islam about polygamy. It was revealed after the battle of Uhud, in which a significant number of Muslim men were martyred and as a consequence, many women were widowed and their children orphaned. To safeguard the new Muslim community, this just and compassionate law was revealed.

Islam requires men to take full care of the orphans' interests and property. But if a man felt that he could not do justice to them as a custodian, then he were advised to marry other women, up to a maximum of four.

Also, the Qur'an conditioned the permissibility of marrying more than one wife with justice and fair treatment. It is a grave sin, according to Qur'an to treat the wives unequally. Any man who wishes to take more than one wife also has to meet the important condition of fair treatment to all his wives. It is a Qur'anic command that anyone who is unable to do so should marry only one wife.

Equal treatment includes all social, economic and physical needs. It is very difficult thing recognizes the Qur'an:

You are never able to be fair and just as between women, even if it is your ardent desire: but turn not away (from a woman) altogether, so as to leave her (as it were) hanging (in the air). (*Surah al-Nisa*, 129).

The Messenger of Allah (Allah bless him and give him peace) said:

A man who marries more than one woman and then does not deal justly with them will be resurrected with half his faculties paralyzed (Sahih al-Bukhari).

This refers to aspects that are within the capacity of a man, such as equal treatment with regard to social, economic and physical needs. As far as the inclination of the heart is concerned, then equal and just treatment to all is beyond the capacity of a man.[21]

People have distorted things and spread misconception about the law of polygamy in Islam. Take, for instance, these words of Dinshaw Faridunji Mulla who is supposed to be an authority on the subject and is cited as such:

A Mohammedan may have as many as four wives at the same time but no more. If he marries a fifth wife, when he has already four, the marriage is not void but merely irregular.[22]

Here Mulla does not bother to explain in what circumstances, for what purposes, and subject to what conditions, the Qur'an chose to allow a strictly controlled and firmly disciplined plurality of wives. Nor has any of the subsequent non-Muslim and Muslim editors of Mulla cared to add to his section titled 'Number of Wives' any commentary on these important aspects of the Islamic law of polygamy. All of them have ignored the fact that the Qur'an strictly disciplined the wholly unrestricted polygamy, prevalent in the pre-Qur'anic era, by subjecting it to very strict conditions. An unconditional permission for an unbridled polygamy is very unjustly attributed by Mulla and others in the Indian courts to a scripture, which clearly says that where bigamy is likely to cause any injustice the man should remain a monogamist.[23]

Authentic studies tell us that in recent years polygamy among the Muslims, whose law conditionally permits it, has been far less than among those whose present law absolutely prohibits it with the force of civil and penal sanctions.

DISSOLUTION OF MARRIAGE

Another aspect of Islamic matrimonial law which has been much distorted is the law on divorce. Many interests have contributed to it. But the ill-educated *maulavis* of the village mosques have done more damage than all of them taken together. They misguide their clientele by transmitting to them their own faulty understanding of a superb divorce law.

The true Islamic law in fact stands for what is now known as the 'breakdown theory' of divorce. The Qur'an has not specified any matrimonial offences. The Prophet (PBUH) of Islam laid down no bars to matrimonial relief. The modern 'breakdown' theory of divorce precludes the courts from going into the causes of breakdown of marriage; the law-giver of Islam did not want the matter to be taken to the court at all, unless it became unavoidable for a wife due to the age-old predominance of man.[24] Under Islamic law an irretrievably broken marriage can be dissolved, extra-judicially, at the instance of either party or by their mutual consent. Depending on whether a marriage is to be dissolved by the husband, or by the wife, or mutually, the divorce process is called *talaq, khul'* and *mubara'at*, respectively.

The process of *talaq*, i.e., divorce by the man, is very simple. A husband who is convinced that his marriage has irretrievably broken down can quietly pronounce a divorce; but it shall not become effective during the period of *'iddat* [nearly three months], during which period he can freely retreat. At the expiry of this period, if he has not revoked the divorce, the marriage is dissolved – but the couple can revive the marriage by a fresh solemnization, provided that the wife agrees. And that is all. However, since the husband cannot be allowed to play hide and seek with his wife by repeatedly pronouncing a divorce and then either revoking it within the permissible period of *'iddat* or offering to remarry the same woman after its expiry, the law provides that a husband can do so only twice in the whole of his life; whenever during his married life he pronounces a divorce for a third time, the marriage is instantly dissolved perpetually, leaving no room either for a revocation of divorce or for a marriage by a fresh solemnization.[25]

The rule of "no marriage with a triply-divorced wife" is meant to be a deterrent for the ambivalent husband; he should know that a third divorce is the last word that he can speak regarding the marital bond. After the third divorce the wife may, and is rather encouraged, to marry another man. At this stage, then, the law thinks of a possible pitiable situation, which this woman may find herself in, viz., incidental failure of her second marriage too leading to divorce, or its dissolution by the death of the second husband. When this happens, it may not be so easy, or even advisable, for the poor woman to seek marriage with a third man. So, the embargo on her remarriage with the first husband is lifted and he is allowed to marry her if she agrees. This again is a pro-wife law meant to meet the extremely pitiable exigency of the dissolution of a woman's second marriage.[26]

This, in fact, is the true law on *talaq*. Unfortunately, ill-educated *maulavis* of the mosques are themselves composing a parody of this humane law through their unlicensed and uncensored counselling. Muslim men in India intending to dissolve their marriage often jump at the third *talaq* in a single pronouncement in sheer ignorance, believing that without this their action would have no effect at all. And our *maulavis*, and the civil courts, give it the real effect of the third *talaq*. Great Muslim jurists of our age have not been wholly oblivious to this misuse of the divorce law under mistaken beliefs and ignorance. Writing in 1943 the Jama'at-e-Islami chief, Maulana Abdul A'la Maududi had said:

Due to want of knowledge, Muslims have been generally given to understand that a *talaq* can be pronounced only through the triple-divorce formula, although it is an innovation and a sin leading to many legal complications. If people knew that triple divorce is superfluous and even a single *talaq* would dissolve the marriage, of course, leaving room for revocation during the next three months and remarriage thereafter, innumerable families could have been saved from disruption.[27]

On the widespread ignorance about the divorce law, Hakim al-Ummat Maulana Ashraf 'Ali Thanavi has clearly decreed that where a man uses the word '*talaq*' thrice just to assert himself, only a single divorce would be effective.[28] He also explains the true procedure of *talaq* at length[29]. Instead of blindly relying on the works of a McNaghten or a Mulla, one should read and enforce the law of *talaq* as expounded by Maulana Maududi, Maulana Thanavi and other Muslim scholars of great learning and stature.[30]

Divorce at the instance of wife may, under Islamic law, take the form of either a *talaq-i-tafwid* or a *khul'*. A Muslim wife can at the time of her marriage reserve in the marriage deed a right for herself to dissolve the marriage in specified circumstances. This is called *tafwid-e-talaq* (delegation of divorce). Irrespective of incorporation of such a clause in the marriage deed, to every Muslim wife is available the right of *khul'* – the attributes of which are, *mutatis mutandis*, the same as of man's right of *talaq*.[31]

The right of divorce, which Islam confers on women, if understood in its true perspective, will indeed be found dazzling. A wife having objective satisfaction that it is no more possible for her to live with her husband has simply to tell him that she wants a divorce. He can, thereupon, attempt persuasion and reconciliation, but cannot force the wife to cohabit. The only thing he can demand is that the wife forgoes her *maher* [which in the case of divorce by *talaq* at his instance he has to play]. If she agrees to it, and the man peacefully relents, there follows a *khul'*, which means a divorce at the instance of the wife. Nothing more is required. Where the man is still reluctant and tries to maintain the marital bond against the wife's wishes, she is free to go to the court announcing a *talaq*. A woman who is forced to go to the court for a decree of *khul'* need not even give the court the reasons why she wants it. Maulana Maududi writes explaining the position clearly:

In the matter of *khul'*, if it is taken to the court, it is not for the court to determine whether she wants separation on a genuine ground or just for the sake of marrying another man. Wife's right to *khul'* is parallel to the man's right of *talaq*. Like the latter, the former, too, is unconditional.[32]

For reasons best known to them, the courts in India have ignored the extremely liberal and pro-women law of *khul'* in Islam as if it were totally non-existent. Ever since then, this institution has remained eclipsed by the judicial ignorance of, and the juristic prejudice against, the law of Islam. In Pakistan [and Bangladesh] the true law of *khul'* has now been restored and enforced.[33]

In addition to *talaq-i-tafwid* and *khul'*, another useful course available to Muslim wives is the law of *faskh*, i.e. judicial divorce to be granted on any of the many specified grounds recognized by law — codified under the Dissolution of Muslim Marriages Act, 1939. Among these grounds are disappearance of the husband, failure on his part to provide maintenance, his inability to do so on account of imprisonment, desertion, impotency, insanity, leprosy, venereal disease, 'option of puberty' and cruelty.[34]

Another important thing is divorce by mutual consent. It is known as *mubara'at*, by which process a couple can jointly dissolve the marriage – of course, extra-judicially – on terms that my be mutually agreed upon. This concept of the *Shari'at* has been introduced into the Special Marriage Act, India, 1954[35] and into the Hindu Marriage Act, 1976.[36] But as a definite law itself it is lying dormant. The law-men in India, who even fail to grasp the clear distinction between *khul'* and *mubara'at*,[37] have been totally ignoring it (*mubara'at*), which is much more progressive and liberal than its parallels under the modern Indian statutes. It is a bilateral agreement between the husband and wife, without the intervention of the court. Unlike *khul'* [which does not hand on the husband's consent] and *talaq* [for which wife's consent is not required], *mubara'at* is a divorce which both the parties my equally look for.

Section 488 of the old Criminal Procedure Code of 1898 furnishes to Indian wives neglected by their husbands in the matter of maintenance, a speedy remedy for securing the same. On certain grounds, including bigamy, it enabled a wife to refuse cohabitation to the husband and yet seek the said remedy. In view of the apparent conflict between the Cr. P.C. law and the *Shari'at* regarding the right of a bigamous husband to seek separate maintenance, a plea for its inapplicability to the Muslims was made, but was turned down by the High Courts of Allahabad[38], Kerala[39] and Mysore[40]. The Madhya Pradesh. High court has, however, accepted the plea, refusing to pass an order of maintenance in favour of a Muslim wife who lived separately from her husband on account of his second bigamous marriage.[41] In several cases, after a maintenance order was granted to a Muslim wife, her husband divorced her by *talaq.* The decision of the courts in such cases was that the maintenance-order ceased to be effective after the expiry of the *'iddat* period observed by the divorced wife as per the rules of Muslim law.[42]

Under the new Criminal Procedure Code of 1973[43], by defining 'wife' as a term including a divorced wife, the remedy was sought to be extended also to the latter.[44] During the debate in Parliament, fearing that the new law would be used to practically supersede the substantive law of Islam on the subject, Muslim leadership secured inclusion of a clause in the Code to the effect that a maintenance-order once granted would be liable to be cancelled if it was shown that the aggrieved wife had already received in full, from her former husband, her post-divorce dues sanctioned by the personal law of the parties.[45]

Islamic law has indeed a very different concept of marriage. The Madras High Court had in fact completely distorted this concept when, in the old case of Packrichi v. Kunacha, it had held that[46] "as marriage recorded in D.F. Mulla's book[47], this wholly erroneous ruling has led to a wide-spread belief that a divorced Muslim wife is a helpless soul after the expiry of her '*iddat*, having no shelter and none whom she can lean on. The fact is that in the Islamic matrimonial culture neither there is an inter-familial transplantation of the girl on her marriage, nor are her parents or guardians perpetually absolved, after that, of their liabilities towards her. In Islam, since marriage is always a dissoluble union, the parents' liability to maintain their unmarried daughter remains only suspended during her married life. On the dissolution of her marriage, whether by her husband's death or by divorce, and in the latter case, whether at her own instance or otherwise, the liability is revived and would continue to be discharged until she got remarried. As stated in the *Fatawa-e-Qadi Khan*[48] and other legal treatises on Islam, a girl who is a *thayiba* (i.e., a widow or a divorce) has in the family of her birth all the rights and status of a *bakira* (i.e., a maiden). As regards an elderly woman having grown up children, the liability to maintain her after the dissolution of her marriage [whether by the death of her husband or by divorce] falls on her children – both male and female – who must discharge it jointly and equally.[49]

As a natural corollary to its concept of marriage and policy on divorce, Islam does not keep the parties tagged to each other for the rest of their lives after the dissolution of a marriage. It encourages both of them [depending on their age] to get remarried—the remarriage of a divorcee, male or female, is not a taboo in Islamic law or culture. The law keeps both parties to a dissolved marriage wholly free to look after their new responsibilities. As regards the female divorcee, Islam does not, for long, think of her in terms of a divorced wife; it thinks of her, once again, as the daughter of her parents, or the mother of her children, as the case may be. Her former husband is, of course, required to pay forthwith her *maher* –

if not already paid. As regards her maintenance, he must provide it for the whole period during which she is not allowed by law to remarry [called '*iddat* in law] – but not till she actually gets remarried. The moment she is free from her '*iddat*, if young, she is a *thayiba* who is now in all respects equal to a maiden girl and returns to the family of her birth; if an elderly women, she happily lives with her children. In either case, she has no stigma of being a divorcee attached to her. This arrangement eminently conforms to Islam's own concepts of marriage and divorce and its unique theory of equality of sexes, which is different from other systems.[50]

The egalitarian spirit of the personal law of Islam is unfortunately lying eclipsed because of the propaganda started by the anti-orientalist British-Indian regime, and now carried on by the vested interests, that under Islamic law women's rights and status are in fact much inferior to men's, and that those who say otherwise are mere apologists. To the impact of this false propaganda misusers of Islamic law have unconsciously added their own contribution. Sanction for this presumed inferior status of females is being ironically attributed to Syedena Muhammad, the enlightened Prophet of Arabia (PBUH) who, in the 7th century A.D. when Europe treated women as chattel, gave them a charter of numerous valuable rights and a guarantee of respectable coexistence with men. This Prophet (PBUH) carried a scripture – the Holy Qur'an – which announced to its men-followers that:

Women have rights against you as you have against them.[51]

It issued a mandate of absolute parity between sexes in respect of the right to work, saying:

For men is what they earn and for women what they earn.[52]

It directed husbands to treat their wives as equal partners in the marital union, thus:

A man who dislikes his wife must know that god might have kept
in the person of the wife many latent benefits for him.[53]

In his 'Farewell sermon' the Prophet (PBUH) warned
men:

Fear God in the matter of women. Their rights are the same over
you as yours on them. So do good to them.[54]

It is high time that our judges and lawyers stop looking
at Islamic Law through the spectacles of the colonial courts
and their past and present rapporteurs. They must understand the Islamic law, its original values and prevent the
widespread misuse of its lofty principles.

NOTES

1. Tahir Mahmood, *Personal Law in Crisis*, New Delhi, 1986, pp. 50.
2. W.W. Hunter, *Indian Mussalmans*, Calcutta, 1871 cited by Tahir
   Mahmood, *op. cit.*, p. 51.
3. *Ibid.*, p. 52.
4. *Ibid.*
5. *Ibid.*, p. 53.
6. *Ibid.*
7. Part I: *Hanafi Law* (2nd revised ed., London, 1875); Part II *Ithna
   Ashari Law* (London, 1869).
8. *Ibid.*, [London, 1930].
9. *Ibid.*, [6th ed. London, 1931].
10. D.F Mulla, *Principles of Mohammedan Law* (Bombay, 1st ed., 1906;
    10th ed., 1933).
11. *Ibid.*, [13th, 14th and 15th editions, 1950, 1955 and 1961, respec-
    tively].
12. *Ibid.*, [16th, 17th, and 18th editions, 1968, 1972 and 1977, respec-
    tively].

13. Tahir Mahmood, *op. cit.*, p. 56.
14. *Vide* the *Mussalman Wakf Validating Act, 1913.*
15. Tahir Mahmood, *op. cit.*, p. 56.
16. D.F. Mulla, *op. cit.*, (18th ed., Bombay, 1977).
17. Quran, Chap. 5: Verse: 6, cited by Tahir Mahmood, *op. cit.*, p. 64.
18. Quran Chap. 4:21, Quran 30: 21, 7: 189, Quran, 2: 187 *vide, ibid.*
19. Quran Chap. 2 : 187.
20. Under the Dissolution of Muslim Marriage Act, 1939 if the husband tampers with the wife's property or prevents her from exercising her rights over it, and if he obstructs her in the observance of the religious profession or practice (as per her school of Islamic law), she may seek a divorce on either of these of these grounds. See the Act, section 2 (viii), clauses (d) and (e).
21. Dr. Asghar Ali Engineer, *Islam and Modern Age*, monthly publication, 2000.
22. *Supra*, note 40 at p. 285, section 255.
23. Quran Chap. 4:3 and Chap. 4:9.
24. Tahir Mahmood *op. cit.*, p. 74.
25. *Ibid.*, p. 75.
26. *Ibid.*, p. 76.
27. A.A. Maududi, *Huquq-al-Zawjayn*, 10(4th ed., 1964) cited by Tahir Mahmood *op. cit.*, p. 76.
28. A.A. Thanvi, IV Behisti Zewar, 29:13 *vide ibid.*, p. 77.
29. *Ibid.*
30. *Ibid.*
31. *Ibid.*
32. *Supra*, note 78 at p. 61 *vide ibid.*, p. 78.
33. Law enacted in Pakistan and Bangladesh after a court decision in Khurshid Bibi *vs.* Mohd. Amin, PLD, 1967 SC 97.
34. See for details, Tahir Mahmood *op. cit.*, p. 79.
35. Section 28, *vide ibid.*, p. 79.
36. Section 13B, added by the Marriage Laws (Amendment) Act, 1976 *vide ibid.*, p. 79.
37. Mulla, in his book, has failed to properly differentiate between *khul* and *mubara'at*. He describe both of them as "dissolution of marriage by agreement" [p. 336, sec. 219(1)], whereas *khul* is in fact a transaction in which the wife may divorce her husband, whether he agrees to it or not. It is analogous to the man's right to *talaq.*
38. Badraddin *vs.* Aisha Begum, 1957 ALJ 300, ruling that the Muslim

Personal law (*Shari'at*) Application Act, 1937 did not make section 488 of the (old) Cr. P.C. inapplicable to the Muslims.

39. Shalulammeedu *vs.* Subaida Beavi, 1970 KLT 4, said that it would be "improper" for the courts to exclude from the benefit of the Cr. P.C. provision "any section of the community born and brought up on Indian soil" [as per V.R. Krishna Iyer, J].

40. Syed Aamed *vs.* Taj Begum, AIR 1958 Mys 128, held that a husband aggrieved by the magistrate's order could seek a suitable remedy in the civil court.).

41. Abdullah *vs.* Chandnibi, AIR 1956 Bhopal 71; Munawar *vs.* Sabir (1970) MPLJ 23.

42. Ahmed Kasim *vs.* Khatun, AIR 1933 cal.27; Mohd. Shamsuddin *vs.* Noor Jahan, AIR 1955 Hyd. 418 Ahmed *vs.* Mst. Begha, AIR 1955 J & K.

43. Under the (new) Code the law of maintenance is found in section 125-127.

44. *Ibid.*, Sec. 125, Explanation.

45. *Ibid.*, Sec. 127(3) (b).
    (The above mentioned cases in the footnotes are cited by Tahir Mahmood *op. cit.*, p. 80-85.

46. (1911) 36 Mad. 385.

47. *Supra*, note 40 at p. 383, sec. 370 cited by Tahir Mahmood *op. cit.*, p. 86.

48. Available in English, tr. by Maulavi Muhammad Yusuf [T.L.L., Cal- . cutta, vols. I-II, 1875].

49. *Supra*, note 55 at 184-85. The texts of Muslim law clearly provides that so long as a person [and this includes a divorced or widowed mother] has a child [male or female] capable of maintaining him or her, no other relation can be compelled to provide maintenance to him or her. [See, e.g., *Fatawa-i-'Alamgiri* as cited in N.E. Baillie, I *Digest of Moohummudan Law*, 104].

50. Tahir Mahmood *op. cit.*, p. 87.

51. Quran, II: 228.

52. Quran IV: 32.

53. Quran, IV: 19.

54. Authentic text of this sermon is available in all biographies of the Prophet (PBUH). See e.g., A.K.S. Najibabadi, *Tarikh-i-Islam*, pp. 242-43 (2nd ed., Karachi, 1957.

3

REFORMS IN MUSLIM COUNTRIES

Major portions of the statutory personal laws enacted in the various Muslim countries represent a mere codification of the established law or, at best, unification of hitherto divergent legal principles. There is, however, no reason to deny the fact that certain provisions in these laws have introduced significant reforms in the traditional law. The principal reforms so introduced in one country or another relate to:

(i) Marriage—age for men and women and difference of age between parties to marriage;

(ii) role of marriage—guardians in the fixation and solemnization of marriage;

(iii) registration and documentation of marriage;

(iv) monetary aspects of marriage—power, dowry and expenses;

(v) polygamy and rights of co-wives;

(vi) maintenance of wife, family and matrimonial home during the subsistence of marriage;

(vii) unilateral divorce rights of parties to marriage and grounds for judicial divorce;

(viii) post-divorce reliefs for the parties—especially for women;

(ix) period of gestation and its implications;

(x) parents' rights relating to custody and guardianship of children – especially of mothers;

(xi) inheritance rights of certain close relatives – surviving spouse, daughters, brothers-sisters, grandfather and descendants of predeceased children;

(xii) choice of the legatee—especially heirs' eligibility to receive a bequest; and

(xiii) validity, tenure and management of family *waqfs*.

Reforms in these areas have been effected – different reforms in different countries – either under the provisions of comprehensive codes (or laws) of personal status or family rights, or by way of sporadic legislation.

The source-materials for all the aforestated reforms have been located by the jurists and the legislators of the Muslim world in the depth, divergence, flexibility and richness of the legal principles within the vast framework of the *Shari'ah*.[1]

In several countries the '*ulama* have approved – or have been closely associated with – the reforms effected. At the same time, some of the reforms in some countries have been opposed and criticized by certain sections of religious leaders and scholars. On some occasions, their objections were accepted and the reforms (proposed or already effected) dropped, repealed or modified.

METHODOLOGY OF REFORM

To achieve the desired legal reforms recourse has been had in various Muslim countries to the Islamic jurisprudential doctrines of *musawat-i-madhahib-i-fiqh* (equality of the schools of Islamic law), *istihsan* (juristic equity), *masalih almursalah* (public interest), *siyasah shar'iyah* (legislative policy of the state), *istidlal* (juristic reasoning), *tawdi* (legislation), *tadwin* (codification) and the like.

The techniques and methodology of reform adopted have included – besides the age-old processes of *ijma'* (consensus of jurists), *qiyas* (analogical deduction of rules) and individual or collective *ijthad* (evolving new legal principles on the basis of the old ones) – some new principles like *tak-*

hayur (eclectic choice out of divergent legal principles within the Islamic law) and *talfiq* (combination of two or more parallel legal rules to evolve a new one).[2]

THE UNCODIFIED LAW

There are, of course, Muslim countries where personal law has not yet been transformed into statutes – the courts find it in the classical legal treatises. Saudi Arabia, for instance, does not have either a civil code or a personal-law statute. As per a directive issued by the country's Supreme Judicial Council far back in 1928, certain specified *Hanbali* texts remain the basic source of the law of personal status, family rights and succession. Sharing the traditional *Hanbali* law with Saudi Arabia, the state of Qatar has also left it uncodified. The Sultanate of Oman has not codified any aspect of personal law, though in recent years it has launched and made remarkable progress with a massive programme of codification of the various branches of law. Of course, it has incorporated in its new Penal Code of 1973 rules for the enforcement of domestic obligations under personal law.

Also in some non-Arab Muslim countries of Asia and Africa – e.g., Gambia, Mali and Nigeria – personal law remains, to a large extent, in its traditional form.[3]

A COMPARATIVE STUDY OF ISLAMIC LAW

The areas of reform in most of the Muslim countries have been Marriage and Divorce. They codified law in such a way that woman do not loose any of their rights pertaining to Marital relationship as also in life after divorce.

CONCEPT OF MARRIAGE

The true concept in marriage in Islam is often badly misunderstood. Marriage among the Muslims is, as per the Qur'an

[IV:21], a 'solemn pact' for the purpose of establishing family life and having children. Though in law it takes the form of a 'contract' ('*aqd*), it is not an ordinary civil contract. The definition of marriage included in the personal law enactments of the Muslim countries reflect various elements of the Islamic concept of marriage, the focus in different countries being on different elements – moral protection of spouses [Algeria], belief in God as the foundation of the family [Indonesia}, life in partnership [Iraq, Syria], family life [Jordan, North Yemen], discharge of family liabilities [Morocco} and equal rights and duties of the spouses [Somalia, South Yemen].[4]

The form of marriage in Islam is unquestionably contractual. The traditional Islamic form of marriage – *ijab* (offer) by one party and *qubul* (acceptance) by the other, exchange in the presence of witnesses personally or through a *wakil* (agent) – is specifically laid down as the basic marriage procedure by the legislative enactment of all those Muslim countries where the marriage law has been fully codified.

STIPULATION IN MARRIAGE CONTRACT

Islam gives to the parties to an intended marriage freedom of mutually stipulating any condition. The basic policy of Islam is not to impose on the parties everything by the force of law; it follows the rules of contractual freedom. The contracting parties can mutually opt out of anything, which the law permits but does not make obligatory. Similarly, they can opt for something special which is neither prohibited nor imposed by the law. This is called *khiyar-al-shart* (option of stipulation). The doctrine of freedom of marital stipulation is specifically recognized by legislation in Jordan, Morocco, North Yemen, Syria and Tunisia.

POLYGAMY

Polyandry is absolutely prohibited in Islam. As regards polygamy, a verse in the holy Qur'an [IV:3] says that though one could have four wives at a time one who cannot treat co-wives with equality and justice should rest content with a single wife, adding that this (monogamy) would be better to keep men away from injustice [or to keep the family limited, as per the interpretation of Imam Shafi'i].[5]

In Jordan, Lebanon and Morocco legislation specifically recognizes the right of every woman to stipulate the time of marriage against her husband's possible second marriage while she remains his wife, violation of this entitles her to seek a divorce. In some other countries this is possible under the general rules called *khiyar-al-shart* (option of stipulation). In Algeria the law provides that an intended second marriage must be 'justified', and the husband must be able to treat co-wives with equality.

In Egypt and Morocco while the law requires every man getting married to provide to the marriage-officials full facts of existing marriage, if any, the first wife can seek a divorce if the second marriage has caused her an injury; in Egypt also the second wife can seek a divorce if she has been deceived into a bigamous marriage.

In Indonesia, Iraq, Malaysia, Somalia, South Yemen and Syria a married man wanting to marry again must obtain prior permission of the court; while in Bangladesh and Pakistan he must seek permission from a quasi-judicial body [an 'Arbitration Council' constituted by a government official with himself as the chairman and one nominee each of the parties as members]. In Indonesia, Somalia and South Yemen the court can allow a bigamous marriage only if the first wife is suffering from barrenness, a physical defect or an incurable disease – and also if she fails to acts as wife in Indonesia or has been imprisoned for over two years in South Yemen. In all these countries the permission for a fresh marriage can be given only after a proper inquiry in one's financial implications.

In Bangladesh, Iraq and Pakistan the first wife can seek a divorce if the second marriage has been unlawfully contracted. In Bangladesh, Malaysia and Pakistan the whole dower, if unpaid, will become immediately payable on account of bigamy. The law in Morocco and North Yemen prohibit bigamy for a man who cannot do equal justice to more than one wife- while those of Jordan, Lebanon and Syria provide that if a man does have two wives he must treat them with equal justice as per the Qur'anic law and cannot accommodate them in the same house except with their consent. In Bangladesh and Pakistan failure to treat co-wives equally is a ground for divorce. In Tunisia bigamy is prohibited and if a bigamous marriage takes place it will be invalid and penalized. In Turkey and Tunisia it has been declared that the Qur'anic conditions for bigamy in the modern social circumstances cannot be fulfilled by anybody.[6]

EFFECTS OF MARRIAGE – GENERAL

Marriage in Islam has no effect on the individual status of the parties. The man and the woman are treated in this respect with a perfect equality. The concept of merger of personalities of the husband and the wife is foreign to Islam. A Muslim wife is neither the "better half" (modern western usage) nor the "half body"(classical Indian concept) of her husband. She retains in marriage her maiden name, her school of law, her independent legal status and her property and proprietary rights. These features of the *Shari'ah* are so firmly established in the Muslim world that the codifiers of personal law did not deem it necessary to re-state in the laws which they have enacted – though in some of them we do find specification of certain rights which wife retains in marriage. The Tunisian law, for instance, declares that the husband shall not be the guardian of his wife's property, and the Indonesian law clarifies that both the parties shall have exclusive control over their respective properties.[7]

MAHER—DOWER OF MARRIED WOMAN

Maher (dower) is an essential element of Muslim marriage. The husband must pay it and it belongs to the wife wholly and exclusively. Marriage is unthinkable without *Maher.*

NAFAQAH—MAINTENANCE OF WIFE

The wife's right to be provided with maintenance by her husband—which in Islam is not absolute—is detailed and enforced by the codified personal laws of nearly all the Muslim countries. In Bangladesh and Pakistan a wife, whose lawful right to maintenance is not fulfilled, can (a) institute a regular civil suit, (b) seek a speedy criminal remedy under the general law and (c) secure redressal of her grievances in this regard through an 'arbitration council'.[8] In Brunei and Malaysia the general laws on maintenance locally in force do not apply to the Muslims, but in both the countries *Shari'ah* court have wide power to secure maintenance due to Muslim wives in accordance with Islamic law with due regard to the traditional rules of wife's *nushuz* (delinquency).[9] Maintenance orders in favour of married women, both regular and interim, can be passed and enforced by the courts in Egypt, Iraq, Jordan, Lebanon, Morocco, North Yemen and Syria – except when a wife has lost her rights to maintenance on account of one or another reason – e.g., unlawful refusal to consummate the marriage or to cohabit later, leaving the matrimonial home without husband's consent or fault, unnecessarily taking up the employment against his wishes and other behaviour that in Islamic law would constitute *nushuz;* two additional grounds for losing the right to maintenance are apostasy in Egypt and being guilty of a penal offence in Iraq.[10] In Somalia and South Yemen the law does not enforce wife's

unilateral rights to maintenance; instead both parties to marriage are required to proportionately contribute to the expenses of married life and matrimonial home except, of
course, when either party has no income or property in which
case the other party will have the full responsibility in the
matter.[11]

TALAQ—DIVORCE BY HUSBAND'S ACTION

Extra-judicial divorce by the action of the husband remains
possible in several Muslim countries. A system of checks and
balances of various kinds has, however, been devised for this
form of divorce. Unintended *talaqs* have now been out-lawed
in a number of Muslim countries. In Egypt, Iraq, Jordan,
Lebanon, Morocco, North Yemen, Sudan and Syria *talaq* is no
more effective or necessarily enforceable if pronounced by a
person who is drunk, insane, imbecile, provoked, shocked,
depressed, ill, superannuated, in sleep or under duress, and
along when it is used as an inducement, threat or vow or is
implied in an ambiguous or metaphorical expression.[12]

Iraq, Jordan and Syria a husband wanting to effect a *talaq* is advised—but not compelled—to approach the court it
shall exhaust all effort to see that the divorce is avoided and
can eventually permit only a single divorce.[13] In Afghanistan,
Algeria, Indonesia, Malaysia, Somalia, South Yemen and Tunisia a *talaq* can be effected by a husband only with the prior
permission or intervention of the court which must first try to
effect a reconciliation, direct or through arbitrators, failing
which it can allow a *talaq*. In Lebanon a *talaq* must be notified to the court by the husband who has pronounced it;
while in Brunei and Egypt it must be duly registered with
civil officials within three and seven days respectively. Under
the law of Bangladesh and Pakistan a *talaq*, after it is pronounced, is to be notified to a local government official to enable him to set up the machinery for reconciliation, and the

talaq remain ineffective for ninety days [or until delivery later if the wife is pregnant] during which period the said machinery will go into action and exhaust all possibilities of reconciliation.[14]

TALAQ-I-TAWFID AND KHUL'— DIVORCE AT WIFE'S INSTANCE

A Muslim wife may derive from her marriage-contract the right to pronounce a *talaq* (called *talaq-i-tawfid*) on specified grounds or even at discretion. This enables married women to dissolve their marriage without the consent of the husband or the intervention of a court or another external agency. The basis of this power of the wife is its *tawfid* (delegation) to her by mutual agreement of the parties incorporated in the contract of marriage. The personal law enactments in Bangladesh, Brunei, Iraq, Jordan, Malaysia, Morocco, Pakistan and Syria enforce the law on delegated divorce.[15] In Morocco such a *talaq* is irrevocable and in Bangladesh and in Pakistan like a *talaq* by the husband it must be notified to local official for the constitution of an 'arbitration council' which will explore the possibilities of avoiding it.

Khul' is an important right of the Muslim wife enabling her to get rid of an unwanted or broken marriage. The right of *Khul'* is available to her under law and, unlike a *talaq-i-tawfid* does not depend on terms of the marriage contract. Without disclosing the reason for her action the wife can get her marriage dissolved by *Khul'* can be effected without the intervention of a court if the husband agrees; if he does not agree the court can pas a decree of *Khul'*. In Algeria, Libya and Morocco the laws recognize *Khul'* and in the first two of these countries the court are expressly empowered to pass a decree of *Khul'* at the wife's instance irrespective of the husband's objection. In Pakistan and Bangladesh the courts have power to pass decree of *Khul* irrespective of the husband's consent.[16]

MUBARA'AH--DIVORCE BY MUTUAL CONSENT

Divorce by mutual consent is different from *khul'* in which the initiative to terminate the marriage is on the part of the wife. The proper term for divorce by mutual consent (in which both the parties desire separation) is *mubara'ah* (mutual freeing). In Pakistan the court have in some cases aptly explained the difference between *Khul'* and *mubara'ah* – these ruling now operate as law both in Bangladesh and Pakistan; in the former country the law on the application of *Shari'ah* referring to *khul'* and *mubara'ah* separately. But in some countries like Jordan and Syria by describing *khul'* as *mukhala'ah* (which expression conveys an element of mutuality), the law mixes up *khul'* with *mubara'ah*- while in Libya the law refers to *mubara'ah* and applies to it the law of *khul'*.[17]

TAFRIQ--DIVORCE BY COURT

The modern concept of the 'judicial separation' (in which marriage remains intact while the parties live separate) is unknown to Muslim law; what is called *tafriq* (separation) *tafriq -i-qada' i* (judicial separation) under the laws of some Muslim countries is in fact judicial divorce. Codified laws in many Muslim countries empower the courts to dissolve a marriage by a decree of divorce [called *faskh, tatliq* or *tafriq*] on a number of grounds including:[18]

1. adultery [Indonesia, Turkey] or leading an immoral life or compelling wife to do so [Bangladesh, Malaysia, Pakistan];
2. addiction with drinking, drugs or gambling [Indonesia, North Yemen];
3. cruelty, injury [Afghanistan, Egypt, Lebanon, Pakistan, Malaysia, Morocco, South Yemen.]
4. disputes, discord, breakdown of marriage [Indonesia,

Jordan, Somalia, South Yemen, Tunisia, Turkey.]
5. desertion, failure to provide maintenance or just and equal maintenance to co-wife, imprisonment for 3-7 years [Afghanistan, Algeria, Bangladesh, Morocco, Malaysia, Somalia, South Yemen, Syria, Turkey]
6. insanity [Afghanistan, Bangladesh, Egypt, Pakistan]
7. interference with wife's religious practice or tampering with her property. [Bangladesh, Malaysia, Pakistan]
8. unknown whereabouts for 1-7 years [Bangladesh, Malaysia, North Yemen, Pakistan, Somalia]

In all these countries the remedy is generally available to the wife. Everywhere before granting a decree of divorce the court has to attempt reconciliation between the parties in all suitable cases – generally through arbitrators and basically in accordance with the procedure laid down by the Qur'an (IV:35)

'IDDAH AND ITS MAINTENANCE (*NAFAQAH*)

A divorce wife must refrain from remarrying for a certain period following the dissolution of a marriage that had been consummated in fact or in law. This period is called *'iddah* of divorce and it laws applies to all forms of termination of marital union. Its duration is not more than three months except in the case of pregnancy at the time of divorce in which case its duration coincides with that of pregnancy. During the *'iddah* of the revocable divorce the woman remain wedded to the man who must, therefore, maintain as his wife. Codified personal laws of all the Muslim countries enforce all these principles:

1. In Iraq, Jordan and Lebanon the period of *'iddah* is to be counted from the date of divorce even though the wife comes to know of divorce later;

2. In Iraq the conduct of woman in *'iddah* during that period will not affect her maintenance rights;

3. In Lebanon a woman divorced on account of her own serious misconduct (nushuz) shall not get maintenance of *'iddah*;

4. In almost all countries rules for fixation of the amount of maintenance of *'iddah* shall be the same as for that during marriage;

5. In North Yemen maintenance of *'iddah* may not be allowed in the case of an Irrevocable divorces unless the wife is pregnant.

MUT'AH–INDEMNITY FOR DIVORCE

Under the laws of some Muslim countries a divorced wife is entitled to receive from her former husband what is called *mut'ah*. This concept has been rendered in to English as 'consolatory gift', 'compensation' and 'indemnity'. *Mut'ah* is, thus basically different from regular maintenance of divorcee. In the case of dissolution of an unconsummated marriage contracted without a specific *maher,* only *mut'ah* is payable and no *maher* or maintenance of *'iddah* can be claimed. This rule is enforced in Jordan, Lebanon, Morocco and North Yemen.[19]

1. In Malaysia to a woman who has been divorced "without just cause" the court can grant, by way of *mut'ah,* a sum that may be "fair and just" – the law being by and large the same Brunei;[20]

2. A woman who has been "arbitrarily divorced" by her husband may be awarded, by way of *mut'ah,* maintenance of one year in Jordan, two years in Egypt and three years in Syria – payable in lump sum or in instalments depending on the financial condition of the husband;[21]

3. In Morocco a husband who divorces his wife at him shall pay her *mut'ah* in conformity with his financial condi-

tions of the husband;[22]

4. In Somalia and South Yemen where the husband is responsible for the termination of marriage by *talaq* or *faskh* the court may grant to the wife up to one year's maintenance- while the wife may lose *maher* if she is responsible for divorce.[23]

DIVORCED WIFE'S *MAHER*:

All unpaid *maher* whatever be its nature become ordinarily payable forthwith on the termination of marriage by *talaq*. In the case of *faskh* (judicial divorce) and *khul'* the husband's liability regarding *maher* is to be determined by the court decree and the parties agreement respectively. The legal rules in this respect are enforced by the laws in several Muslim countries some significant provisions of which are as follows:[24]

1. In Bangladesh and Pakistan in all cases of judicial divorce wife's right to *maher* (if otherwise admissible under the law) remains intact;

2. In all cases where *maher* is not "specified" but is otherwise payable "proper" *maher* (*maher-i-mithl*) shall be paid in all countries.

3. Where the divorce wife claims a higher amount to have been specified as her *maher* but cannot prove it, while the husband quotes an amount as specified *maher* but cannot prove it, while the husband quotes an amount as specified *maher* which means unusually low, "proper" *maher* shall be payable in Egypt, Jordan, Lebanon and Syria;

4. Where an unconsummated marriage is dissolved on the ground of Impotency or sexual deformity of either party, no *maher* is payable in Jordan and Syria.

5. Where an unconsummated marriage is dissolved while *Maher* is specified, half of it will be payable in Iraq, Jordan and Syria.

6. In Jordan where a marriage is dissolved on account of the wife's apostasy, no *maher* will be payable.

RESIDENCE AND COSTS FOR DIVORCED WIFE HAVING CHILDREN

After a divorce the divorced mother ordinarily retains her normal right to the custody of her children. This is so since in Islam a mother is the mother of her children and not their father's wife. A change in her marital status does not therefore in itself affect her rights in regards to her children. As a divorced mother may be deprived of her marital home, there must be a place where she can live with her children to look after them. Laws in several countries take care of it.

In Egypt for a divorced wife who has in her custody children born of the dissolved marriage the husband must provide either a proper and independent house or rent for such a house; in case the matrimonial home used by the couple before divorce is a rented one the divorced mother and her children will have a lien over it after the divorce—in all such cases the divorcees having the right to residence so long as she has the lawful custody of children; also in Algeria and Malaysia divorced wives having children in their custody must be provided accommodation by their former husbands.[25]

Maintenance of children in the custody of the divorced mother is always to be paid by their father; he must also pay her remuneration for suckling and keeping custody except of agreed upon to the contrary in a divorced by mutual consent.

REMARRIAGE OF DIVORCED WOMEN

Remarriage during *'iddah* following a divorce (whether revocable or irrevocable) or husband's death is not permissible for the woman; once the *'iddah* expires she is free to remarry. As regards remarriage with the same man who has obtained a divorce), Muslim law classifies the effect of divorce in this regard into two categories—*bainunah-i-sughra* (small parting) and *bainunah-i-kubra* (great parting)—the former leaving and the latter not leaving room for a fresh marriage between parties. A first and a second *talaq* by man's action create, when it becomes effective, *bainunah-i-sughra*; while the third *talaq* crates *bainunah-i-kubra* as soon as it is pronounced. Divorce in any other form-- *faskh, tatliq, talaq–i-tawfid*, in any other form –*faskh, tatliq, tafriq, khul', talaq-i-tawfid,* etc., creates *bainunah-i-kubra*; only in some exceptional cases [e.g., divorced on the ground of temporary inability to provide maintenance] will a judicial divorce create small parting.

All these legal rules are stated in the laws of Iraq, Jordan, Lebanon, Morocco, North Yemen, Somalia and Syria.[26]

DISSOLUTION OF MARRIAGE BY DEATH

A woman whose husband dies must observe *'iddah* of death for four months and ten days or the duration of the pregnancy whichever is longer. So should a woman whose husband dies while she is observing *'iddah* of a revocable divorce (dies while she is observing *'iddah* of a revocable divorce (but not if the divorce was irrevocable in which case *'iddah* of divorce shall be completed). Once the *'iddah* of death is over the woman is a *thayiba* free to marry again. These rules of Muslim law form part of the codified laws in Algeria, Indonesia, Iraq, Jordan, Lebanon, Morocco, North Yemen, Somalia, South Yemen, Syria and Tunisia.[27]

All unpaid *maher* of the widow becomes immediately payable on the dissolution of her marriage by her husband's death- as confirmed by the enactments in Jordan and Syria. The widow's *maher* is a debt and like the other debts of the deceased is to be paid before the law of succession is applied to the estate of the deceased. In Bangladesh and Pakistan a widow who ha her husband's property in her possession at the time of his death can lawfully retain it by way of a lien until her unpaid *maher* has been paid out of the property of the deceased; in a number of cases this legal rule ha been applied and explained.[28]

INTESTATE AND TESTAMENTARY SUCCESSION

1. CLASSIFICATION OF HEIRS

The law of intestate succession (*fara'id* or *mawarith*) is an important chapter of the Islamic personal law. The holy Qur'an contains mandatory provisions in this regards [IV: 7/12,33,176]. The Sunni doctor of law treated the Qur'anic law on inheritance as an amending law and engrafted it into the pre-Islamic customary law. On the other hand the Shi'ah Ithna 'Ashari jurists built on the Qur'anic foundations a completely new structure of succession law. Within the various Sunni schools of law there is divergence of juristic opinion in regard to some details of the law of inheritance; while the law of inheritance under the Shi'ah Zaidi school by and large agrees with the Shafi'i law. The Sunni schools of law there is divergence of jurist opinion in regards to some details of the law of inheritance; while the law classify heirs into three classes: (i) *dhu faraid* [preferential heirs, mostly women, specified in the Qur'an with their fixed fractional shares]; (ii) *'asabat* [agnatic heirs]; and (iii) *dhu al-arham* [uterine heirs]. Viewed together these classes include mainly (a) surviving spouses, (b) parents and grand parents, (c) children and lower agnatic descendants, (d) brothers and sisters by all kinds of blood (full, half and uterine), and (e) nephew and paternal uncles (by full/half blood) and their agnatic male descendants. Within each of the classes the rule "nearer in degree excludes the remoter" determine the actual heir. On the other hand, if class (i) heirs do not exhaust the estate while there id no class (ii) heirs, the residue reverts by the process of *radd* (return) prorata to class (i) heirs accepts the surviving spouse.

Class (iii) heirs [including mainly son's daughter's children, false grand parents, daughters descendants, nephew by uterine blood, nieces and female paternal cousins] inherit when there is no heir of classes (i) and (ii) other than spouses, taking the estate subject to the internal rule of exclusion.

The Ithna 'Ashari law of inheritance is much simpler and indeed closer to the Qur'anic injunctions. It classifies heirs into three classes different from those at Sunni law, viz. (i) parents, children and lower lineal descendants; (ii) grandparents, bothers and sisters and nephews and nieces; (iii) uncle and cousins.

Class (i) excludes classes (ii) and (iii) and class (ii) excludes class (iii) while the surviving spouse always inherits, taking a fixed Quranic shares.

In Algeria, Egypt, Morocco, North Yemen, Syria and Tunisia the codified laws of inheritance have basically retained the three-fold Sunni classification of heirs. On the other hand, the law in Iraq is based on Ithna 'Ashari classification of heirs. In Somalia and Turkey, too, the modern laws of inheritance are closer to, though not wholly same as, the Ithna 'Ashari law. New rules concerning inheritance rights of certain heirs have been introduced in many of these countries and also in Jordan, Kuwait, Bangladesh and Pakistan. However the concept of heir apparent, women's limited estate, ancestral property and coparcenary, which are foreign to Islamic law, have not been introduced by legislation in any Muslim countries. All property remains absolute and heritable.[29]

II. SHARE OF THE SURVIVING SPOUSE

The traditional rule that the principle of *radd* [pro rata distribution of the remainder of the estate to Qur'anic heirs] would never be applicable to the surviving spouse has been subjected to reform in Algeria, Egypt, Jordan, Sudan, Syria, Somalia and Tunisia.[30] In the first five countries where no other heir of classes (i), (ii) and (iii) is alive the surviving spouse now gets the whole estate in preference to the rule of escheat – the same principle having been established by the courts in Bangladesh and Pakistan. In Somalia the whole estate goes to the spouse where no other heir recognized by the present Somali law (which has considerably restricted the list of heirs) is in existence. In Tunisia the rule of *radd* has been introduced and made applicable to the spouse along with the other Qur'anic heirs.

III.   SHARES OF DAUGHTER AND SON'S DAUGHTER

Sons and the daughters of the praepositus co-existing inherit together under all the schools of law- each son taking a share double that of each daughter. In the absence of a son, daughters take fixed shares- a single daughter one half and two or more of them two-third of the estate, the remainder going to the other Qur'anic and agnatic heirs entitled to inherit as per the rules. So, a daughter may have to share the estate not only with the male Qur'anic and agnatic heirs but also with a son's daughter or sister of the deceased. These rules have been subjected to significant reform in Iraq, Tunisia and Somalia.[31]

In Iraq in the absence of a son daughters now take the remainder of the estate after the fixed Qur'anic shares have been allotted to the surviving spouse (wife: 1/8, husband: ¼) and parents (1/6 each) – in the absence of these other heirs they get whole estate excluding the brothers, sisters, nephews, nieces, uncles and cousins of the deceased). In Tunisia daughters now excludes all collateral heirs – e.g., a brother or the paternal uncle of the deceased, so that if there is a residue after all the surviving Qur'anic heirs have taken their fixed shares it will go to the daughters; the principle applying also to another Qur'anic heir—sons-daughters—if she is otherwise eligible to inherit. In Somalia too daughters excludes all collateral's and in the absence of parents, children and grandchildren take the whole estate.

IV.   SHARES OF BROTHERS AND SISTERS

At the traditional law daughters and son's daughters always exclude brothers of the deceased by full or half blood but not always such of the deceased. When there is no brother by full or half blood, the sister by full or half blood takes the residue of the estate, if any, after the daughters and other Qur'anic heirs take their shares [while in the same situation brothers by full or half blood would be excluded by the daughters and the sons daughters]. Legislation in North Yemen, Syria and Tunisia specifically enforce this rule; while in Iraq a newly introduced provision says that in the matter of exclusion from inheritance sisters by full blood will always be treated on par with brothers by full blood.[32]

According to the domination Hanafi opinion (in force in Bangladesh and Pakistan) among the agnatic heirs brothers and sisters of the deceased by full blood are excluded by the grand father inheriting in the absence of the father and children or son's children – though he and they stand in the same degree of relationship to the deceased. Other schools of Islamic laws (Maliki, Shafi'i, Zaidi) in such a situation bracket the grandfather and brothers-sisters giving him a number of options enabling him and the brothers and sisters to inherit together.

FAMILY *WAQFS*

Translating into action the famous saying 'charity begins at home' the *Shari'ah* allowed making a *waqf* (endowment) in favour of one's family and relatives. *Waqf ala 'l-aulad* or *waqf-i-ahli* is a particular kind of *waqf* in which the settler may settle property in perpetuity for the benefit of his family members and future generations of his descendants, etc. Classical law recognized this kind of *waqf* on par with public *waqfs*.

Legislative protection of the institution of the family *waqfs* on popular demand-the resulting laws had come in force in Bangladesh, Pakistan and South Yemen.[33]

In some other Islamic countries there has been an opposite trend in respect of family *waqfs*. In Egypt family *waqfs* were first restricted in their tenure and operation and then completely abolished; and later all non-charitable *waqfs* were abolished also in Libya, Syria and Tunisia – while in Kuwait and Lebanon legislation made family *waqfs* revocable. In Kuwait such *waqfs* must be restricted to not more than two series of beneficiaries, and in Lebanon they are to be compulsorily terminate if they are uneconomic, irreparably damaged or extensively fragmented due to increase in the number of beneficiaries.

NOTES

1. Tahir Mahmood, *Personal Law in Islamic Countries*, New Delhi, 1987, p. 11.
2. *Ibid.*, p. 13.
3. *Ibid*, p. 14.
4. *Ibid*, p. 272.
5. *Ibid*, p. 273.
6. *Ibid*, p. 274.
7. *Ibid*, p. 276.
8. Bangladesh-Pak 1961, read with Criminal Procedure Code 1898:488, Ref. Tahir Mahmood, *op. cit.*, p. 278.
9. Brunei 1955, 136; Malaysia 1984:159-70 (Ref. *ibid.*, p. 279).
10. Egypt 1920:1; 1929 : 11B, 16; Iraq; 1959:23-33, Jordan 1976; 66-77; Lebanon 1917; 92-101; Moscow 1958: 115-119; N. Yemen 1978: 41-47, Syria 1953:74-84 (Ref. *ibid.*, p. 279).
11. Tunisia 1956:31-32; Somalia 1975:31; S. Yemen 1978:41-47; Syria 1953: 74-82 (Ref. *ibid.*, p. 279).
12. (Ref. *ibid*, p. 281) Egypt 1924:1, 4; Iraq 1959:34-36; Jordan 1976:90-94; Moscow 1958, 51, 54, N. Yemen 1978, 59-60; Sudan 1935: 3-5; Syria 1953; 92, 94

13. Iraq 1959:39; Jordan 1976:101; Syria 1953:88 (Ref. *ibid.*, p. 282).

14. Banglad̥esh-Pakistan 1961:7 (Ref. *ibid.*, p. 282).

15. Bangladesh 1961:8; Brunei 1955:146; Iraq 1959:34; Jordan 1976:87; Malaysia 1984; 50 Morocco 1958:67, Pakistan 1961:8; Syria 1953:87(2).

16. Algeria 1984:54; Libya 1972:12-19A; Morocco 1958: 61-65.

17. Syria 1953:95-104, Jordan 1976:102-112, Libya.

18. Afghanistan 1971; Algeria 1984:153; Bangladesh 1939:2; Egypt 1929:6-14 & 1920: 4-5,9; Indonesia 1974:9; Iraq 1957: 40-45; Jordan 1976:113-134; Lebanon 1974:119-126; Libya 1972:4-11; Malaysia 1984:82; Morocco 1958: 53-59; N. Yemen 1978:42-56; Somalia 1975:42-44; S. Yemen 1974:24-31; Syria 1953:105-112; Tunisia 1956:25, 32; Turkey 1926:124-138.

19. Jordan 1976:55; Lebanon 1917:84; Morocco 1958:60; N. Yemen 1978:34.

20. Brunei 1955:148; Malaysia 1984:56.

21. Egypt 1929:18 A; Jordan 1976:134; Syria 1953:117.

22. Morocco 1958:60.

23. Somalia 1975:44; S. Yemen 1974:30.

24. Bangladesh 1939:5, Egypt 1929:18; Iraq 1959:21; Jordan 1976:48-57, Lebanon 1917: 82-87; Morocco 1958:72-75; N. Yemen 1978:77-85; Somalia 1975: 48-52; Yemen 1974:31-36; Syria 1953: 121-127; Tunisia 1956: 34-36.

25. Egypt 1929:18C; Algeria 1984:51; Malaysia 1984:71.

26. Iraq 1959:38; Jordan 1976:99-100; Lebanon 1917:117-118; Morocco 1958: 70-74; N. Yemen 1978; 68; Somalia 1975: 15, 38-39, Syria 1953: 6, 119-120.

27. Algeria 1984:59; Indonesia 1975:39; Iraq 1959:48-49; Jordan 1976:139-146; Lebanon 1917: 143-144; Morocco 1958:72-75; N. Yemen 1998:77-85; Somalia 1975:48-52; S. Yemen 1974:31-36; Syria 1953:121-127;Tunisia 1956:34-36.

28. See e.g. Maina Bibi (1924) 52 IA 155.

29. Tahir Mahmood, *op. cit.*

30. Algeria 1984:167; Egypt 1943:30; Jordan 1976:181; Sudan 1925:1; Syria 1953:288; Somalia 1975:160; Tunisia 1959:143 A.

31. Iraq 1959:91 (2); Tunisia 1956; 143A; Somalia 1975:161-163.

32. N. Yemen 1976:22; Syria 1953: 278; Tunisia 1956:105-106; Iraq 1959:89 (4).

33. Abdul Fata's case (1894) 22 1 A 76; Bangladesh-Pakistan *Waqf,* Validating Acts, 1913-1930, South Yemen (Aden) Mohammedan *Waqfs* Ordinance 1939.

4

TERRITORIAL DIVERSITIES AND PERSONAL LAWS IN INDIA

It is a mere myth to say that people in India follow their personal laws because they follow different religions, having their own laws. But the fact is there are different laws not only because of different religions but also because of regions and locales people live in. These are called local—regionally different—customary laws. The customary laws govern the communities even if they belong to same religion. Thus laws differs from region to region and from religions to community.

This is the problem with regard to having a Uniform Civil Code throughout India. I will illustrate my point in detail showing the diversities in different regional Family laws in different parts of the country.

GOA, DAMAN AND DIU

On our western coast is the Union Territory of Goa, Daman and Diu, where the Portuguese civil law—governing family law and succession—is still applicable. The rulers in Portugal were busy extending their own laws to their overseas colonies on the subcontinent. This was how the Portuguese Civil Code of 1867, the two later Portuguese Decrees on Marriage and divorce of 1910, and the 1946 Decree on Canonical Marriages had one after another came into force in Goa, Daman and Diu.[1] The other centres of Portuguese in India, Dadra and Nagar Haveli, was also the recipients of the civil laws of Portugal. The Portuguese law had survived in Goa, Daman and

Diu until now.

The Hindus of Goa, now in majority, are, for instance, still governed by the Portuguese family and succession laws, subject to some ancient Hindu traditions protected by the old Gentle Hindu Usages Decree of 1880. The Hindu legal traditions protected by this Decree relate to marriage, divorce, adoption and joint family belongs to 19th century regime of Hindu law under which divorce was almost an impossibility, adoption of or by females was unknown and joint-family property had, under any circumstances whatsoever, no more than maintenance right to offer to women.[2] The general Hindus elsewhere enjoy the liberal divorce policy of the Hindu Marriage Act of 1955, modernized adoption law of the Hindu Adoptions and Maintenance Act of 1956 and the property law enforced by the Hindu Succession Act, 1956.

The second largest community in Goa, Daman and Diu are the Christians and in respect of marriage law they are governed by either the Portuguese law of civil marriages or the 1946 Imperial Decree on Canonical marriages. The matrimonial laws applicable to the Christians in rest of India are the Indian Divorce Act, 1869 and the Christian Marriage Act, 1872, which are very different from that applicable to the Goan Christian. In respect of succession, all Goan Christians are governed by the local Portuguese law, the Indian succession Act of 1925 being wholly inapplicable in the territory.[3]

As regards the Goan Muslims since the Muslim Personal Law (Shariat) Application Act of 1937 does not still apply in that Union Territory, they are governed by the Portuguese family and succession laws. The Goan Muslims are thus governed partly by Portuguese law and partly by ancient Hindu usage.

PONDICHERRY

In this Union Territory all local Hindus, Christians and Muslims are found divided into two groups- the Renoncants and other; the former being still governed by the French Civil Code and the later by the India laws. The four Hindu law enactments of 1955-56 and the Dissolution of Muslim Marriages Act, 1939 are applicable to the others and these clauses are not applied to the Renoncants.[4]

JAMMU AND KASHMIR

Here most of the central laws do not apply, Parliaments legislative power being restricted by virtue of special constitutional provisions.[5] As regards personal laws the local versions differ on many points from their central counter parts. However, after the extensive amendments of 1976 the Kashmir legislature enacted its new Hindu Marriage Act in 1980, under which at least the law of marriage-age and marriage-guardianship very much differs from its parallel under the present version of the central Act.[6]. The Hindu Succession Act, 1956 does have a local substitute in Kashmir, but it has not repealed the Buddhist Succession Act, 1943 of Ladakh.

This predominantly Muslim state has not yet adopted the Muslim Personal Law (*Shari'at*) Application Act of 1937 [which puts the civil courts under an obligation to apply Muslim law to Muslims in respect of family relations and inheritance]. Kashmir customary law which, thus, prevails over the written *Shari'at* law, is notorious for its perplexities and equities. Most customary concepts of valley – including those relating to female *khananashini* and male *khanadamadi* are more or less unheard of by the Muslims elsewhere. Wholly uncodified until today, the customary law of Kashmir is known to the courts through Dogra's inaccurate Code[7] and Ganjoo's all the more unreliable Digest[8] of Kashmiri customs. Repeated attempts to get enacted a local law on the lines of the central *Shari'at* Act in the valley have so far proved abortive. So Kashmiri Muslims follow their local customs while their fellow co-religionists elsewhere in this country are bound by the provisions of the central *Shari'at* Act of 1937. Kashmiri application of customary laws in preference to personal law has the support of the State High Court which finds nothing wrong and unconstitutional in it.[9]

There is the J&K Muslim Dower Act, 1920 – enabling the civil courts to slash the amount to specified dower when its payment is claimed. Under the J&K Dissolution of Muslim Marriages Act, 1943, the law of 'option of puberty' is quite different from that under the Central Dissolution of Muslim Marriages Act, 1939 – the former faithfully conforming to and the latter substantially deviating from, the traditional Hanafi law on the subject. By a recent local law, registration of all Muslim marriages has been made compulsory in the state of Jammu & Kashmir while in other states like West Bengal, Bihar, Assam and Orissa laws on registration of Muslim marriages, there is no such special law for the Muslim.

The Special Marriage Act, 1954 has no local substitute in J&K so that the only choice for the Kashmiris – to whatever religion they belong – in the matter of family law and succession is their personal law. In this state there is no parallel of Article 44 of the Constitution of India (relating to Uniform Civil Code) in the Constitution of Jammu and Kashmir which is still in force.

SOUTH INDIAN STATES

Inapplicability of the Central Muslim Personal Law (*Shari'at*) Application Act of 1937 is not in vogue only in the State of Jammu and Kashmir. States like Tamil Nadu, Andhra Pradesh and Kerala also have locally amended the said central law. In the state of Kerala Hindu law of property, too, differs from that in force in the rest of the country. They have replaced the age-old *Mitakshara* joint family system by a 1975 local legislation.[10] Elsewhere in the country, *Mitakshara* joint family is still regulated by the restrictive provisions of the Hindu Succession Act, 1956. Kerala has also abolished all kinds of Malabar laws [of the matrilineal type] governed by the Marumakkatayam, Aliyasantana, Nambudri and other matrilineal laws.[11] Interestingly, all these laws remain operative in Tamil Nadu, Andhra Pradesh and Karnataka by force of statutes.[12] This makes the Kerala Hindus different in respect of their legal system from those of the other south Indian states.

Strangely, the Muslims in Kerala have retained their Marumakkatayam system which is undoubtedly based on un-Islamic customs and is not shared by non-Keralite Muslims of India. Similarly, the Christian Succession Acts of Travancore and Cochin have survived the local joint family abolition legislation of 1975. These laws discriminate between the Keralite and non-Keralite Christians.

EASTERN INDIA

In Nagaland, the local customs and usages enjoy protection of the Constitution. Accordingly, the Tribal customary law is protected there either by the force of legislation or by judicial precedent. In some other East-Indian states including Meghalaya, Mizoram and Sikkim the story is the same as in Nagaland.[13]

GROUP DIVERSITIES

Under the Indian Succession Act of 1925, the government of every state is authorised to issue a gazette-notification in order to exempt from the application of that act any particular race, sect or tribe.[14] This authorization has, in the past, been exercised in favour of Christians of Coorg[15], certain Christian races of Assam[16] and several Christian tribes[17] of Bihar and Orissa.[18] These laws protected against the generality of the personal law statutes, evolved during the British rule, have continued to enjoy the same status even after independence with the birth of the two privileged classes under the constitution—viz. the 'Schedule Castes' and 'Schedule Tribes'. Here all the four Hindu-law enactments of 1955-56 are wholly inapplicable to each of the Scheduled Tribes. Inapplicability of some of these acts to certain tribes in Assam, Bihar and Orissa has been judicially confirmed.

CUSTOM-BASED DIVERSITIES

Specific Hindu, Buddhist, Jain and Sikh customs enjoy full legal protection under the provisions of the concerned enactments themselves. Among the customs and customary institutions that remain so protected are:

1. those violating statutory rules relating to *sapinda* relationship and prohibited degrees in marriage;[19]
2. customary marriage-rites replacing *saptapadi*;[20]
3. customary divorce; and [21]custom of adopting major and married children[22].

Communities, tribes, groups and families whose customs are legally protected would often be concentrated in particular states, regions and smaller territorial units. In certain specified matters rules of marriage and adoption laws may differ from state to state in the country from district to district in a particular state. The statutory law would protect legal diversities at all these levels.

Further the term 'law' in Article 13 of the Constitution is specifically extended to custom and usage having the force of law.[23] On the contrary, some courts have even unduly stretched the scope of the term 'custom' as used in the Hindu-law enactments of 1955-56. Classical Hindu law is known by its two broad versions—*Mitakshara* and *Dayabhaga*—and the former has four geographical compartments, namely, Varanasi, Mithila, Dravida and Maharashtra compartments.[24] According to the special rules of adoption under the Vyavahara Mayukha [this rule is followed in Maharashtra region of *Mitakshara* school]. By this analogy, in matters relating to marriage, divorce, age and marital status of adoptees, locally prevailing versions of Hindu law in South, North and Eastern India can also be pleaded as protected custom and usage.

Under the Muslim Personal Law (*Shari'at*) application Act, 1937 custom and usage relating to wills, legacies and adoption enjoy statutory protection against the contrary provisions of Islamic law. This discriminatory provision, which was incorporated into the Act at the behest of Quaid-e-Azam Muhammad Ali Jinnah in search of purely political gains.[25] It has been faithfully retained in India until now. At present whatever Act is applicable in India including the predominantly Muslim territories of Lakshadweep and Malabar [Kerala] there remain confusion in respect of the law applicable to the Muslims.

NOTES

1. For Hindus, The Hindu Usage Decree, 1880 which protected some old traditions still remained intact.
2. The arrangement was most unsatisfactory.
3. Art. 29 – "The non-catholic natives of Goa who are not Hindu may deserve the provisions of this law which shall apply to them in so far as they are not contrary to their religion. In the same manner their own usages shall be safeguard.
4. See. e.g., the Hindu Marriage Act, 1955, 2 (2A); Hindu Succession Act, 1956, Sec. 2 (2A); Hindu Minorities and Guardianship Act, 1956, Sec. 3 (2A).
5. Art. 370.
6. See Lecture III, cited by Tahir Mahmood.
7. S.R. Dogra, *Code of Tribal Customs in Kashmir* (1938).
8. N.K. Ganjoo, *A Digest of the customary law of Kashmir* (1956).

9. See, e.g. Khatji vs. Abdul Razak, AIR 1977 J & K 44.

10. Kerala Joint Hindu Family Abolition Act, 1975.

11. *Ibid.,* note 144.

12. *Ibid.*

13. Art. 371 A.

14. Sec. 3.

15. Sec. 3.

16. *Gazette of India,* 1868, p. 1094.

17. Khasias & Jyaitengs of Khasia & Jaintia Hills. See *Gazette of India,* 1877, p. 512.

18. Mundas & Oraons. See I PLJ 225 (226).

19. Hindu Marriage Act, 1955, Sec. 5, Clauses (iv) (v).

20. *Ibid.,* Sec. 7.

21. *Ibid.,* Sec. 29(2).

22. Hindu Adoptions and Maintenance Act, 1956, Sec. 10, Clauses (iii) and (iv).

23. Art. 13 (3) (a).

24. Tahir Mahmood, *Personal Law in Crisis,* New Delhi, 1986, p. 41.

25. Some Nawabs and Zamindars of India, who had their own customs relating to will and adoption, did not want Muslim law to be applied to them so as to curtail their customary powers in that respect. Muhammad Ali Jinnah got their interest protected by means of a provision (now found in Sec. 3 of the Act) that in these matters a Muslim could only voluntarily adopt (for himself and his minor children and future generations) the Islamic Law.

5
MODEL *NIKAHNAMA*

The recent development in Muslim Personal Law is the issuance of the Model *Nikahnama* which symbolizes a change in the approach towards Muslim social issue of marriage and shows more concern and awareness about the rights of Muslim women. This gave a sort of impetus to the new thinking on the true Islamic Law which actually safeguarding women's rights.

The Model *Nikahnama*, which is also known as Bhopal Declaration by the Muslim Personal Law Board, raised several questions about the need as well as its credibility. While drafting the *Nikahnama*, the Board members wanted to end controversies existing across the country because of different *Nikahnamas* being used. However, it raised more doubts than it settled. Some people say it is a total disappointment; the board has only discouraged the Triple Divorce, which actually is a sinful form of divorce; it could have pronounced it as illegal under Islamic Law.

Women activists also have voiced objections: the Board has, they say, not taken clear stand against this sinful practice. It is also pointed out that Model *Nikahnama* is indifferent to the issues such as polygamy, minimum marriage age for Muslim women, alimony of divorced wife and omission of *Khul'* women's right to divorce is discriminatory in nature. Worse, the *Nikahnama* has taken away the right to approach a secular court.

There may be some substance in all these criticisms, but one thing should not be ignored. The Model *Nikahnama* is also a positive development as this has resulted in more debate and many activists have come out openly declaring that they will draft their own Model *Nikahnama.*

Indirectly, it has created social awareness about the need to give greater importance to the rights of women. And legally, as well as on the basis of religious principles, this *Nikahnama* is not binding on anybody. Maulana Kalbe Sadiq, president, AIMPLB said that it is just a guide for those who wish to be guided. It is not obligatory to have it.

Some critics say that because it is not enforceable in the court of law, the *Nikahnama* will not serve any purpose. It will not make any reform. The government, they argue, should come out with a *Nikahnama* based on Islamic tenets which should have legal validity.

Prof. K.A. Sidiq Hasan, Secretary of Jamaat-e-Islami, Hind, who took part in the AIMPLB meet, does not, however, agree with this view. It cannot be left to the government, he says, that "we could not expect a fair legislation from the government." But there is need for reform. Many an enlightened people are agreeable to it. But in a diversified society like India, where the Muslim community is culturally so scattered and so different from each other in manner and customs that Kerala Muslim has nothing in common with his Kashmiri counterpart, except faith. In such an intricate scenario imposing a common code is a Herculean task, and if things are pushed beyond a certain point. These may blow up.

Should we, then, a question arises, leave things at that? No, reforms have been done in among Muslim countries to meet the present day needs and conditions. We have to do something worthwhile to improve the position of our women. The *Nikahnama*, whatever the critics may say, is a step in that direction. It has many flashiness of hope. One is that the AIMPLB has by making the declaration has emerged as the top, unified Muslim body. Comprising clerics of various Islamic streams, enlightened men and women, it can push through this and other *Shari'ah* issues.

Secondly, the Declaration has, as noted above, generated a healthy debate. Dr. Asghar Ali Engineer in a learned article 'A hope or disappointment?' see optimism in the Declaration. He says the Model *Nikahnama* is not a revolutionary measure but at least it is one step forward in the right direction. Another ray of light here is, thanks to the efforts of the Muslim women NGO's in sixties and seventies, functioning and campaigning for change in Muslim Personal law, the AIMPLB has changed its approach towards many an issue, especially to the ones relating to women. Earlier the Board worked to protect the Muslim personal law. Now it has started to reform it. Change and reform are signs of life. That is as such a pretty healthy development towards women's problems. But Dr. Engineer rises the question that why the *'ulama* took so long to tender this advice to avoid this sinful form of divorce? This form of divorced has been banned in all Muslim countries including Pakistan and Bangladesh. It was only the Indian *'ulama* who refused to ban it and wanted, ironically, to continue it in the name of divine law. This sinful form of divorce is not permitted by the Quran and not even by the Hadith. On the contrary, the Prophet (PBUH) strongly condemned it. According to one Hadith, when it was reported to the Prophet (PBUH) that someone has divorced his wife thrice in one sitting, his face turned red with anger and he is reported to have said that he is playing with Allah's laws in my own life time. (Dr. Asghar Ali Engineer, *Rights of Women in Islam*). The Quran while disapproving *talaq* as it breaks husband-wife relations and Allah has created love and compassion between them (30:21) has shown just methods of divorcing if the conditions compelled to do so (4:35 and 2:229). Then the presence of witnesses is a must for divorce (65:2). The triple divorce violates all the Quranic injunctions.

It is, for this reason that Ahl-e-Hadith, the Shi'ahs and the Bohras do not accept it and among Sunnis, too, Hanbalis and Malikis generally do not permit it.

Triple divorce should be abolished and if it is not possible to do so right away due to internal differences, strong campaign should be launched against it and also penalize those Muslims who resort to it.

The AIMPLB should take initiative to codify the Muslim personal law in the spirit of the Islamic *Shari'ah*. The *'ulama* and well known Muslim lawyers should draft a comprehensible bill in this respect, but well within *Shari'ah* framework, and give it to the government to enact it through Parliament. Islam was most fair to women and gave them well defined rights. But selfish men have deprived them of their Islamic rights. This was done in the medieval times. Now things have changed. Women should be given back their rights. How? A comprehensive codification will help their cause. One can see how other Muslim countries have done it.

6
CONCLUSION

In the Indian context the Muslim Personal law is, as indicated in chapter 2, actually an Anglo-Mohammedan law and there is urgent need for its reform and codification. Many Muslim countries have brought several changes in the *Shari'ah* laws in view of the present day social challenges. They have made significant changes in their (Islamic) laws as far as marriage, women's rights, divorce, etc., are concerned. However, in India the orthodox '*ulama* said that any Muslim country changes any verse of Holy Quran to suit "if the morbid desire of the Muslim ruler or political party in some Muslim country changed the verse of the holy *Quran*, it does not mean that Muslims all over the world must accept the changed verse of holy Quran on the ground that a Muslim country has amended it. Any logic, which goes against the letter and spirit of the Shariat, can never be accepted." Such arguments misled the community. In fact no Muslim country has changed or can dare to change the verses of the holy *Quran*. They have made necessary changes in Shariat which is not divine and which can be changed.

The Muslim critics of Uniform Civil Code take shelter under constitutional provisions too. Article 25 says, "Subject to public order, morality and health and to the other provisions of this part, all persons are equally entitled to freedom of conscience and the right freely to profess, practice and propagate religion." In view of the freedom of conscience guaranteed in this article, some people argue, there can be no room for a common civil code which may tantamount to taking away the religious freedom of any community and force people to act against their conscience. Thus any attempt to reform Muslim Personal Law or to introduce a Uniform Civil Code through an act of Parliament, is against the ideal of secularism. They criticize Article 44 which advocates a common Civil Code for all the citizens. Dr. Asghar Ali Engineer has examined these questions very objectively and sensitively. Dr. Engineer feels that India being a pluralist country for ages it caters to different religions. There are several castes that follow different customary laws even though they belong to the same religion. Our customary laws change with the regions. Therefore, it is wrong to say that Hindu, Muslim and Christian are homogenous communities. Their laws, customs and traditions vary from region to region. Also apart from major religious and caste traditions, there are a pretty large number of tribal traditions and practices. So imposition of UCC on the minorities who are not willing to change or accept would lead to violation of democratic values.

There is a strong argument that if the Hindu personal law is reformed, why not the Muslim personal law/ Well, the cases are different. Not many people seem to appreciate that most of the reforms done in the Hindu personal law are already there in the Muslim personal law. Take, for instance, right to marriage, divorce, inheritance and property for women. But this is not my case that there is no need of reforms in the Muslim personal law. There are many things to be done in the domain of gender justice and elsewhere. But how these things ought to be done is important.

At present the main factor against implementation of UCC is the post-Babri Masjid demolition atmosphere. The minorities, specially Muslims have developed a sense of insecurity and have become more conscious about their identity. Things should be handled with care. Let the Muslims change their life. They know their problems and are keen to solve them. Outside interference disturbs them. The present study has made a strong case for this sort of approach—non-interference from outside. And it has also said in so many words as to how the Muslims should take care of their problems in the domain of personal law.

In the Indian context, we have explained, that Anglo-Mohammedan law or the so called Muslim personal law should be completely discarded. The Islamic scholars should formulate actual *Shari'ah* law. Now one should stop propagating that *Shari'ah* is divine and so cannot be tempered with. The *Shari'ah,* which is followed in Muslim countries all over, is actually formulated by the theologians. And they have formulated it in the light of their existing social circumstances in the past. Today we need to formulate it as per our social circumstances and requirements.

Contextually, let us take up the case of women. The principle of Islam grants equal status to women. Today women are much more aware and participate in social and economic activities. They are now professional in different fields. Many women have even taken up male jobs—and very successfully. Therefore, the laws of marriage, divorce and inheritance must be reformulated.

Today the main problem in Muslim personal law is polygamy, i.e. Muslims having four wives. Secondly, there is the practice of triple divorce where a husband divorces his wife by pronouncing the word *Talaq* thrice in one sitting. Such *Talaq* is considered valid even if it is pronounced in the state of anger, inebriation or jokingly. And finally, there is maintenance issue where a woman is entitled to three months maintenance after divorce. Also she is entitled to her marriage dower, '*Mehr*' and time to *mataa'.* (After Shah Bano case the Muslim husbands were exempted from payment of maintenance for life or until death of their divorced wives.)

Let us try to comprehend these complex issues in the

light of the discussions already undertaken in the present study. Take the case of triple divorce, which is so prominent among the Indian Muslims. It is far from Islamic—in fact it is a sinful act already banned in all other Muslim countries except India. Recently the All India Muslim Personal Law Board advised that this form of divorce should be avoided. Our 'ulama can play an effective role in eradicating this sinful practice which is not accepted and considered valid by Shia Muslim sect and also by the followers of Hanbali school of thoughts in Sunni sect.

We should not be constrained by what our predecessors thought and did. We should begin to think afresh in our own experiential context and in the light of the values and principles laid down by the Qur'an. Imam Abu Hanifa, the founder of Hanafi school, used to say that if two of his disciples disagreed with him he would listen to them as two holding an opinion are more likely to be correct. This has to be borne in mind while dealing with *Shari'ah* formulations. However, it is often ignored and *Shari'ah* is treated as immutable. Whenever opinions differ, the issue should be hotly debated amongst the jurists. Imam Abu Hanifa would listen to debates patiently and after having heard each side would come out with a balanced formulation. Very often, however, even after the Imam's formulation, opinions continued to differ and people would stick to their own judgments. This process continued for more than thirty years before it was completed.

The words of *hadith* as reported are not always the words of Prophet (PBUH) himself. It is how in companions of the Prophet (PBUH), with whom the tradition originated, understood him. This means the tradition reaching us is based on the companions' understanding of what the Prophet (PBUH) said or did. Thus the *Shari'ah* formulations depend a great deal on the human factor. First, how those are extracted from the Qur'an and *Hadith*. Secondly, what is the context of the Quranic verses? Thirdly, what is the authenticity of the tradition, whether it is weak or forged or authentic? Acceptance and rejection of the *Hadith* would also depend on the person concerned. Fourthly, even if the tradition is authentic how did the companion of the Prophet (PBUH) reporting it understood it?

Muslims ordinarily believe that, in reality, Shariat law is democratic and even generous towards women. A Muslim woman is entitled to inherit, hold and acquire property in her own name. In marriage she is a free agent and cannot be forcibly married against her will. She has the right to divorce called *Khul'*. She is entitled to the custody of her children in preference to her husband. In marriage, she is to be treated as an equal partner. Certain jurists claim that a Muslim husband has no right to inflict his will on a reluctant wife. "She cannot be compelled to cook her husband's food and can demand payment for service, she can even demand payment for suckling the children of the marriage."

It is also seen that most of the Muslim countries have effected reforms in their personal laws. These laws are based on Islam but modern reforms have made them gender just. In all the countries which we have discussed in the chapter on reforms in other Muslim countries, though polygamy is not totally abolished, it is restricted and codified in such a way that it is not that easy to go for second marriage. But as far as triple divorce is concerned it is abolished completely all over the Muslim countries including Pakistan and Bangladesh. Therefore in India Muslim personal law needs urgent reform in respect of polygamy and triple divorce.

The recently approved Model *Nikahnama* has, as discussed above, raised several questions about the need as well as its credibility. While drafting the *Nikahnama*, the Board members wanted to end controversies existing across country because of different *Nikahnamas* being used. However, it raised more controversies than it solved. The board has only discouraged the triple divorce. It could have pronounced it as illegal under Islamic Law. The Model *Nikahnama* is indifferent to the issues such as polygamy, minimum marriage age for Muslim women, alimony of divorced wife, etc. There is omission of *Khul* women's right to divorce so it is discriminatory in nature.

It has generated healthy debate and many activists have come out openly declaring that they will present their own blueprint fro reforming the Muslim personal law.

Despite all this, the *Nikahnama*, as discussed above, has many positive features. The AIMPLB has taken a right step, however small it might be, in the right direction. Those Muslim scholars and social activists who have the good of people, especially Muslim women, in their agenda, will come forward and take more such steps to give them what is their due according to the true principles of Islam.

ANNEXURES

1

UNIFORM CIVIL CODE DEBATE

The word 'Uniform' here has so far been thoughtlessly taken as a synonym for the word 'common'. There is, however, a difference between 'common' and 'Uniform' – the former meaning 'one and the same in all circumstances whatsoever', and the latter meaning 'same in similar conditions'. Ignoring this, people ordinarily believe that the idea behind the Directive of Article 44 is replacement of all the personal laws by a Westernized 'Civil Code'. This is not a correct reading of the Article. Nor can we make a right reading of the Article unless we understand the concept of Uniform Civil Code after taking into serious consideration the diversity in our personal laws throughout India.

MAJORITY AND MINORITY IDENTITIES

'By asserting that the Constitution has promised UCC and not the reform of Personal Law of one community, what was being implied was that the minorities [read Muslim] were being given special privileges by being allowed to retain their personal laws.'

This, privilege given to the minority communities [read Muslim], that is, retaining their personal law, makes the Muslims stand out not as a part of the common national community comprising citizens. The assertion that the Hindu Code Bill was the first step towards UCC also feeds into this discourse. The Hindu code Bill is configured as a common code for the majority community. When the common code of the majority is taken as the first step in the making of UCC, those governed by this Code, so it would appear, are members of a common national community and therefore proper citizens. The UCC in this instance becomes the negation of the identities of the minorities.

The UCC as signifying unity in the community of the nation, the UCC as means of modernizing pre-modern customs, the UCC as a threat to the 'particularity' of politicize religious identities of the minorities, the UCC as discursive strategy to carve out the identities of 'majority' and 'minorities' communities in their relation to the state, the UCC as being partly synonymous with the HCB – these are some of the multiple meanings that the UCC has acquired through the latter part of the independence struggle and in the first few formative years of the independence. Clearly, none of these meanings when seen in the context of gender equality tantamounts to equate with equal rights between men and women in the family.

THE UCC CONTROVERSY BEFORE 1947

The debate in the Constituent Assembly on what was at that time Article 35 and which later became Article 44 of the Constitution is instructive. Mohammad Ismail from Madras moved that the following proviso be added to the Article; 'provided that any group, section or community of the people shall not be obliged to give up its own personal law in case it has such a law'. (*Constitution Assembly Debates*, vol. vii, p.540). His contention was that the right to follow personal law was a part of religion and culture and that if anything was done affecting the personal law, it would be an interference with the ways of those people who have been observing those laws for generations and ages. Mahboob Ali Baig moved an amendment suggesting the addition of the following proviso: 'provided that nothing in this article shall affect the personal law of the citizen.' His argument was that so far as the Mussalmans were concerned, their laws of succession, inheritance, marriage and divorce were completely dependent upon their religion. A heated argument between M. Ananthasayanam Ayyannger and Mahboob Ali Baig reflects an element of tension in that debate. B. Pocker, a Muslim member from Madras supported the amendment moved by Mohammad Ismail. He said that the Constituent Assembly had no mandate to interfere with the religious right and practices of the Muslim community. Naziruddin Ahmad moved that the following proviso be added to Article 35: 'provided that the personal law of any community which has been guaranteed by the statute shall not be changed except with the previous approval of the community ascertained in such manner as the Union Legislature may determine by law.' Naziruddin Ahmad had no doubt that a stage would come when the civil law would be uniform but believed that the power to make the civil code uniform was in advance of the time. He was of the view that the goal should be to secure a uniform civil code but that it should be gradual and with the consent of the people concerned. He concluded by saying that 'we should proceed not in haste but with caution, with experience, with the statesmanship and with sympathy'. Though Naziruddin Ahmad's amendment was negative, his underlying approach has held sway all these years.

The three most important speeches in the Constituent Assembly on the question of a Uniform Civil Code were those made by K.M. Munshi, Alladi Krishnaswami Ayyar and Dr. B.R. Ambedkar. K.M. Munshi made it clear that the Constituent Assembly had already accepted the principle that the freedom to practice and propagate religion did not bar the making of any law regulating or restricting any secular activity, which may be associated with religious practices or for social welfare and reform. (Religion And Society, December 1979) "In India family laws are called personal laws. The laws are personal in that they related to the sphere of personal relation but also in that they are person–specific. The specificity flows primarily from religious affiliation, through local custom is also important. As a result, family laws are hived off from the main body of civil law, codified separately for four communities–Hindus, Muslims, Christians, and Parsis–based on their religious prescriptions. In reality, the four codes are a mix of scriptural sanctions, heterogeneous customs and practices, and most important precepts forwarded and established through the political manoeuvrings of powerful spokespersons from these communities. Thus the laws necessarily reflect patterns of social political dominance based on religion, caste and gender.

"Personal laws define the relationship between men and women with the family and control and direct marriage, divorce, maintenance, guardianship of children, adoption, succession and inheritance. All four codes concern women intimately, and all treat women as subordinate to and dependent on male kin. The male is considered the head of family, and women do not have equivalent rights, especially to property.

"Personal laws are codified separately for the four religious communities—that is, they are not just customary or communal law, but also statutory law based on religion. As a secular nation–state, India maintains these religious alongside secular laws, civil, criminal, all of which are administered by the same legal judicial apparatus."

Since the 1930s the contradictions in different personal laws have given rise to demands for a Uniform Civil Code based on secular and egalitarian principles to replace personal laws. But there has also been considerable public opinion in favour of retaining the different personal laws, with great resistance to state interference. This debate has plagued the Indian state and, in recent years, evoked bitter conflicts even within the women's movement.

The question of personal law reform came to the fore before the Rau Committee (1941-46) which was formulating the code of Hindu law. In the Constitution Assembly, the common code became popular and the UCC become especially contentious as an instrument of national unity (rather than for securing women's rights). One group in the Constitution Assembly favoured the inclusion of UCC as a fundamental right for breaking down barriers of communities. Another group opposed it. The compromise led to its inclusion among the directive principles. But several questions remained. First right to religion, especially of minorities, was protected as a fundamental right against state intervention. But it was not clear whether personal laws were included in 'religion'. Second, protection against sexual discriminations was included as a fundamental right, but it was not clear how gender equality could be secured against discrimination against personal laws.

In the first Congress government of Independent India, Prime Minister Jawaharlal Nehru and law Minister B.R. Ambedkar favoured the Uniform Civil Code as an instrument of modernization, secularization, and national unity. But given the immediate political context, they concentrated on reforming Hindu Personal law first and proposed a comprehensive Hindu Civil Code. It had supporters and opponents. In the course of debate both sides invoked the UCC (Everett 19981; Parasher 1992). The latter's aim was to derail the Hindu Civil Code but in the process personal laws (especially for Muslim) became marked as an area of minority privilege. The debate heightened the minority fear that the UCC would be an instrument of homogenization. Besides this, while issues of national integration dominated the debate on the Hindu Civil Code its implications for gender relation within the family also attracted attention. Thus in this period the Uniform Civil Code acquired many layers of meanings. It signified women's right as citizens of a modern secular state but against the threat of particularistic and traditional values of religion, culture and family. It came to represent the unity and secularity of the nation and a means of modernizing premodern customs. But politicized religious identities perceived it as a threat to their religion and identity. Most important, Hindu personal law reform helped create a majority that was seen as being subjected to the discipline of citizenship and a majority that the state granted the indulgence of community authority (Mukhopadhay 1998). This last argument became a ticking time bomb in the hands of the Hindu right with the rise of aggressive majoritarianism in the 1980's.' [*Policy Research Report on Gender and Development*, working paper series no. 9 – *Toward a feminist Politics? The Indian women's Movement in Historical Perspective*—Samita Sen, pp. 28, 31 and 32].

DEMISE OF 'UNITY IN DIVERSITY' : THE UCC IN 1980S

In the 1980s, the UCC reappears as a subject of national debate. Another feature of this decade is that the reappearance of the UCC coinciding with a period in the history of the post-colonial state in the India marked by a crisis of identities. This crisis of identities refers to the escalation of communal conflicts, the resurgence of majority and minority fundamentalisms, caste wars, and regional separatist movement (in Assam, Darjeeling District and South Bihar) in this period and political mobilization seems also to have increasingly relied on particularistic identities and loyalties. This crisis has been attributed to the failure of 'secularism' as it construed in the Indian context. A discussion of how secularism has been construed in India will help to place on the UCC in proper context.

Indian secularism does not represent the separation of religion in politics, and the attenuation of communal-based identities. The concept of *Sarva Dharma Samabhav* is, in fact, the cornerstone of the Indian variant of secularism. It was developed and followed through by the Congress party that led India to independence and held power at the centre for long since independence. This discussion about secularism was not merely a preface to the UCC in the eighties. It was integral to the debate on the UCC because it was within the unifying impulse of secularism that Article 44 of the Constitution was conceived.

Shah Bano controversy played major role in the debate on UCC. After the Shah Bano judgment there were two important developments. The first development was the debate in the press and political mobilizations for and against the judgement. The second development was the enactment of the Muslim (Protection of Rights on Divorce) Bill in Parliament, which also generated debate in the press, as well as mobilization for and against it. The relevance of the debate lied in the fact that it was about a whole gamut of attitude to Muslim law, Muslim women, as also the position of the community as a whole, its way of life and its right to exit as a religious community in a secular state. However, two things mentioned in the judgment attracted greater attention. First that provision in section 125 (which is part of the Criminal Code and is applicable to everybody irrespective of one's religious affiliation) for maintenance in order to prevent destitution of a divorced wife. Second, that the state should enact a UCC to promote national integration.

The issue of community-based personal law versus UCC was joined at levels by disparate political constituencies often representing conflicting interests. The Muslim body inside and outside Parliament objected to the mention of the UCC in the con text of the judgment: they feared that the talk about UCC was another way of talking about uniformity and imposition of majority laws on minorities. The Hindu lobby argued for a UCC on the ground that as 'citizens' of the same country all people should be subject to uniform laws, and uniform institutions. The fact that the judgment mentioned the need for a UCC in the context of maintenance case in which the parties happened to be Muslim led to the erroneous belief that only Muslim oppressed women and, therefore, should be scrapped in favour of UCC. This gave the feeling that Hindus were not governed by personal laws and their laws indeed were Indian and secular. This successfully obscured the fact that all family laws on maintenance were a farce which required changing.

NATIONAL CULTURE AS HINDU-CULTURE : THE UCC IN 1990S

As the fervour of the Shah Bano controversy abated, and the Muslim Women (Protection of Rights on Divorce) Bill entered the Indian statute book, the demand for a UCC also ebbed. In the nineties three different constituencies emerged, each of which had a stake in the UCC. The first constituency was representative of a section of the women's movement. The second was of the state officials at the different levels of the judicial and legal system. And the third and perhaps the most significant, represented the spokespersons of the BJP who spoke for the Hindu right wing, and for whom the UCC 5represented the cornerstone of a larger political project. Communal riots erupted all over the country in 1990s. Political uncertainty and instability were fuelled by the collapse of two central governments within a period of three years. Discussion of UCC = national integration = bridging disparate loyalties = uniformity took the centre stage. This was nothing short of imposing Hindu personal law on one and all. The BJP played a big role there. [*Gender, State and Nation,* pp. 198, 199, 203, 204, 205, 207]

SUPREME COURT DIRECTIVE ON UCC

The fifth decade of independence witnessed a further erosion of secular principles. The problem was escalated after the demolition of Babri Masjid at Ayodhya on 6 December 1992. The demolition and the riots that followed were indicators of an aggressive majoritarianism. The gulf between the Hindu and Muslim communities widened. The hope that had been expressed in the Constituent Assembly that after independence when there would be political stability then we could go for a Uniform Civil Code came crumbling down. Ironically, the demand, which was meant to be a symbol of India's claim to modernity became a weapon in the hands of regressive and communal forces to beat down the minorities.

Along with these political developments, the judicial trends set by the Shah Bano judgment, echoing communal undertones also got consolidated during this period. The wide media coverage, which followed these judgments, resulted in further collapse of the just parameters of the gender discourse. The most significant development here was the decision of the Supreme Court in a case concerning polygamy of Hindu men after conversion to Islam. While the issue before the Court was bigamy of a Hindu man and validity of his marriage contracted prior to conversion, the Court addressed the issue of Uniform Civil Code in the context of nation, national integration and minority identity.

The judgments in the period under reference have led even legal scholars, who had earlier advocated Uniform Civil Code to re-examine their positions. They have forced human rights activists and women's rights advocates to take a more restrained and conscious position in order to clearly distinguish their demand from that of the right wing communal forces. [*Women and Law in India*, Flavia Agnes, pp. 111, 116, 120, 121]

THE SUPREME COURT AND THE UCC : A DEBATE

The issue of Uniform Civil Code is governed by three distinct undertones, i.e. gender equality, national integration and concept of modernity. The gender concern groups demand for a Uniform Civil Code so that it could eliminate the woes and sufferings of Indian women in general and Muslim women in particular. They believe that the latter cannot voice their concern and fight for their rights. As such, they say, the state should intervene and enact a uniform code to bestow gender justice upon minority women.

The demand for Uniform Civil Code made by the politicians voices the concern of national integration and communal harmony. They are most communalists and project the Muslims as the 'other', different from 'us'—Hindus and the nation. It is indeed a matter of grave concern that this position, advocated by the Hindu right wing, received a boost through judgments pronounced by the Courts of a secular and pluralistic state. The Shah Bano controversy, demolition of the Babri Masjid, the rise of the Hindu rightwing, the attacks on Christians, the gruesome sexual violence upon Muslim women during the recent Gujarat carnage, have all been factors that have necessitated a re-examination of the earlier call for a UCC. Many progressive groups and some women's organizations no longer support this demand.

Surprisingly, even the BJP itself has abandoned it. There is strong reaction from Muslim groups. Every time the Supreme Court makes a comment, what one sees in the Media are images of *purdah* clad Muslim women and opinions of Muslim religious leaders opposing the demand. Regrettably, in most of the debates on the issue, often its core element is ignored and the UCC is projected as a case against the Muslim minority. Look at the Sarla Mudgal case, 1995: the core issue before the court was conversion and bigamy by a Hindu man. Neither Muslim law nor rights of Muslim women were issues before the court. The court was examining the rights of two Hindu wives and validity of two marriages by a biga-mous Hindu husband – the first one under the Hindu law and the subsequent one contracted after a fraudulent conver-sion to Islam. The parties to the litigation were all Hindus. But, unfortunately, the judgment and the media publicity that followed focused primarily on UCC in the context of nation, national integration and minority identity.

WHAT DOES ARTICLE 44 DEMANDS?

Whenever any debate touched UCC, the Article 44 of the Constitution comes up to the fore. People say all sorts of things and use the Article to bolster their cases. Contextually, let see what does Article 44 stand for? What does it demand? The answer to the queries are simple. There is no ambiguity anywhere in the language used here. But still we mix up things and got confused, specially on the point that the Arti-cle 44 does not direct any law-making body to enact a uni-form civil code straight away. It only says that the state shall endeavour to secure a uniform civil code for the citizens throughout the territory of India.

An eminent British expert of Hindu law once said about it: Civil code, throughout the world, suggests a great deal of private law, including contract and tort. There are many countries in the world, which have no civil codes at all. In many other countries there is in force a civil code which con-tains all sorts of civil laws (as opposed to penal laws) except family and succession laws. In very few countries there is a civil code which covers also laws of family relations and suc-cession. Family and succession laws are contained in special statutes standing separate from the local civil codes if there are any in force almost everywhere.

Let us examine our case in the light of these facts. The Article 44 appears in Part IV of our Constitution, which provides 'Directive Principles of State Policy'. The governing and decisive Article in this part is Article 37 which clarifies the following three points:

1. the principles contained in Part IV *shall not be enforceable by any court;*
2. these principles will be, nevertheless, fundamental in the governance of the country; and
3. it shall be the duty of the State *to apply these principles in making laws.*

Article 44 does not ask clearly the legislature to enact a civil code; it contains a principle which state can apply in making civil laws. Ordinarily, the principle of uniformity, to be applied in making civil laws, is fundamental in governance of the country; but if, for any valid and important reason, the state cannot apply the principle of uniformity while making civil laws, no court in the country can in any way have the principle enforced. The Constitution leaves it entirely and exclusively to the wisdom of the state when, how, in what way, and to what extent, it can and should apply the principle of uniformity in making civil laws.

How can the state endeavour to secure uniformity of civil laws? And to what extent? The demands of Article 44, whatever they are, and the modalities for its implementation both are to be determined in tune with the provisions of Part III of the Constitution guaranteeing Fundamental Rights, including right to equality before law and equal protection of laws, civil liberties, freedom of individuals to profess and practice their respective religions, freedom of religious communities to manage their own affairs, and the right of sections of citizens to preserve their cultures. [Articles 14-29].

Article 44 talks of uniform civil code for the citizens throughout the territory of India. If a legislature of a particular state enacts a code, obviously it cannot be applied throughout the territory of India; nor will any other state will be bound to re-enact it locally. For instance, if the Maharashtra Legislature enacts a new marriage law and makes it applicable to all Maharashtrians in that state people will be governed by the new law, but they will remain subject to the central laws or uncodified personal laws in the rest of the country. Will this amount to securing a uniform civil code through out the territory of India? Enactment of a uniform civil code at the state level is, thus, as per the Constitution, clearly a contradiction in terms.

ARTICLES ON FUNDAMENTAL RIGHTS VS. ARTICLE 44

Both Fundamental Right and Directive Principles of State Policy are fundamental to the governance of the country, but the fundamental rights are enforceable by resort to judicial remedies while the directive principles are not justifiable in that sense. The distinction is significant but not one that creates a chasm or cleavage between the two or destroys their mutual complimentarity. Fundamental rights and directive principles are equally relevant in judging the validity of affirmative and ameliorative social legislations. It is clear from the decisions of the Supreme Court that legislations enacted in pursuance of the Directive Principles of State Policy are more readily upheld. However, the courts do not and cannot invalidate legislations or administrative actions on the ground that these contravene the Directive Principles of State policy. Fundamental Right are precise norms cast in a legal mould. (*Religion And Society*, December, 1979)

A CHECKLIST OF CONSTITUTIONAL PROVISIONS

1. Article 13 (1): saying that all 'laws in force' since the pre-Constitution days as are inconsistent with the fundamental Rights shall be void to the extent of such inconsis-

tency;

2. Article 13 (2): directing the state in future not to make any law that takes away or abridges a Fundamental Rights shall be void to the extent of such inconsistency;

3. Article 14: containing broad equality clause;

4. Article 15: directing the state not to discriminate against any citizens on the ground only of religion, race, caste, sex or place of birth or any of them; *without prejudice to its power of making special provisions for women and children and for socially and educationally backward classes* (including (schedule castes and schedule tribes).

5. Article 25(1): guaranteeing the right freely to profess, practice and propagate *religion.*

6. Article 25(2): explaining the right to freedom of religion *shall not affect* the State's power to regulate or restrict *secular activity associated with the religious practice* and to provide for social welfare and reforms;

7. Article 26(B): guaranteeing every "religious denomination" *the right to manage its own affair in the matter of religion;*

8. Article 29 (1): guaranteeing to all sections of citizens the right to *conserve* the *distinct culture,* if any;

9. Article 38: directing the state "to strive to promote people's welfare" by securing and effectively protecting a social order under which, inter alia, justice shall inform all institutions of national life;

10. Article 44: directing the state 'to endeavour to secure for the citizens a uniform civil code throughout the territory of India.

11. Article 246: empowering Parliament and the state legislatures to make laws in the areas which since the pre-Constitution days fall in the domain of personal laws;

12. Article 372: declaring that, subject to other provisions of the Constitution period shall remain in force unless law-

fully altered, repealed, amended [or adapted] by a competent authority.

PART III: FUNDAMENTAL RIGHTS

Article 13: Laws inconsistent with or in derogation of the fundamental rights

1. All laws in force in the territory of India immediately before the commencement of his constitution, in so far as they are in inconsistent with the provisions of this part, shall, to the extent of such inconsistency, be void.
2. The state shall not make any law which takes away or abridges the rights conferred by this part and any law made in contravention of this clause shall, to the extent of the contravention, be void.
3. In this article, unless the context otherwise requires:
   (a) 'law', includes any Ordinance, order, bye-law, rule, regulation, notification, custom or usage having in the territory of India the force of law;
   (b) "law in force" includes laws passed or made by a legislature or other competent authority in the territory of India before the commencement of this constitution and not previously repealed, not withstanding that any such law or any part thereof may not be then in operation either at all or in particular areas.
4. Nothing in this article shall apply to any amendment of this Constitution made under Article 368.

Article 14: Equality before law

1. The State shall not discriminate against any citizen on grounds only of religion, race, Caste, sex, place of birth or any of them.
2. Nothing in this article shall prevent the State from making any special provision for women and children.

3. Nothing in this article or in clause (2) of Article 29 shall prevent the State from making any socially and educationally backward classes of citizens or for the Scheduled Caste and the Scheduled Tribes.

Article 17: Abolition of untouchability

'Untouchability' is abolished and its practice in any form is forbidden. The enforcement of any disability arising out of 'untouchability' shall be an offence punishable in accordance with law.

Article 25: Freedom of conscience and profession, practice and propagation of religion

(1) Subject to public order, morality and health and to the other provisions of this part, all persons are equally entitled to freedom of conscience and the right freely to profess, practice and propagate religion.

(2) Nothing in this article shall affect the operation of any existing law or prevent the State from making any law
  (a) regulation or restricting any economic, financial, political or other secular activity which may be associated with religious practice;
  (b) providing for social welfare and reform or the throwing open of Hindu religious institutions of a public character to all classes and sections of Hindus.

Explanation I. The wearing and carrying of Kirpans shall be deemed to be included in the profession of the Sikh religion.

Explanation II. In sub-clause (b) of clause (2), the reference to Hindus shall be construed as including a reference to persons professing the Sikh, Jain or Buddhist religion and the reference to Hindu religion institutions shall be construed accordingly.

Article 26: Freedom to manage religious affairs

Subject to public order, morality and health, every religious denomination or any section thereof shall have the right:

(a) to establish and maintain institutions for religious and charitable purposes;
(b) to manage its own affairs in matters of religion;
(c) to own and acquire movable and immovable property; and
(d) to administer such property in accordance with law.

Article 29: Protection of interests of minorities

(1) Any section of the citizens residing in the territory of India or any part thereof having a distinct language, script or culture of its own shall have the right to conserve the same.

PART IV : DIRECTIVE PRINCIPLES OF STATE POLICY

Article 38: State to secure a social order for the promotion of welfare of the people

1. The State shall strive to promote the welfare of the people by securing and protecting as effectively as it may a social order in which justice, social, economic and political, shall inform all the institutions of the national life.
2. The State shall, in particular, strive to minimize the inequalities in status, facilities and opportunities, not only amongst individuals but also amongst groups of people residing in different areas or engaged in different vocations.

III. PERSONAL LAWS AND THE FUNDAMENTAL RIGHTS

Those parts of the pre-Constitution personal laws-both codi-

fied and uncodified applicable to whichever community—
that have not today been touched by any 'competent authority' [qualifying for that job under article 372 of the Constitu-
tion] remain in force, as before, by virtue of the main provision of the said article. Though, in theory, there is no constitutional embargo on the legislative power of the State in respect of these laws, the policy of the successive governments
at the Centre has led to their continue exemption from direct
reform. Of course, all these laws have been made subservient
to those few legislative measures [e.g. the laws relating to
child marriage and dowry] which have been enacted for the
entire Indian citizenry. Besides these laws, new personal
laws have been enacted by Parliament for the majority community and the Sikh, Jain and the Buddhist minorities –
bracketing all of them under the newly evolved jurisprudential expression "Hindu' [not used in religious sense]. The
traditional laws of all these communities not covered by
these new enactments remain in force as before.

So, in the area of personal laws there are now in force in
this country:

(1) the pre-1950 laws of Muslims, Christians, Parsis and Jews
    [some of them Codified];
(2) the post –1950 codified laws of Hindus, Budhdhists,
    Sikhs and Jains.

MUSLIM LAW AND JUDICIAL REFORMS

Distinct family laws govern most of India's major religious
groups—Hindus, Muslims, Christians, Parsis and Jews—as
well as many so-called tribal groups (Hindu law governs
Sikhs, Jains and Parsis). Muslim leaders pressed for the retention of legal pluralism far more than the leaders of other
religious groups did soon after Indian independence, especially during the debates of the Constituent Assembly. Con-

cerns about the recognition of distinct religious identity were most strongly felt among Muslims in the aftermath of the formation of Pakistan.

While the legislature introduced major changes in Hindu law in the 1950's, major policy makers claimed that they were leaving changes in the laws of the religious minorities to their representatives, who in practice were typically conservative religious and political elites. The conservatism of such elites made major changes in these laws seems unlikely. Nevertheless, some changes took place in Muslim law and in India's other family laws gave women greater rights as compared with the ones enjoyed by them in the last generation. The judiciary was the main agent of change, although legislatures and some religious leaders and religious institutions also played come roles. However, changes were slower in Muslim community.

Of the three Acts pertaining to Muslim Personal Law in India, the Dissolution of Muslim Marriage Act of 1939 governed the grounds on which Muslim women could get judicially mediated divorce. Another law, the Muslim women's (Protection of Rights on Divorce) Act, governed the rights of Muslim women to post-divorce maintenance after it was passed in 1986. The other Act, the Muslim Personal Law (*Shari'at*) Application Act of 1937, stated that the Sharia would apply to Muslims in family matters without specifying the rules it recognized, although the 'Islamic laws' applied in different regions of the world vary considerably. The silence of this Act left much of the content of India's Muslim law to the judiciary's discretion.

Indian legislatures gave the content and implementation of Muslim law little attention after independence. Not one of the one hundred and eighty two official Law Commissions of the post-colonial period assessed the functioning of Muslim law or considered possible changes in Muslim law. Only a few legislative changes were introduced in Muslim law through the instrumentality of the pieces of legislation mentioned above after independence.

•

2

THE HINDU SUCCESSION (AMEND.) BILL, 2004
[ANNEXURE TO SECTION I]

PARLIAMENT OF INDIA
RAJYA SABHA
DEPARTMENT RELATED PARLIAMENTARY STANDING
COMMITTEE ON PERSONNEL, PUBLIC GRIEVANCES,
LAW AND JUSTICE

SEVENTH REPORT
ON
THE HINDU SUCCESSION (AMENDMENT) BILL, 2004
(PRESENTED TO THE RAJYA SABHA ON 13TH MAY, 2005)
(LAID ON THE TABLE OF THE LOK SABHA ON 13TH MAY, 2005)

RAJYA SABHA SECRETARIAT
NEW DELHI
MAY, 2005/VAISAKHA, 1926 (SAKA)

CONTENTS

(ii) List of the witnesses who appeared before the Committee; and

(iii) Views/suggestions of individuals/organisations on the Hindu Succession (Amendment) Bill, 2004 and comments of Government thereon;

* To be appended at printing stage.

COMPOSITION OF THE COMMITTEE (2004-05)

1. Shri E.M. Sudarsana Natchiappan, *Chairman*

RAJYA SABHA

2. Dr. Radhakant Nayak
3. Shri Balavantalias Bal Apte
4. Shri Ram Nath Kovind
5. Shri Ram Jethmalani
6. Dr. P.C. Alexander
7. Shri Tariq Anwar
8. Shri Raashid Alvi
9. Vacant
10. Vacant

LOK SABHA

11. Dr. Shafiqurrahman Barq
12. Smt. Bhavani Rajenthiran
13. Shri Chhatar Singh Darbar
14. Justice (Retd.) N.Y. Hanumanthappa
15. Shri Shailendra Kumar
16. Smt. Kiran Maheshwari
17. Shri Dahyabhai V. Patel
18. Shri Brajesh Pathak
19. Shri Harin Pathak
20. Shri V. Radhakrishnan

21. Shri Vishwendra Singh
22. Shri Bhupendrasinh Solanki
23. Prof. Vijaya Kumar Malhotra
24. Kumari Mamata Banerjee
25. Shri S.K. Kharventhan
26. Shri Shriniwas D. Patil
27. Shri A.K. Moorthy
28. Shri Ramchandra Paswan
29. Vacant
30. Vacant
31. Vacant

SECRETARIAT

Shri Tapan Chatterjee, Joint Secretary
Shri Surinder Kumar Watts, Deputy Secretary
Shri H.C. Sethi, Under Secretary
Shri Vinoy Kumar Pathak, Committee Officer

INTRODUCTION

I, the Chairman of the Department Related Parliamentary Standing Committee on Personnel, Public Grievances, Law and Justice having been authorized by the Committee to present the Report on its behalf, do hereby present this Seventh Report on the Hindu Succession (Amendment) Bill, 2004*.

2. In pursuance of the rules relating to the Department Related Parliamentary Standing Committees, the Chairman, Rajya Sabha referred** the Hindu Succession (Amendment) Bill, 2004 as introduced in the Rajya Sabha on 20th December, 2004 for examination and report.

3. The Committee considered the Bill in five sittings held on 3rd & 17th February, 19th & 27th April and 10th May, 2005.

4. The Committee heard the oral evidence of the Secretary, Ministry of Law and Justice, Legislative Department in its sitting held on 3rd February 2005.

5. The Committee heard the views of the prominent NGOs and eminent experts on the Bill (Annexure-I) in its sittings held on 16th February and 19th April, 2005.

6. In its sitting held on 27th April, 2005 the Committee took up clause-by clause consideration of the Bill.

7. In its sitting held on 10th May, 2005 the Committee considered the draft report on the Bill and adopted the same.

8. In the said sitting, the Committee also decided that the evidence tendered before it may be laid on the table of both the Houses of Parliament.

9. In the course of its deliberations, the Committee has made use of the background note on the Bill received from the Ministry of Law and Justice (Legislative Department); Hindu Succession Act, 1956; 174th Report of the Law Commission of India on 'Property Rights of Women : Proposed Reforms under the Hindu Law'; suggestions received from organizations/experts; comments of the Ministry on the views received from organizations/experts.

10. For facility of reference and convenience, observations and recommendations of the Committee have been printed in bold letters in the body of the Report.

11. On behalf of the Committee, I would like to acknowledge with thanks the contributions made by experts/organizations who deposed before the Committee and submitted their valuable suggestions on the Bill.

NEW DELHI: E.M. SUDARSANA NATCHIAPPAN
May, 2005   Chairman
                                     Committee on Personnel, Public
                                     Grievances, Law and Justice

CHAPTER I

INTRODUCTORY

1.0 The Constitution of India enshrines the principle of gender equality in its Preamble and Parts III, IV and IVA pertaining to Fundamental Rights, Fundamental Duties and Directive Principles respectively. The Constitution not only grants equality to women, but also empowers the State to adopt measures of positive discrimination in favour. of women. However, there exists a wide gap between the goals enunciated in the Constitution and the ground reality in respect of the position of women in the socio-economic fabric of India.

1.1. Gender disparity manifests itself in various forms, especially with regard to effective rights in property. To quote from *Mulla: Principles of Hindu Law*[1]:

"The law of inheritance was of later growth and, in general, applied only to property held in absolute severalty as distinguished from property held by the joint family. The fundamental conception of the Hindu joint family is a common male ancestor with his lineal descendants in the male line. Even under early Hindu law, the rights of sons were recognised and they acquired equal interest with the father in the ancestral property as coparceners." *(page 277).*

1.2. The 174th Report of the Law Commission of India on 'Property Rights of Women: Proposed reforms under the Hindu Law', states that the discrimination against women is particularly in relation to laws governing the inheritance/succession of property amongst the members of a joint Hindu family.

HISTORICAL OVERVIEW

1.3. The disparity in the property rights on the basis of gender is deep rooted and can be traced back to the ancient times. Traditional Hindu inheritance laws evolved from the ancient texts of *Dharmashastras* and the various commentaries and legal treatises on them. In particular, the *Mitakshara* and the *Dayabhaga* legal doctrines, dated around the twelfth century AD govern the inheritance practices among the Hindus. *Day-*

abhaga prevails in eastern India comprising West Bengal and the adjoining areas, whereas in most of northern and parts of western India *Mitakshara* law is prevalent. In other parts of western India, the *Mayukha* school is prevalent while in parts of southern India, the *Marumakkatayam, Aliyasantana* and *Nambudri* systems prevail.

1.4. Amongst Hindus, broad distinction can be made between two types of property, *i.e.*, ancestral/joint family property and separate/self acquired property. Joint family property is generally inherited from the male line of descent and also consists of property that is jointly acquired or is acquired separately but merged into the joint property. The Law Commission Report (*Ibid*) states as below:

Under the *Mitakshara* law, on birth, the son acquires a right and interest in the family property. According to this school, a son, grandson and a great grandson constitute a class of coparceners, based on birth in the family. No female is a member of the coparcenary in *Mitakshara* law. Under the *Mitakshara* system, joint family property devolves by survivorship within the coparcenary. This means that with every birth or death of a male in the family, the share of every other surviving male either gets diminished or enlarged *(para 1.3.2; page 2)*.

The *Mitakshara* law also recognises inheritance by succession but only to the property separately owned by an individual male or female. Females are included as heirs to this kind of property by *Mitakshara* law *(para 1.3.3; page 2)*.

Under the *Dayabhaga* law, succession rather than survivorship is the rule. Neither sons nor daughters become coparceners at birth nor do they have rights in the family property during their father's lifetime. However, on his death, they inherit as tenants-in-common. Daughters also get equal share along with their brothers. Since this ownership arises only on the extinction of the father's ownership, none of them can compel the father to partition the property in his lifetime and the latter is free to give or sell the property without their consent. As females could be coparceners, they could also act as *Kartas* and manage the property on behalf of the other members in the *Dayabhaga* school *(para 1.3.4; page 2)*.

1.5. In the face of such multiplicity of succession laws diverse in their nature, property laws continued to be complex and discriminatory against women. The social reform movement during the pre-independence period raised the issue of gender discrimination and a number of ameliorative steps were initiated. The principal reform that was called for, and one which became a pressing necessity in view of changed social and economic conditions, was that in succession there should be equitable distribution between male and female heirs and the Hindu women's limited estate should be enlarged into full ownership. As per the Law Commission Report *(Ibid)*, the earliest legislation bringing females into the scheme of inheritance is the Hindu Law of Inheritance Act, 1929. Subsequently, the Hindu Women's Right to Property Act, 1937 brought significant changes in the law of partition, alienation of property, inheritance and adoption. Although better rights were given to women in respect of property, it was found to be incoherent and defective in many respects and gave rise to a number of anomalies. In 1941, the Hindu Law Committee was set up under the Chairmanship of Shri B.N. Rau, which strongly recommended that a complete code of Hindu law be prepared, covering inheritance, marriage and other aspects. The Hindu Code Bill as framed by the Committee was introduced in the Legislative Assembly in April 1947. However, in the face of stiff resistance from various orthodox sections of the society, the Bill was shelved in 1951. The then Prime Minister of India, expressed his unequivocal commitment to carry out reforms to remove disparities and disabilities suffered by Hindu women. Finally, after much effort, the Hindu Succession Act, 1956 was enacted and came into force on 17th June, 1956. According to *Mulla (Ibid)*:

Fragmentary legislation in the form of number of uncoordinated rules did not prove a satisfactory remedy.... A uniform and comprehensive system of inheritance recognising equable distribution between male and female heirs and contained in a series of coherent propositions carefully considered and authoritatively stated was, therefore, a long felt desideratum. *(page 278-279).*

CONSTITUTIONAL PROVISIONS GUARANTEEING GENDER EQUALITY

1.6. The framers of the Indian Constitution took note of the adverse condition of women in society and a number of provisions and safeguards were included in the Constitution to ward off gender inequality. In this context, Articles 14, 15(2), (3) and 16 of the Constitution can be mentioned. These provisions are part of the Fundamental Rights guaranteed by the Constitution. Part IV containing Directive Principles of State Policy further endorses the principle of gender equality which the State has to follow in matters of governance. Similarly, Part IVA of the Constitution enshrining the Fundamental Duties states that:

"It shall be the duty of every citizen of India - *(e)* ....; to renounce practices derogatory to the dignity of women; ...."

THE HINDU SUCCESSION ACT, 1956

1.7. The Hindu Succession Act, 1956 (HSA) amends and codifies the law relating to intestate succession among Hindus and aims to lay down a uniform law of succession whereby attempt has been made to ensure equality of inheritance rights between sons and daughters. It applies to all Hindus including Buddhists, Jains and Sikhs. It lays down a uniform and comprehensive system of inheritance and applies to those governed by the *Mitakshara* and the *Dayabahga* schools as well as the various schools existing in South India such as *Murumakkattayam, Aliyasantans, Nambudri,* etc.

The HSA reformed the Hindu personal law and gave woman greater property rights, allowing her full ownership rights instead of limited rights in property. The daughters were also granted property rights in their father's estate. In the matter of succession to the property of a Hindu male dying intestate, the Act lays down a set of general rules in sections 8 to 13. Sections 15 and 16 of the Act contain separate general rules affecting succession to the property of a female intestate.

SUCCESSION TO PROPERTY OF A MALE INTESTATE

1.8. As per succession to property of a male intestate laid down by the Act, the two systems of inheritance to the separate or self-acquired property, which hitherto prevailed under *Mitakshara* and *Dayabhaga* schools, are abolished and a uniform system came into operation as propounded in section 8 of the Act. The three classes of heirs recognised by *Mitakshara, i.e., Gotraja Sapindas, Samanodakas* and *Bandhus* and the three classes of heirs recognised by *Dayabhaga, i.e., Sapindas, Sakulyas* and *Bandhus* cease to exist in case of devolution taking place after the coming into force of the Act. The heirs are divided, instead, into four classes or categories. These are:

1. heirs in Class I of the Schedule;
2. heirs in Class II of the Schedule;
3. agnates; and
4. cognates

1.9. The Schedule to the Act provides the following twelve relations as Class I heirs:

(i)   son;
(ii)   daughter;
(iii) widow;

(iv)   mother;

(v)   son of a pre-deceased son;

(vi)   daughter of a pre-deceased son;

(vii) son of a pre-deceased daughter;

(viii) daughter of a pre-deceased daughter;

(ix)   widow of a pre-deceased son;

(x)   son of a pre-deceased son of a pre-deceased son;

(xi)   daughter of a pre-deceased son of a pre-deceased son; and

(xii) widow of a pre-deceased son of a pre-deceased son.

1.10. Of these, mother, widow, son and daughter are primary heirs. In the absence of Class I heirs, the property devolves on Class II heirs and in their absence first on agnates and then on cognates.

CRITIQUE OF HSA FROM A GENDER PERSPECTIVE

1.11. Some sections of the Act came under criticism evoking controversy as being favourable to continue inequality on the basis of gender. One such provision has been the retention of the *Mitakshara* coparcenary with only males as coparceners. As per the Law Commission Report, coparcenary constitutes a narrower body of persons within a joint family and consists of father, son, son's son and son's son's son. Thus ancestral property continues to be governed by a wholly patrilineal regime, wherein property descends only through the male line as only the male members of a joint Hindu family have an interest by birth in the coparcenary property. Coparcenary property, in contradistinction with the absolute or separate property of an individual coparcener, devolve upon surviving coparceners in the family, according to the rule of devolution by survivorship. Since a woman could not be a coparcener, she was not entitled to a share in the ancestral property by birth.

1.12. However, attempt was made to partially remove this

disparity. Section 6 of the Act, although it does not interfere with the special rights of those who are members of a *Mitakshara* coparcenary, recognises, without abolishing joint family property, the right upon the death of a coparcener, of certain of his preferential heirs to claim an interest in the property that would have been allotted to such coparcener if a partition of the joint family property had in fact taken place immediately before his death ('notional' partition). To elaborate this further, the share of the deceased male in the joint property and the shares of his heirs are ascertained under the assumption of a 'notional' partition (*i.e.,* as if the partition had taken place just prior to his death). Thus, section 6 of the Act, while recognising the rule of devolution by survivorship among the members of the coparcenary, makes an exception to the rule in the proviso. According to the proviso, if the deceased has left him surviving a female relative specified in Class I of Schedule I, or a male relative specified in that Class who claims through such female relative, the interest of the deceased in the *Mitakshara* coparcenary property shall devolve by testamentary or intestate succession under this Act as mentioned above, and not by survivorship.

1.13. Notwithstanding these facts, the direct interest in the coparcenary held by male members by virtue of birth remains unaffected. It affects only the interest they hold in the share of the deceased. A son's share in the property in case the father dies intestate would be in addition to the share he has on birth. A man has full testamentary power over all his property, including his interest in the coparcenary.

1.14. Thus, non inclusion of women as coparceners in the joint family property under the *Mitakshara* system as reflected in section 6 of the Hindu Succession Act, 1956 relating to devolution of interest in coparcenary property has been under criticism for being violative of equal rights of women guaranteed under the Constitution in relation to property rights.

This meant that females cannot inherit ancestral property as males do. If a joint family gets divided, each male coparcener takes his share and females get nothing. Only when one of the coparceners dies, a female gets a share of his interest as an heir to the deceased.

1.15. It has been further observed that as per the proviso to Section 6 of the Act, the interest of the deceased male in the *Mitakshara* coparcenary devolve by intestate succession firstly upon the heirs specified in Class I of Schedule I. As mentioned above, under this Schedule, there are only four primary heirs, namely, son, daughter, widow and mother. For the remaining eight, the principle of representation goes up to two degrees in the male line of descent as mentioned in para 6 (v), (vi), (x) and (xi). But in the female line of descent, it goes only upto one degree as mentioned in para 6 (vii) and (viii). Thus, the son's son's son and the son's son's daughter get a share but a daughter's daughter's son and daughter's daughter's daughter do not get anything.

1.16. Further, as per section 23 of the Act, married daughter has been denied the right to residence in the parental home unless widowed, deserted or separated from her husband and female heir has been disentitled to ask for partition in respect of dwelling house wholly occupied by members of the joint family until the male heirs choose to divide their respective shares therein. These provisions have been identified as major sources of disabilities thrust by law on women.

1.17. Another source of controversy was the establishment of the right to will away property. A man has full testamentary power over all his property, including his interest in the coparcenary. As per the Law Commission Report, ".... The Act gave a weapon to a man to deprive a woman of the rights she earlier had under certain schools of Hindu law."

The legal right of Hindus to bequeath property by way of will was conferred by the Indian Succession Act, 1925.

STATE AMENDMENT ACTS

1.18. To overcome these lacunae and make the law gender neutral, a number of State Amendments as mentioned below have been made in the Act effecting changes in the law relating to *Mitakshara* coparcenary declaring the daughter to be a coparcener in a Joint Hindu family:

(i) The Hindu Succession (Andhra Pradesh Amendment) Act, 1986;
(ii) The Hindu Succession (Tamil Nadu Amendment) Act, 1990;
(iii) The Hindu Succession (Karnataka Amendment) Act, 1994; and
(iv) The Hindu Succession (Maharashtra Amendment) Act, 1986.

1.19. On the other hand, with the enactment of the Kerala Joint Hindu Family System (Abolition) Act, 1975, the State of Kerala has totally abolished the right to property by birth of males and put an end to the Joint Hindu family system. The consequence of the derecognition of the members of the family, irrespective of their sex, who are governed by the *Mitakshara* law, is that they have become tenants-in-common of the joint family property and became full owners of their share.

EXAMINATION BY THE LAW COMMISSION OF INDIA

1.20. As per the Background Note of the Ministry, the Law Commission of India made a *suo motu* study of sections 6 and 23 of the Hindu Succession Act, 1956 and submitted its 174th Report to the Union Government in May, 2000. In July 2001, the National Commission for Women also made certain recommendations suggesting amendments to the aforesaid Act, which had been referred to the Law Commission of India for study and report.

1.21. The Law Commission of India after holding wide ranging consultations gave its recommendations in its 174th Report (*Ibid*) relating to amendments to the Hindu Succession Act, 1956 in the form of a draft Bill titled the Hindu Succession (Amendment) Bill, 2000. The Central Government after consulting the State Governments and other concerned Ministries/Departments of the Government of India decided to accept the recommendations of the Law Commission of India. Accordingly, the Hindu Succession (Amendment) Bill, 2004 has been introduced in the Rajya Sabha on the 20th of December, 2004.

STATEMENT OF OBJECTS AND REASONS OF THE HINDU SUCCESSION (AMENDMENT) BILL, 2004

1.22. The Statement of Objects and Reasons of the aforesaid Bill is as follows:

The Hindu Succession Act, 1956 has amended and codified the law relating to intestate succession among Hindus. The Act brought about changes in the law of succession among Hindus and gave rights which were till then unknown in relation to women's property. However, it does not interfere with the special rights of those who are members of Hindu *Mitakshara* coparcenary except to provide rules for devolution of the interest of a deceased male in certain cases. The Act lays down a uniform and comprehensive system of inheritance and applies, *inter alia*, to persons governed by the *Mitakshara* and *Dayabhaga* schools and also to those governed previously by the *Murumakkattayam*, *Aliyasantana* and *Nambudri* laws. The Act applies to every person who is a Hindu by religion in any of its forms or developments including a *Virashaiva*, a *Lingayat* or a follower of the *Brahmo*, *Prarthana* or *Arya Samaj*; or to any person who is Buddhist, Jain or Sikh by religion; or to any other person who is not a Muslim, Christian, Parsi or Jew by religion. In the case of a testamentary disposition, this Act does not apply and the interest of the deceased is governed by the Indian Succession Act, 1925.

Section 6 of the Act deals with devolution of interest of a male

Hindu in coparcenary property and recognises the rule of devolution by survivorship among the members of the coparcenary. The retention of the *Mitakshara* coparcenary property without including the females in it means that the females cannot inherit in ancestral property as their male counterparts do. The law by excluding the daughter from participating in the coparcenary ownership not only contributes to her discrimination on the ground of gender but also has led to oppression and negation of her fundamental right of equality guaranteed by the Constitution. Having regard to the need to tender social justice to women, the States of Andhra Pradesh, Tamil Nadu, Karnataka and Maharashtra have made necessary changes in the law giving equal right to daughters in Hindu *Mitakshara* coparcenary property. The Kerala Legislature has enacted the Kerala Joint Hindu Family System (Abolition) Act, 1975.

It is proposed to remove the discrimination as contained in section 6 of the Hindu Succession Act, 1956 by giving equal rights to daughters in the Hindu *Mitakshara* coparcenary property as the sons have. Section 23 of the Act disentitles a female heir to ask for partition in respect of a dwelling house wholly occupied by a joint family until the male heirs choose to divide their respective shares therein. It is also proposed to omit the said section so as to remove the disability on female heirs contained in that section.

The above proposals are based on the recommendations of the Law Commission of India as contained in its 174th Report on 'Property Rights of Women: Proposed Reform under the Hindu Law'.

1.23. The Bill was referred to the Department Related Parliamentary Standing Committee on Personnel, Public Grievances, Law and Justice on 27 December 2004 for examination and report.

CHAPTER II

CLAUSE-WISE CONSIDERATION OF THE BILL

2.0 The Hindu Succession (Amendment) Bill, 2004 seeks to make two major amendments in the Hindu Succession Act,

1956. First, it is proposed to remove the gender discrimination in section 6 of the original Act. Second, it proposes to omit section 23 of the original Act, which disentitles a female heir to ask for partition in respect of a dwelling house, wholly occupied by a joint family, until the male heirs choose to divide their respective shares therein.

2.1 The Committee undertook clause-by-clause consideration of the Bill in the presence of Secretary, Legislative Department, Secretary, Department of Legal Affairs and the representatives from these respective Departments.

2.2. This clause seeks to substitute section 6 of the Hindu Succession Act, 1956 with a new section. The table below reproduces the aforesaid section of the Act, alongwith the amendments as introduced by the Bill:

The Hindu Succession Act, 1956	The Hindu Succession (Amendment) Bill, 2004
6. Devolution of interest in coparcenary property— When a male Hindu dies after the commencement of this Act, having at the time of his death an interest in a *Mitakshara* coparcenary property, his interest in the property shall devolve by survivorship upon the surviving members of the coparcenary and not in accordance with this Act:	2. For section 6 of the Hindu Succession Act, 1956 (hereinafter referred to as the principal Act), the following section shall be substituted, namely:- '6. *(1)* On and from the commencement of the Hindu Succession (Amendment) Act, 2004, in a joint Hindu family governed by the *Mitakshara* law, the daughter of a coparcener shall:
Provided that, if the de-	*(a)* also by birth become a coparcener in her own right; the same manner as the son here;

ceased had left him surviving a female relative specified in class I of the Schedule or a male relative specified in that class who claims through such female relative, the interest of the deceased in the *Mitakshara* coparcenary property shall devolve by testamentary or intestate succession, as the case may be and not by survivorship.

Explanation 1 – For the purpose of this section, the interest of a Hindu *Mitakshara* coparcener shall be deemed to be the share in the property that would have been allotted to him if a partition of the property had taken place immediately before his death, irrespective of whether he was entitled to claim partition or not.

Explanation 2. – Nothing contained in the proviso to this section shall be construed as enabling a person who has separated himself from the coparce-

(b) have the same rights in the coparcenary property as she would have had if she had been a son;

(c) be subject to the same liabilities and disabilities in respect of the said coparcenary property as that of a son,

and any reference to a Hindu *Mitakshara* coparcener shall be deemed to include a reference to a daughter:

Provided that nothing contained in this sub-section shall apply to a daughter married before the commencement of the Hindu Succession (Amendment) Act, 2004.

(2) Any property to which a female Hindu becomes entitled by virtue of sub-section *(1)* shall be held by her with the incidents of coparcenary ownership and shall be regarded, notwithstanding anything contained in this Act or any other law for the time being in force in, as property capable of being disposed of by her by will or other testamentary disposition.

(3) Where a Hindu dies after the commencement of the Hindu Succession (Amendment) Act,

nary before the death of the deceased or any of his heirs to claim on intestacy a share in the interest referred to therein.

2004, his interest in the property of a Joint Hindu family governed by the *Mitakshara* law, shall devolve by testamentary or intestate succession, as the case may be, under this Act and not by survivorship, and the coparcenary property shall be deemed to have been divided as if a partition had taken place and,-

(a) the daughter is allotted the same share as is allotted to a son;

(b) the share of the pre-deceased son or a pre-deceased daughter, as they would have got had they been alive at the time of partition, shall be allotted to the surviving child of such predeceased son or of such predeceased daughter; and

(c) the share of the pre-deceased child of a pre-deceased son or of a pre-deceased daughter, as such child would have got had he or she been alive at the time of the partition, shall be allotted to the child of such pre-deceased child of the pre-deceased son or a pre-deceased daughter, as the case may be.

Explanation.- For the purpose of this sub-section, the interest of a Hindu *Mitakshara* coparcener shall be deemed to be the share in the property that would have been allotted to him if a partition of the property had taken place immediately before his death, irrespective of whether he was entitled to claim partition or not.

(4) After the commencement of the Hindu Succession (Amendment) Act, 2004, no court shall recognize any right to proceed against a son, grandson or great grandson for the recovery of any debt due from his father, grandfather or great grandfather on the ground of the pious obligation under the Hindu law, of such son, grandson or great-grandson to discharge any such debt;

Provided that in case of any debt contracted before the commencement of the Hindu Succession (Amendment) Act, 2004, nothing contained in this sub-section shall affect-

(a) the right of any creditor to proceed against the son, grandson or great-grandson, as the case may be; or

(b) any alienation made in respect of or in satisfaction of, any such debt, and any such right or alienation shall be enforceable under the rule of pious obligation in the same manner and to the same extent as it would have been enforceable as if the Hindu Succession (Amendment) Act, 2004 had not been enacted.

Explanation.- For the purposes of clause (a), the expression "son", "grandson" or "great-grandson" shall be deemed to refer to the son, grandson or great-grandson, as the case may be, who was born or adopted prior to the commencement of the Hindu Succession (Amendment) Act, 2004.

(5) Nothing contained in this section shall apply to a partition, which has been effected before the commencement of the Hindu Succession (Amendment) Act, 2004.'

AMENDED SECTION 6(1) AS PROPOSED BY THE BILL

2.3. This section seeks to make the daughter a coparcener by birth in a joint Hindu family governed by the *Mitakshara* law, subject to the same liabilities in respect of the said coparcenary property as that of a son.

2.4. Proviso to section 6(1) states that nothing contained in this sub-section, i.e., making daughter coparcener in the *Mitakshara* Hindu joint family property, shall apply to a daughter married before commencement of the Hindu Succession

(Amendment) Act, 2004. As stated in the Background Note furnished by the Legislative Department, it is proposed to give benefit of the provision of this Bill to married daughters, only after the commencement of the proposed amending legislation.

SUGGESTIONS OF THE LAW COMMISSION

2.5. The States of Andhra Pradesh, Tamil Nadu, Maharashtra and Karnataka have amended the provisions of the HSA effecting changes in the *Mitakshara* coparcenary of the Hindu undivided family, by making the daughter a coparcener, whereas the State of Kerala has totally abolished the right by birth and put an end to the Joint Hindu Family system. The Law Commission, in its 174th Report, 2000, stated that it was first inclined to recommend adoption of the Kerala model in its entirety, which appeared to be fair to women. But, on further examination, it became clear that if the joint Hindu family is abolished and there are only male coparceners, then only they would hold as tenants in common and women would not get anything more than what they are already entitled to by inheritance under section 6 of the HSA. So, the Commission was of the view that it would be better to first make daughters coparceners like sons so that they are entitled to and get their share(s) on partition or on the death of the male coparcener and hold thereafter as tenants in common.

2.6. On the issue of distinction between already married and unmarried daughters, the Law Commission Report stated as below:

The Commission wanted to do away with the distinction between married and unmarried daughters, but, after a great deal of deliberation, it was decided that it should be retained as a married daughter has already received gifts at the time of marriage which, though not commensurate with the son's share, is often substantial.

Keeping this in mind, the distinction between daughters already married before the commencement of the Act, and those married thereafter, appears to be reasonable and further would prevent heart burning and tension in the family. A daughter who is married after the commencement of the Act will have already become a coparcener and entitled to her share in the ancestral property. So, she may not receive any substantial family gifts at the time of her marriage. Hopefully, this will result in the death of the evil of dowry system.

VIEWS/OPINION SUBMITTED BEFORE THE COMMITTEE

2.7. Divergent views emerged on the proposed amendment of the HSA. Various memoranda were received, reflecting these views. While deposing before the Committee, one of the witnesses was of the opinion that the proposed Bill would enhance the share of daughters by making them coparceners, on the same basis as sons in the *Mitakshara* coparcenary. But in doing so, it will alter the share of other Class I female heirs of the deceased, such as the deceased's mother and widow. In States where the wife is not entitled to a share on partition, making daughters coparceners will not only reduce the widow's share to less than that under the unamended HSA, it will reduce it to less than a daughter's share. This is because the deceased man's 'notional' share in the coparcenary, in which the widow gets a part, will decline. Thus, while the amendment will benefit daughters, it will disadvantage the widows. The deceased's mother's share will be affected similarly, the extent depending on whether or not the state entitles her to a share on partition in the *Mitakshara* joint family property. In this context, the Law Commission Report, while commenting on the four Hindu Succession (State Amendment) Acts i.e., Andhra Pradesh, Tamil Nadu, Karnataka and Maharashtra, states that these Acts have conferred equal coparcenary rights on sons and daughters, thus preserving the right by birth and extending it to daughters also in the *Mitak-*

shara Coparcenary. This has the indirect effect of reducing the widow's successional share because if the number of co-parceners increases the interest of the husband will decrease.

2.8. Further, it was argued by some of the witnesses who appeared before the Committee, that the *Mitakshara* coparcenary is an archaic institution – a leftover of a bygone era. Its retention, as proposed in the Bill, will leave many inequalities and anomalies, especially on the ground of gender, and disadvantage some categories of women. Therefore, it was opined that the *Mitakshara* coparcenary system should be abolished altogether. That would bring about uniformity across all categories of property and all categories of Class I female heirs.

2.9. Commenting on the proviso to this section, one of the experts stated that while these rights will apply to all daughters in the long run, at the time of amendment, it is discriminatory towards daughters who are already married. In fact, the married daughters' share (like that of the widow in Tamil Nadu, Andhra Pradesh and Karnataka) will decline. There appears no persuasive justification for the blanket exclusion of married daughter. Even if the parents have given her gifts in marriage, these are seldom equivalent in value to inheritance shares and rarely include immovable property. On the same lines, it was argued by some others that this provision was unjust, not only because many women may not have received a share in the property at the time of marriage, but also because the amount that may have been received or expenditure incurred at the time of marriage, can certainly not be equated to equal rights in property.

2.10. On the other hand, opinion emerged that creating any right in favour of a married daughter in the Hindu Undivided Family property would disturb peace in the family and bring in litigation from a married daughter, as she would be under pressure from her in-laws' to get her share from the parental property by means of partition.

COMMENTS OF THE MINISTRY

2.11. Commenting on this sub-section, the Ministry stated as below:

The Government considers that abolition of the Hindu *Mitakshara* Coparcenary system will affect the sentiments and religious feelings of cross sections of the Hindu society and may adversely affect the preservation and sanctity of the age old system. Hence, the suggestion is not acceptable to the Government.

2.12. In respect of proviso to this section, the Ministry responded that any change in the existing law may elicit some criticism and may be unsuitable to certain people. However, a general policy perspective to bring in equal rights to women in coparcenary property, cannot be avoided. Further, when a Bill changing a system has to be brought in, it has to demarcate the difference by a cut off date. It should be in the larger interest, causing minimum inequality. The opinion furnished by the Ministry in this regard is reproduced below:

In so far as extending the amendments to married women, it is worthwhile to mention here that Law Commission of India, in its 174th Report, has adequately considered the matter ... married daughters have already received substantial gifts from the parents and that the family has already spent considerable money on marriage expenses,..... The proposal to apply the law to unmarried daughters is just and reasonable and will cause minimum disturbance to the settled transactions and less family disputes and unrest. Hence, the Government does not consider that any change in the Bill is called for.

RECOMMENDATIONS OF THE COMMITTEE

2.13. The Committee suggests that in the amended section 6,

sub section (1), clause(a), the words '*also*' and '*here*' may be deleted.

2.14. In section 6, sub section (1), clause (c), the words '*and disabilities*' may be deleted and the words '*of a coparcener*' be inserted after the word '*daughter*' in line 9, to make the meaning more clear.

2.15. The Committee takes note of the fact that a distinction has been made between married and unmarried daughters while granting them the status of coparceners in the *Mitakshara* joint family system. Daughters married before commencement of the Hindu Succession (Amendment) Act, 2004 will not get the benefit of this amendment. Divergent views were expressed regarding inclusion of daughters married before commencement of the aforesaid Act, into the new scheme of things. It was submitted before the Committee that in the long run these rights will apply to all daughters, though they are at present excluded, giving rise to dissatisfaction among a section of the general public.

In view of the foregoing, the Committee recommends that Government should work out some means to compensate the already married daughters, who are not likely to get the status of coparceners in the *Mitakshara* joint family property. In the absence of such a measure, a whole generation of women, contemporary to the passage of this important enactment, will lose out their property rights, while their fellow sisters, just by the virtue of being unmarried, will get the full benefit.

The Committee, in this context, recommends that for those undivided Hindu joint family governed by the *Mitakshara* system, where partition has not taken place at the time of commencement of the Act, the already married daughters should be given the status of coparceners. This way, a large section of already married women could be brought under the purview of the Bill, without the fear of increased litigation.

GENERAL OBSERVATIONS OF THE COMMITTEE

2.16. The Committee is of the view that Hindu Succession (Amendment) Bill, 2004 is a step in the right direction. Laws reflect the face of society and its evolution over the time. To respond to the needs of a dynamic social system, laws have to be changed and amended, at regular intervals. In this context, the Committee feels that the aforesaid Bill, brought forth after nearly fifty years of enactment of the Hindu Succession Act, 1956, has a historical relevance and can go a long way in establishing gender parity in the property laws, governing the Hindu society.

At the same time, the Committee takes note of the fact that the joint family system is a unique feature of the Indian society. Though not impervious to various inadequacies and anomalies, the joint family system has been in existence since time immemorial and is continuing, with many changes in its structure and ideology, to keep pace with the changing needs of the time. While noting the concern regarding discrimination against women in the patrilineal, patriarchal joint family set up, the Committee comprehends that strong public sentiment is attached with the joint family system. Moreover, it is beyond the scope of the present Bill to consider any step regarding abolition of the joint family system in the Hindu households. As regards the demand to abolish the *Mitakshara* joint family system, the Government may initiate a detailed study, to examine the relevance of such a system in the present context and take steps accordingly.

As far as the basic objective of the Bill to remove gender discriminatory practices in the property laws of the Hindus, the Committee welcomes the amendment in section 6 of the Bill, whereby daughters have been given the status of coparceners in the *Mitakshara* joint family system. However, the Committee feels that the position of other Class I female heirs should not suffer as a result of this move. In this context, the

Committee recommends that Government should examine this concern and make suitable provisions to ensure that no injustice is done to the other female heirs, especially the widows.

AMENDED SECTION 6(2) AS PROPOSED BY THE BILL

2.17. This part of the Bill seeks to give full testamentary power to a Hindu female in respect of her coparcenary ownership in the joint family property.

RECOMMENDATION OF THE COMMITTEE

2.18. The Committee suggests that the words '*will or other*' in line 14 of the Bill may be deleted. Testamentary disposition itself means *will*. Therefore, the use of both the words, which are synonymous, are not called for.

AMENDED SECTION 6(3) AS PROPOSED BY THE BILL

2.19. This part seeks to lay down that after commencement of the proposed legislation, if a male Hindu dies, his interest ('notional' share) in the property of a joint Hindu family governed by the *Mitakshara* law shall devolve by testamentary or intestate succession, as the case may be, as per the provisions of the Hindu Succession Act, 1956 and not by survivorship.

2.20. Section 8 of the Hindu Succession Act, 1956 lays down general rules of succession in case of a Hindu male dying intestate, whereby his interest would devolve firstly to the relatives specified in Class I of the Schedule, and in the absence of Class I heirs to the Class II heirs, thereafter to the agnates and lastly to the cognates. Class I heirs include twelve categories of relatives, of whom there are only four primary heirs, namely, mother, widow, son and daughter. The remaining eight represent one or the other person who would have been a primary heir, if he or she had not died before enactment of the Bill. Of these, the son's son's sons and son's son's daughters have been included as Class I heirs, but a daughter's daughter's sons and daughter's daughter's daughters have been placed as Class II heirs. This aspect of the Hindu Succession Act has been criticized as a source of infirmity and gender discrimination.

VIEWS SUBMITTED BEFORE THE COMMITTEE

2.21. It was submitted before the Committee that the proposed Bill leaves this provision untouched and does not seek to amend this sub-section, which violates the principle of gender justice and equality. In this context, one of the memoranda submitted to the Committee stated as below:

There are inequalities in the HSA in generational depth, to which heirs of predeceased sons and predeceased daughters have claims in a man's 'notional' share. The heirs of the predeceased son are traced to two generations after him, and include both children and widows; those of the predeceased daughter go to only one generation after her, and exclude the husband. The 2004 Bill leaves this inequality intact.

2.22. Another submission on the same lines was also made before the Committee. To quote from the memoranda received:

The rules of succession of a deceased coparcener's share also discriminate against women as can be seen in the Schedule to section 8 of the Hindu Succession Act, 1956. Under the Act, if one of the primary heirs is already dead, their heirs inherit. Thus, for example, if the son or daughter has already died, their children can inherit the property of their grand parents. However, though the principle of representation goes up to two degrees in the male line of descent, in the female line of descent it goes only upto one degree. Accordingly, the deceased's son's son's sons and son's son's daughters get share, but a deceased's daughter's daughter's son and daughter's daughter's daughter does not get anything. These distinctions between male and female heirs should be removed.

GENERAL OBSERVATION OF THE COMMITTEE

2.23. The Committee is of the view that within the scope of the present Bill, all measures should be adopted to ensure that gender discrimination in matters of inheritance of joint family property are uprooted, so that the amendments proposed by the Bill bring about far-reaching changes in the Indian society. The Committee agrees with the observation made by the Law Commission in this regard that this sub-section of the Bill contains gender bias, whereby the principle of representation among Class I heirs goes upto two degrees in the male line of descent, but in the female line of descent, it goes upto only one degree. Further, though the Bill seeks to make substantial amendment in section 6 of the Hindu Succession Act, 1956, the proposed proviso to sub-section 3 has been left untouched.

RECOMMENDATION OF THE COMMITTEE

2.24. In view of the foregoing, the Committee recommends that the Schedule to section 8 of the Act should be amended accordingly, to endorse the principle of gender justice and equality. The Schedule may be re-drafted as below:

THE SCHEDULE

HEIRS IN CLASS I AND CLASS II

Class I

1. Son;
2. Daughter;
3. Widow;
4. Mother;
5. Son of a pre-deceased son;

6. Daughter of a pre-deceased son;
7. Son of a pre-deceased daughter;
8. Daughter of a pre-deceased daughter;
9. Widow of a pre-deceased son;
10. Son of a pre-deceased son of a pre-deceased son;
11. Daughter of a pre-deceased son of a pre-deceased son;
12. Widow of a pre-deceased son of a pre-deceased son;
13. Son of a pre-deceased daughter of a pre-deceased daughter; and
14. Daughter of a pre-deceased daughter of a pre-deceased daughter

Further, the Ministry should examine whether the four categories of heirs mentioned in Class II, i.e., (i) son's daughter's son (ii) son's daughter's daughter (iii) daughter's son's son and (iv) daughter's son's daughter, can be identified as Class I heirs.

The Committee is of the view that the proposed change would take care of the anomalies mentioned in the aforesaid proviso and remove grievances of a large section of the people who has been pointing out that this proviso is a major source of infirmity.

AMENDED SECTION 6(4) AS PROPOSED BY THE BILL

2.25. This part of the Bill seeks to abrogate the concept of *pious obligation*. It states that the right to proceed against a son, grandson or great-grandson for the recovery of any debt due from his father, grandfather or great-grandfather, on the ground of pious obligation, will not be recognised by any court after commencement of the Hindu Succession (Amendment) Act, 2004.

2.26. The Committee deliberated at length on the issue relating to '*pious obligation*'. As per the concept of a Hindu joint family under the *Mitakshara* school of law, it was ordinarily joint, not only in estate but in religious matters as well. According to *Mulla: Principles of Hindu Law (vol. II, page 277):*

The law of heirship had close connection with the doctrine - 'He who inherits the property, also offers the *pinda*. It was based upon the principle of consanguinity.

2.27. During oral evidence of experts before the Committee, strong views emerged in the context of continuation of the joint family system. It was reiterated that the principle of 'pious obligation' is integral to the concept of joint family system and the abrogation of one leads to the disintegration of the other. To quote from the proceeding of the meeting dated 27 April 2005:

Once there is the abolition of pious obligation, naturally there is no joint family at all.... He (*son*) is giving the *pinda* at a particular time; he is also clearing all the debts of the family; he is managing the joint family and seeing to it that all his sisters are married properly... he also sees to it that all his younger brothers are settled in life properly.... If there is a debt incurred by the family, that debt would be cleared by the joint family.... If you want the daughter to have certain rights in the property, she should also have certain liabilities.

2.28. Further, as per the principles of 'pious obligation', the debts of a deceased coparcener will devolve upon his heirs in the coparcenary, i.e., son, grandson and great grandson. The rights of a creditor of the deceased would not be affected by his death. In this context, it is pertinent to mention here that the Kerala Joint Family System (Abolition) Act, 1975 abrogated the doctrine of pious obligation of the son. However, the other four State Amendment Acts mentioned *supra* (generally referred to as the Andhra model) which conferred coparcenary rights on unmarried daughters are silent in this regard except that the daughter as a coparcener is bound by the common liabilities and presumably can become a *karta* in the joint family.

VIEW OF THE LAW COMMISSION

2.29. The Law Commission, in its 174th Report, recommended a combination of the Andhra and Kerala models, the synthesis of which, it was believed, would be in keeping with justice, equity and family harmony. Thus, it has been recommended to abrogate the doctrine of pious obligation while making the daughter coparcener in the full sense.

VIEWS SUBMITTED BEFORE THE COMMITTEE

2.30. On this issue, one of the witnesses expressed the following opinion:

Firstly, we feel that the religious obligations and economic factors should be separated. The issue of *pinda* should be separated from the issue of clearing debts. The issue of clearing debt is an economic one, while the issue of *pinda* is a religious one.

2.31. Further:

... as far as pious obligation is concerned.... If you want the daughters to be given equal right as coparceners, then there can be equal sharing of economic burden. As far as pious obligation is concerned, daughters should also have the right to give the *pinda*. They should not be deprived of religious rights. If they are given all obligations, they must also have the obligation of economic burden.

RECOMMENDATION OF THE COMMITTEE

2.32. The Committee suggests that the word '*solely*' should be added before the words *on the ground of the pious obligation* in line 37 of the Bill. There may be other conditions for which the son may be proceeded against in case of father's debt, for example, if he has got rights on the estate of his father. So, insertion of the word '*solely*' will ensure that it is only the concept of *pious obligation*, which has been abrogated as a condition to proceed against the son, grandson or great-grandson.

GENERAL OBSERVATION OF THE COMMITTEE

2.33. The Committee observes that the Hindu Undivided Family system is a unique feature of the Indian society and the concept of pious obligation acts as a thread which binds the family together and prevents it from disintegration. Pious obligation includes both spiritual as well as material aspects and makes the heir(s) responsible/liable for spiritual duties, like performing the last rites of the deceased, paying back debts accrued by the deceased and also fulfilling other responsibilities left incomplete in respect of the joint family. Once pious obligation is abrogated, the concept of joint family also suffers a blow.

However, the Committee is conscious of the changing socio-economic scenario whereby nuclear families have become a viable alternative in the context of urbanisation. Mobility of the population due to the needs of the present day, such as for education and employment, cannot be overlooked. The concept of joint family should also evolve and shed off the features which have become anachronistic. The concept of joint family no longer involves joint residence. Similarly, the concept of pious obligation, whereby son, grandson and great grandson were responsible to fulfill their responsibilities towards the joint family, can be done away with. Instead, a much more practical concept would be to make all the primary heirs liable/responsible to fulfill all such duties. The Committee feels that Section 6(1)(c), which states that daughters who have been made coparceners, will be subject to the same liabilities in respect of the said coparcenary property, as that of a son, would take care of the concern of the Committee.

AMENDED SECTION 6(5) AS PROPOSED BY THE BILL

2.34. This part mentions that nothing contained in the amended section 6 shall apply to a partition, which has been effected before commencement of the Hindu Succession (Amendment) Act, 2004.

2.35. During the course of deliberation on the Bill, the Committee pondered on the concept of 'partition' as referred to in the aforesaid part. When the Secretary (Legislative Department) was asked as to the validity of partition effected through oral means, he replied that it depends upon the facts of the particular case. The Secretary stated as below:

Sub Section (5) (*of the Bill*) says that nothing contained in this section shall apply to a partition, which has been effected before commencement of the Act. So, people may not have a chance of effecting registered partition or going to the court and getting it registered.

2.36. Further, the Secretary, Department of Legal Affairs stated as below:

... under the present legal position, it is not necessary that a partition should be registered. There is no legal requirement. There can be oral partition also.

RECOMMENDATION OF THE COMMITTEE

2.37. The Committee recommends that the term 'partition' should be properly defined, leaving no scope for any arbitrary interpretation. Partition, for all practical purposes, should be registered or should have been effected by a decree of the court. In cases where oral partition is recognised, it should be backed by proper documentary evidence.

Subject to above, clause 2 is adopted.

CLAUSE 3

2.38. This clause seeks to omit section 23 of the Hindu Succession Act, 1956. Section 23 of the Act reads as under:

Section 23. Special provision respecting dwelling houses:- Where a Hindu intestate has left surviving him or her both male and female heirs specified in Class I of the Schedule and his or her property includes a dwelling house wholly occupied by members of his or her family, then, notwithstanding anything contained in this Act, the right of any such female heir to claim partition of the dwelling house shall not arise until the male heirs choose to divide their respective shares therein; but the female heir shall be entitled to a right of residence therein:

Provided that where such female heir is a daughter, she shall be entitled to a right of residence in the dwelling house only if she is unmarried or has been deserted by or has separated from her husband or is a widow.

2.39. According to *Mulla: Principles of Hindu Law (Vol. II, page 450)*:

The object of the special provision is to prevent female heirs and, particularly a daughter of the intestate, from creating a situation in which partition of the family house may entail a forced sale of it or otherwise cause hardship to the son or sons of the intestate where it may not be possible for the son or sons to buy off the share of the female heir who insists on actual partition of it.... It would seem that the right of a female heir to demand partition may be deferred and remain in abeyance under this section till the lifetime of the male heirs enumerated in Class I of the Schedule or the last survivor of them, unless a partition of the dwelling house is sought by any one of them before such time.

VIEWS OF THE LAW COMMISSION

2.40. The Law Commission while examining the aforesaid section of the Act in its 174th Report, commented as below:

Another apparent inequity under the Hindu Succession Act as per Section 23, is the provision denying a married daughter the right to residence in the parental home unless widowed, deserted or separated from her husband and further denying any daughter the right to demand her share in the house if occupied by male family members. This right is not denied to a son. The main object of the section is said to be the primacy of the rights of the family against that of an individual by imposing a restriction on partition.

2.41. However, the Law Commission quoted a recent Supreme Court judgment whereby it was endorsed that the idea of this section is to prevent fragmentation and disintegration of the dwelling house at the instance of the female heirs to the detriment of male heirs in occupation of the house, thus rendering the male heir homeless/shelterless.

2.42. The Law Commission, in its 174th Report, stated that once a daughter is made a coparcener on the same footing as a son, her right as a coparcener should be real in spirit and content. To quote from the Report:

We are also of the view that Section 23 of the Hindu Succession Act, 1956, which places restrictions on the daughter to claim partition of the dwelling house, should be deleted altogether. We recommend accordingly.

VIEWS SUBMITTED BEFORE THE COMMITTEE

2.43. Views from cross sections of the society were received by the Committee, which widely differed in their interpretation of the proposed omission of this section in the Bill. While some sections acclaimed this proposed amendment, the others opined that this is violative of the traditional Hindu laws.

COMMENTS OF THE MINISTRY

2.44. The Ministry in its reply stated as below:

India is bound to implement the U.N. Convention on Elimination of

Discrimination Against Women (CEDAW). Article 14 of the Constitution guarantees equality before law and equal protection of the law within the territory of India. Clause (1) of article 15 of the Constitution, *inter alia*, provides that the State shall not discriminate against any citizen solely on the ground of sex. Hence, the proposal to remove the gender discriminatory provisions in the Hindu Succession Act, 1956 is constitutionally valid and is aimed at giving equal rights to women in Hindu *Mitakshara* Coparcenary property. Omission of section 23 of the Act will enable Hindu women to seek partition of dwelling house occupied by the family members as at present, only in case the male members choose to seek partition, the female members would be entitled to have the partition of the dwelling house. The amendments are a much needed social reform and meet the demands of the Hindu women's community. Hence, the suggestion to drop the proposal cannot be accepted.

GENERAL OBSERVATION OF THE COMMITTEE

2.45. The Committee feels that this amendment will remove one of the major anomalies in the inheritance rights, as propounded by the Hindu Succession Act, 1956. It will make the daughters, who have been made coparceners in the joint Hindu family system, equal claimant in respect of dwelling house. Objection has been raised in certain quarters that if the proposed amendment is enacted, it would give rise to fragmentation in the joint family property. The Committee feel that such apprehension is unfounded and endorses inequality between the sexes. If restriction on partition is to be imposed by giving primacy to the rights of the family, against that of an individual, it should be applicable to both the sons and daughters alike. Thus omission of the section 23 of the aforesaid Act is in keeping with the changing needs of the time.

Clause 3 is adopted without any change.

CLAUSE 4

2.46. This clause of the Bill seeks to give the right of testamentary disposition to both the men and women in case of any property, which is capable of being disposed of by him or by her, in accordance with the provisions of the Indian Succession Act, 1925. The following table shows the amendment in section 30 of the Act:

The Hindu Succession Act, 1956	The Hindu Succession (Amendment) Bill, 2004
Section 30. Testamentary succession. - Any Hindu may dispose of by will or other testamentary disposition any property, which is capable of being so disposed of by him, in accordance with the provisions of the Indian Succession Act, 1925 (39 of 1925), or any other law for the time being in force and applicable to Hindus. *Explanation.-* The interest of a male Hindu in a *Mitakshara* coparcenary property or the interest of a member of a *tarwad, tavazhi, illom, kutamba* or *kavaru* in the property of the *tarwad, tavazhi, illom, kutamba* or *kavaru* shall, notwithstanding anything contained in this Act or in any other law for the time being in force, be deemed to be property capable of being disposed	4. In section 30 of the principal Act, for the words "disposed of by him", the words "disposed of by him or by her" shall be substituted.

of by him or by her within the meaning of this section.	

2.47. In this context *Mulla: Principles of Hindu Law (vol. II, page 465),* states that under *Mitakshara* law, no coparcener, not even a father, can dispose of by will his undivided coparcenary interest even if the other coparceners consent to the disposition, the reason being that at the moment of his death the right of survivorship (of the other coparceners) is in conflict with the right to will. Then, the title by survivorship, being the prior title, takes precedence. However, the aforesaid section of the Hindu Succession Act, 1956 abrogated that rule of *Mitakshara* law, which lays down in explicit terms that such interest is to be deemed to be property capable of being disposed of by will, notwithstanding anything contained in any provision of the Act or any other law for the time being in force. It introduced into the statute the concept that any Hindu may dispose of, by will, any property capable of disposition (this includes his undivided interest in a *Mitakshara* coparcenary property) in accordance with the provisions of the Indian Succession Act, 1925. Thus, it guarantees the coparcener's right to will away his interest in the joint family property.

VIEWS OF THE LAW COMMISSION

2.48. The Law Commission's 174th Report states that the right to will away property was traditionally unknown to Hindus. To quote from the Report:

The legal right of Hindus to bequeath property by way of will was conferred by the Indian Succession Act, 1925. None of the clauses of 1925 Act apply to Hindus except wills... coparcener under *Mitakshara* law had no power to dispose of his coparcenary interest by gift or bequest, so as to defeat the right of the other members. The coparcenary system even restricted the rights of the Karta to alienate property, thereby safeguarding the rights of all members of the family, including infants and children, to being maintained from the joint family property.

2.49. The Law Commission's above Report states that the Act gave a weapon to a man to deprive a woman of the rights she earlier had under certain schools of Hindu law. This is ironical as this testamentary right is often inversely related to the right of his daughter by succession. It can also defeat a widow's right. There is, thus, a diminution in the status of a wife/widow. The Law Commission observed that both the Kerala and Andhra models of Amendments fail to protect the share of the daughter, mother or widow from being defeated, by making a testamentary disposition in favour of another, or by alienation. To quote from the Report:

As noticed earlier, quite often fathers will away their property so that the daughter does not get a share even in his self-acquired property. Apart from this, quite often persons will away their property to people who are not relatives, thus totally depriving the children and legal heirs who have legitimate expectation. Consequently, there has been a strong demand for placing a restriction on the right of testamentary disposition. But after due deliberation, the Commission is not inclined to the placing of any restrictions on the right of a Hindu deceased to will away property.

VIEWS SUBMITTED BEFORE THE COMMITTEE

2.50. While deposing before the Committee, one of the experts was of the view that the notion of Hindu family is already being undermined by allowing the concept of will to exist.

2.51. As per a memorandum submitted to the Committee, the Bill leaves untouched a person's unrestricted testamentary rights over his/her property. In principle, this right is gender-neutral since both the sexes enjoy it, but in practice (given male bias in our society) the provision can be used to disinherit female heirs. In fact, the man can will away not only his separate property but also his 'notional' share in the coparcenary. This could totally disinherit the widow in States where she gets no share on partition. Partial restriction on testamentary rights is thus important so that female heirs inherit at least part of the property through intestate devolution. Opinion has, thus, been expressed that testamentary rights should be partially restricted (e.g. restrictions on half or 1/3rd of the property, which would devolve intestate) while allowing full freedom of will in the rest.

GENERAL OBSERVATION OF THE COMMITTEE

2.52. The Committee takes note of the fact that partial restriction to testamentary rights has been demanded from certain quarters. It is of the opinion that the Ministry may examine in detail the feasibility of such a move and take steps accordingly.

Subject to above, clause 4 is adopted.

CHAPTER III

MISCELLANEOUS ISSUES

3.0 While deliberating on the Bill, the Committee considered the principal Act, i.e., the Hindu Succession Act, 1956 and suggested certain modifications/changes as discussed below.

SECTION 4(2) OF THE PRINCIPAL ACT

3.1. This section states as below:

For the removal of doubts it is hereby declared that nothing contained in this Act shall be deemed to affect the provisions of any law for the time being in force providing for prevention of fragmentation of the agricultural holdings or for the fixation of ceilings or for the devolution of tenancy rights in respect of such holdings.

VIEWS PERTAINING TO THIS SUB-SECTION

3.2 Divergent views on the interpretation of this sub-section emerged. According to *Mulla: Principles of Hindu Law (Vol. II, page 299)*:

It is sometimes said that the Act does not apply to agricultural lands but that would not be a correct proposition. Sub Section (2) relates only to certain specified matters and subject to that, the provisions of the Act must govern succession to agricultural lands too.

Considerable legislation by various States, aimed at prevention of fragmentation of agricultural holdings and securing their consolidation, and for the purpose of fixing ceilings and devolution of holdings, has found place on the statute-book in recent years and this section is not intended to override or disturb such legislation. Land policy in different States, though founded on the concept of a socialist welfare state, cannot be expected to be uniform and sub-section (2), therefore, leaves such legislation relating to agricultural land undisturbed... it may be said that this provision detracts from the fundamental objective of uniformity of legislation. However, the explanation is that what is aimed at is a uniform law for all Hindus and not necessarily a uniform law for all forms of property.

3.3. One of the memoranda submitted to the Committee argued that agricultural land is the most important form of rural property in India; and ensuring gender-equal rights in it is important, not only for gender justice but also for economic and social advancement.

3.4. Further, analysing this section of the Act, the memorandum argued as below:

˙nterest in tenancy land devolves according to the order of devolu-t˙on specified in the tenurial laws, which vary from State to State. Broadly, the States fall into three categories, (i) in southern and most of central and eastern States, tenurial laws are silent on devolution. So, inheritance can be assumed to follow the 'personal law'. (ii) in a few States, tenurial laws explicitly note that the HSA or 'personal law' will apply. (iii) in the north-western States of Haryana, Punjab, Himachal Pradesh, Delhi, Uttar Pradesh and Jammu & Kashmir, the tenurial laws do specify the order of devolution, and one that is gender-unequal. Here (retaining vestiges of the old *Mitakshara* system) primacy is given to male lineal descendents in the male line of descent and women come very low in the order of heirs. Also, a woman gets only a limited estate, and loses the land if she remarries (as a widow) or fails to cultivate it for a year or two. Moreover, in UP and Delhi, a 'tenant' is defined so broadly that this unequal order of devolution effectively covers all agricultural land.

3.5. Another memorandum received by the Committee states as below:

The proposed changes do not address the crucial issue of women's equal rights in agricultural land. We, therefore, recommend an amendment, which states clearly that the HSA granting women equal rights in property, will apply to agricultural land and will override any laws to the contrary. We, therefore, recommend that the existing section 4(2) of the Hindu Succession Act, 1956, be deleted.

3.6. It was further argued that a clause should be introduced in the Act to the effect that the amended Hindu Succession Act would override any gender discriminatory clauses in State tenurial laws, currently in place.

COMMENTS OF THE MINISTRY

3.7. The subject "Land, that is to say, rights in or over land; land tenures including the relation of landlord and tenant and collection of rents; transfer and alienation of agricultural land; land improvement and agricultural loans; colonization" is a subject falling under the State List in the Seventh Schedule to the Constitution of India. Hence, in case a State legislation occupies the field, the provisions of sub-section (2) of section 4 of the Hindu Succession Act, 1956 clarify that the State

Law shall prevail in the matter of succession also. The petitioners should address the State Governments to get necessary amending law passed by the State Legislatures. Any deletion of sub-section (2) of section 4 will not change the legal position.

3.8. As regards the question of providing a provision regarding overriding effect on tenurial laws, the proposed legislation, being a concurrent subject and tenurial laws being a State subject, the State Legislatures may have to be approached for making necessary laws in the matter. The remedy lies in pursuing the matter with the State Governments, to put the tenurial laws in consonance with the provisions of the HSA, 1956. Omission of section 4(2) may not achieve the purpose.

GENERAL OBSERVATIONS OF THE COMMITTEE

3.9. The Committee takes note of the fact that objections have been raised from various quarters regarding continuation of section 4(2) of the Act. In this context, while deliberating on the Bill, the Committee made reference to the Government of India Act, 1935. In the Concurrent List, i.e., List III, Entry 7 of the aforesaid Act regarding succession, states "Save as regards agricultural land". But in the Constitution of India, entry 5 of List III pertaining to Concurrent List, does not mention "Save as regards agricultural land". Similarly, what is stated about devolution in Entry 21 in List II of the 1935 Act, is also omitted in Entry 18 of List II of the Constitution of India. To quote from the deliberation of the Committee:

Therefore, this proviso helps to have pre-Constitutional powers, that is powers conferred by the Act of 1935. No doubt, it was necessary at that time because there were land reforms... this provision was needed for protecting the interests of land reforms and agricultural reforms.

3.10. The Committee feels that in the present day circumstances, where legislations have been undergoing progressive changes, there is no need to retain this sub-section, which becomes a barrier in establishing gender equality. Keeping in view the above-mentioned facts, the Committee recommends that Government may consider incorporating this amendment in the present Bill, deleting section 4(2) from the original Act. Otherwise, a subsequent amending legislation may be brought in to address this issue.

SECTIONS 14, 15 AND 16 OF THE PRINCIPAL ACT

3.11. Section 14 of the principal Act deals with 'Property of a female Hindu to be her absolute property';

Section 15 pertains to 'General rules of succession in the case of female Hindus'; and

Section 16 mentions 'Order of succession and manner of distribution among heirs of a female Hindu'.

GENERAL OBSERVATION OF THE COMMITTEE

3.12. While deliberating on the clauses of the Bill, the Committee expressed the view that the aforesaid sections of the Act have lost their relevance in view of the proposed amendments in the present Bill. These sections should be re-examined and reframed so that the provisions enunciated by these do not run contrary to the Amendment Bill. The Ministry may look into the matter and take appropriate steps accordingly.

SECTION 24 OF THE ORIGINAL ACT

3.13. This section seeks to prevent certain sections of widows from inheriting property of the intestate if she has remarried. According to this section:

Certain widows re-marrying may not inherit as widows—Any heir who is related to an intestate as the widow of a predeceased son, the widow of a predeceased son of a predeceased son or the widow of a brother shall not be entitled to succeed to the property of the intestate as such widow, if on the date the succession opens, she has re-married.

3.14. According to *Mulla: Principles of Hindu Law (Vol II, page 453)*, the following can be stated:

The reason is that a widow succeeds as the surviving half of her husband, and she ceases to be so by remarriage.

GENERAL OBSERVATION OF THE COMMITTEE

3.15. While deliberating on the clauses of the Bill, the Committee expressed the following views on the aforesaid section of the Act:

... the right of a widow who remarries is denied, whereas, the right of a widower who remarries is protected....We are making a distinction between a widower who remarries and his right is not affected. But the widow who remarries is denied the right.

3.16. In the light of what has been stated above, the Committee is of the view that Government should examine the justification behind maintaining the aforesaid section of the Act in the context of modern times, whereby focus is on maintaining gender equality and making the laws of the land gender neutral. The Committee feels that the aforesaid section may be omitted from the body of the Act. Government may include this amendment in the present Bill or else a subsequent legislation may be brought in, to cover all such issues, not covered under the present Bill.

NOTES

* Published in the *Gazette of India* (*Extraordinary*), Part-II, Section 2, dated the 20 December, 2004.

** Rajya Sabha Parliamentary Bulletin, Part II (No 41884), dated the 27th December, 2004.

[1] *Mulla Principles of Hindu Law,* Eighteenth Edition, by Satyajeet A. Desai (vol. II); *Butterworth's India,* New Delhi, 2001.

3

LAW ON MARRIAGE AND FAMILY
[ANNEXURE 1 TO SECTION II]

1. MARRIAGE

1. Choice of spouses:
   Marry those among you who have no spouses;
   Or the virtuous among your slaves;
   If they are indigent God will enrich them by His grace;
   And God is well informed.

   (24: 32)

2. Those of you who have not the means,
   Wherewith to marry free believing girls:
   They should marry believing slave-girls.
   But wed them with the consent of their custodians:
   And give them their due as per the law.

   (4:25)

2. PROHIBITED DEGREE IN MARRIAGE:

1. Marry not former wives of your ascendants;
   (Existing relationship of this nature are saved) indeed it
   was shameful and odious, and an abominable custom.

   (4:22)

2. Prohibited to you for marriage are-
   Your mothers and daughters;
   Your sisters and paternal and maternal aunts;
   Your nephews and nieces;
   Your foster mothers and foster sisters
   Your step daughters in your custody born of a women

with whom your marriage was consummated (there being no such prohibition if the marriage was not consummated): and former wives of your lineal descendants: and two sisters as co-wives (existing relations are
saved): verily God is oft-forgiving, most merciful.

3. There shall be no hindrance for Muslims in marrying
wives

Of adoptees.

And proper dissolution of the former marriage.

And God's law is meant to be followed.

(32:37)

4.(a) Also prohibited are those who are already married.
(Except in the case of prisoner of war)

(b) Thus God commands you:

Except the aforesaid, marriage with all women is lawful
Providing you properly take them as wives,
Desiring solemnity of marriage and not lust.

3.   RELIGION OF PARTIES

(1) (a) Do not marry non-believing girls.

Except if they have given up disbelief;

Indeed a believing slave girl is better than a non-
believing girl

Even though you be enamoured by the latter.

(b) And do not marry your girls to non-believing men,

Except they given up disbelief;

Indeed a believing slave man is better than a non-
believing free man:

Even though he has enamoured you.

(II: 221)

(2) This day have been lawful for you all good things,
And female married to you from amongst those who
were given a book before you:
If you take them properly for the purpose of marriage:

Desiring chastity, not lewdness.
And having no foul intentions.

4.   NUMBER OF WIVES

If you fear that you will not be able to deal justly with
orphans;
Marry those other women whom you like two or three or
four;
But if you fear that you cannot do justice to them,
Then take only one wife (or even a slave girl),
That will be more suitable to prevent you from injustice.

(IV: 3)

5.   DOWER

(1)   Give to the wives their dower as gift;
      But if they on there own remit a part of it,
      You can take it and enjoy it with cheers.

(IV: 4)

(2)   As you derive benefit from your wives,
      Do give them their stipulated dower
      But there is nothing wrong if after dower is stipu-
      lated,
      You mutually agree about it otherwise;
      Verily God is all knowing, all wise.

(IV: 24)

6.   CONJUGAL RELATIONS

(1)   O believers!
      It is not lawful for you to treat women as your
      inherited property;
      And do not harass them with a view to getting back,
      Part of what you have given them:
      (Except when they have been guilty of open lewd-

ness)
If you dislike something in them;
May be that what you dislike,
God may have kept in it a great deal of guard.

(IV: 19)

2. (a) Men are protectors of women,
As God has given the one more strength than the other;
So the righteous and the pious women would guard,
What God would have them guard.
(b) As regards women on whose part you fear dis-loyalty
And ill-conduct,
Admonish them, refuse them co-habitation and turn away from them.
But if they behave with you,
Then do not seek a device with them

(IV: 34)

7.   RECONCILIATION

If you fear a breach between the spouses;
Appoint one arbiter from his family,
And one arbiter from her family;
If they wish for peace,
God will bless their reconciliation,
Verily God is all knowing and well informed.

B.   DISSOLUTION OF MARRIAGE

8.   WIDOWHOOD

If any of you die and leave behind widows
They shall wait for four months and ten days
When they have completed their term;
There will be nothing wrong,

If they act for themselves in a respectable way,
And God is well aware of all your deeds.

(II: 234)

(1)   There is nothing wrong if you propose to them.
Or hold it within your hearts;
God knows if you cherish them in hearts;
But do not enter with them into a secret agreement:
Except in a respectable way,
And do not try to marry them,
Until they have completed the prescribed period

(II: 240)

(2)   Those of you who die and leave behind widows,
They shall bequeath for their widows a year ex-
penses and residence,
But if they go out of that residence
There is no blame on you,
If they act for themselves in a respectable way:
And God is exalted in power and wise.

(LXV: 1)

9.   DIVORCED BY HUSBAND

(1)   When you divorce the wives,
Divorce them for the period of their *iddah* and
count *iddah;*
And fear your God your Lord:
Do not turn them out of their houses,
(except when a women has been guilty of open
lewdness)
nor shall they go out,
these are the laws of God,
those who violate them wrong themselves;
you do not know,
that after all this God may create a new situation.

(LXV: 1)

(2) And wives are nearing completion of their iddah,
Then resume cohabitation with them in a reasonable
way,
Or part company with them in a reasonable way;
And take two just persons from amongst you as witnesses,
And thus establish evidence before god;
This is enjoined for those who believe in God,
And in the day of judgment,
And those who fear God,
For them he finds a way out.

(LXV; 2)

(3) Divorce is permissible only twice;
Thereafter there must be either co-living on equitable terms,
Or separation with kindness.

(4) When you divorce women and thereupon they near
completion
Of their *iddah,*
Then live with them on equitable terms;
Or part company on equitable terms.
But do not retain them with a view to harming
them,
Or taking undue advantage;
He who does so wrongs his own soul.

(II: 231)

10. DOWER OF DIVORCED WIFE

(1) If you decide to replace wife with another,
While you have given her even a margin of gold:
Do not take back anything from her;
And do not try to so by slander and cruelty.

(IV:20)

(2) How can you take it back,

While you have had mutual co-living,
And while you have given them a solemn covenant.

(IV: 21)

11.   *IDDAH* OF DIVORCED WIVES

(1)   Divorced women shall wait before remarriage for
      three
      Menstrual courses;
      It is not lawful for them to hide what God has kept
      in their wombs
      If they believe in God and in the Day of Judgment;
      During the period of *'iddah* their husband shall
      have a right to revoke the divorce.
      Provided that they indeed desire reconciliation.

(II: 228)

(2)   For those women who have entered menopause *id-
      dah* period is three months,
      And the same is the law for those women who have
      not begun menstruation;
      For the pregnant women the *iddah* period last until
      delivery;
      Those who fear God for them he makes things easy.

(LXV: 4)

(3)   O people when you marry women,
      And then divorce them before consummation;
      You do not have to count their *iddah*,
      In such a case give the a gift,
      And separate from them respectably.

12.   REMARRIAGE OF DIVORCEES

(1)   When you have divorced women and they have
      completed their *iddah*,
      Do not prevent them from marrying other men,
      If they and those men mutually agree as per the le-

gal rules;
This is the command for all those,
Who believe in the Day of Judgement.

(II:232)

(2) If a man has divorced his wife finally,
She is no more lawful to him;
Except if she has married another man and he too
has divorced her
in which case there will be nothing wrong if they
reunite,
provided that they are sure that they can keep to
limits of God;
this is the Law of God which He clearly ordains,
so you can understand.

(II:230)

13. MAINTENANCE OF DIVORCED WIVES

(1) For divorced women there shall be maintenance on
equitable terms;
This is the law for those who fear God.

(II:241)

(2) Let the divorced women live as you do as per your
means;
Do not be cruel to them so as to impose restriction
on them;
And if they are pregnant support them financially
until delivery;
And if they are suckling your child give them their
due;
And mutually discuss things in a reasonable way,
And if you cannot mutually agree let another
woman suckle the child.

(3) Let the affluent spend according to his means;
And the man with restricted resources according to

his,

God puts no burden on any person beyond what he has given him;

After indigence God may grant affluence.

14. DIVORCED BY MAN BEFORE CONSUMMATION

(1) You may divorced women before consummation
While their dower is yet to be fixed;
But give them a gift;
The wealthy according to his means,
And the poor according to his means.

(II: 236)

(2) And if you divorce them before consummation,
While their dower has been fixed;
Half of the stipulated dower may be deducted;
The women may forgo what is payable;
And the husband may forgo his rights of deduction;
if he forgoes it will be nearest to good,
And do not forget to behave mutually with kindness,
Verily God can well see what you do.

(II: 237)

15. DIVORCED BY WIFE

(1) It is not lawful for you to forcefully keep women
Treating them as your property,
And do not harass them with a view to getting back part of the dower,
(Except when they have committed open lewdness)

(IV: 19)

(2) If a woman is scared of cruelty or desertion by husband,
There is nothing wrong if they arrange an amicable mutual settlement;

Such settlement is best,
Though one looks to one's own benefit:
Be kind and fear God, knows all that you do.

(IV: 128)

(3) It is not lawful for you,
That you demand return from the women,
Anything of what you have given them,
Except when both of you fear,
That you cannot keep to the limits of God,
There is nothing wrong if she redeems herself with it;
This is the law of God, which must not be violated,
He who violates it is wrong doer.

(II: 229)

16. CUSTOM OF *ILA*

(1) As regards those who take a vow of countenance for their wives,
They can wait and watch for not more than four months;
Then if they resume cohabitation,
God is most forgiving most merciful.

(II: 226)

(2) But if they are firm on dissolving the marriage,
God hears and knows everything.

(II: 227)

17. CUSTOM OF ZIHAR

(1) (i) God does not turn into your mothers,
Those of your wives whom you call your "mothers"
Nor can any be their mother except those who have given them birth;
The words that they use are iniquitous and false;

And of course, God is most forgiving.

(ii) But if they are firm on dissolving the marriage
God hears and knows everything.

18. SUCKLING AND WEANING

(a) The mothers shall suck to their offspring for two
years.
If the father desires that she complete the term:
But he shall bear the cost of their food and clothing
on equitable terms.

(b) No soul shall have a burden laid on it greater than it
can bear;
No mother shall be treated unfairly on account of
her child nor any father on account of his child;
Same will be the law for the heirs.

(c) If the parents decide on weaning by mutual consent
and consultation,
There is nothing wrong in it.

(d) There is nothing wrong also,
If they give the child to the care of a foster mother,
Provided that they pay for it equitably.

(e) And fear God;
Do not forget that God is watching all that you do.

(II: 233)

19. ADOPTION

(1) God does not treat your 'adoptees' as your sons;
These are nothing more than mere words spoken by
you;
But God tells you the truth and shows the right way.

(2) Relate them to their natural fathers, this is truer in
the sight of God.

(XXXIII: 4-5)

20. RIGHTS OF PARENTS

(1) Be kind to the parents.

(VI: 151)

(2) (i) Your God decrees that you worship none but and be
kind to your parents;
If either or both of them become old in your life,
Say not a word of disrespect to them,
Nor revile them,
And speak to them kind words.

(ii) Behave with them with utmost humility,
and seek for them Gods mercy;
as they cherished you during childhood.

(XVII: 23-24)

(3) God has so enjoined on man for his parents,
As in travail upon travail did his mother bear him;
And in two yea he was weaved;
So he should thank God and his parents,
God is the ultimate goal.

(XXXI: 14)

II. LAW ON PROPERTY AND SUCCESSION

A. CARE OF PROPERTY

21. PROPERTY OF THE ORPHANS

(1) Let the orphan enjoy the property;
Do not tamper with it,
And do not misappropriate with yours;
This will indeed be a serious wrong.

(2) Those who wrongfully eat up an orphan's property,
Verily they play with fire;
And they will meet the consequences.

(IV:10)

(3) As regards female orphans,

Whom you do not give their due,
And yet wish to take as wives;
And as regards children who are weak;
You must firmly do justice to all these orphans;
There is no good deeds of yours but,
Of which God is indeed fully aware.

(IV: 127)

22.   GUARDIANSHIP AND CUSTODY OF PROPERTY

(1)   Property shall not be given to the weak of understanding,
So they shall be maintained out of it;
And spoken to in kindness.

(IV: 5)

(2)   (i)   The orphans should be watched until they reach majority,
Then if they are find mature,
Their property should be handed over to them.

(ii)   The guardian must not extravagantly consume property;
Nor should it be hurriedly spent while the owner is minor.

(iii)   An affluent guardian shall claim no remuneration.

(iv)   When the property is handed over to the owner, take witness to it.

(IV: 6)

B. TESTAMENTARY SUCCESSION

23.   BEQUEST TO PARENT AND RELATIVE

It is prescribe for you,
When death approaches any of you,
While he is leaving behind property;
Bequeath well for parents and next of kin as per usage;

This is incumbent on the God-fearing.

(II: 181)

24. CHANGING TERM OF BEQUEST

Then if someone thinks that the testator has been partial or unjust,
And thereupon he effects a settlement between the legatees.
He does nothing unlawful;
Verily God is oft-forgiving most merciful.

(II: 182)

25. WITNESS TO BEQUEST

(1) O believers! When death approaches any of you,
While bequeathing take two just witnesses from amongst yourselves,
Or from amongst others if you apprehend death while on journey.
Those witnesses may be detained in public,
So that they swear in the name of God saying;
That they shall not meddle with truth for money,
Even for the sake of a near relative,
And shall not hide truth; and that if they do so,
They may be treated as wrongdoers.

(V: 109)

(2) If it is established that the witnesses have done wrong,
To confront them can stand up two other witnesses,
From amongst those who enjoy better credibility,
They shall swear in the name of God saying,
That their evidence is superior to that of the former,
That if they could be treated s evildoers.

(V: 110)

(3) (a) These rules are meant to ensure setting up proper evidence,

Let witnesses know that their evidence can be rejected;
In favour of that given by others,

(b) Fear God and listen to him,
Verily God does not guide the delinquent.

(V: III)

C. INTESTATE SUCCESSION

26. BASIC RULES-

(1) Men inherit from their parents and near relatives;
And women inherit from their parents and relatives;
Whether the heritage is big or small;
And the shares of inheritance are prescribed.

(IV: 7)

(2) Heirs in the property of parents and relatives are
Determined by law,
So are the rights of married women;
All of them must be given their shares;
Verily God shall be witness to everything.

(IV; 33)

(3) And where at the time of division of estate,
There are other relatives, orphans and indigents;
Provide them bare necessities of life out of the estates;
And decide for them reasonably;
They are to be treated like those children.
For whom no property has been left;
Fear God and decide wisely.

(IV: 8-9)

27. SHARE OF CHILDREN AND PARENTS

(1) (i) God so direct you in respect of your children, that
for the male there shall be share equal to that of
two females;

    (ii) And where there be females only –two or more;
        for them is two-third of the heritage;
    (iii) And where there is only one female for her is half
(2) (i) As regards parents for either of them,
        is one-sixth of the heritage,
        Where the deceased has left the child.
    (ii) And where there is no child and parent have to
        inherit, for the mother there shall be one-third.
(3) All of those shares will be out of wHat is left,
    After payment of legacies and debts.
(4) Your parents and children are nearest beneficiaries,
    And their shares are ordained by God;
    Verily God is all –knowing all wise.

                                              (IV: 11)

28. SHARE OF SPOUSES

(i)   For the husband in his wife's property,
        There shall be one-half where there is no child;
        And a quarter where there is a child;
        Of what remains after payment of legacies and debts.

(ii) For the wife in her husbands property,
        There shall be a quarter where there is no child;
        And one-eighth where there is a child,
        Of what remains after payment of legacies and debts.

                                              (IV: 12)

29. SHARES OF BROTHER AND SISTERS

(i)   where a deceased man or women,
        is not survived by children and parents,
        while he or she has left a brother or sister,
        either of them shall get one-sixth;
        and when there number is more than two,

they shall share between them one-third;
of what remains after payment of legacies and debts,
without prejudice to any one.

(ii) This is ordained by god;
And God is all knowing, most forbearing.

(IV: 12)

(4) God so direct you,
In respect of a deceased leaving behind no ascendant or descendant,
If it was a man dying childless but survived by a sister;
Where there are two sisters they take two-third of estate;
And if there are both brothers and sisters,
The male shall get twice as much as female,
And god knows all things.

(IV:176)

[ANNEXURE II TO SECTION II]

SURAH ALI-I-IMRAN (3); VERSE 59

The similitude of Jesus
Before Allah is as that of adam;
He created him from dust,
Then said to him: 'Be": and he was.

SURAH AL NISA (4): VERSE 1

O mankind! Reverence
Your Guardian-Lord,
Who created you
From a single person,
Created, of like nature,
His mate, and from them twain
Scattered (like seeds)
Countless men and women
Fear Allah, through Whom
Ye demand your mutual (rights),
And (reverence) the wombs
(That bore you): for Allah Ever watches over you.

SURAH AL NISA (4): VERSE 34

Men are the protectors
And maintainers of women,
Because Allah has given
The one more (strength)
Than the other, and because
They support them
From their means.

Therefore the righteous women
Are devoutly obedient, and guard
In (the husband's) absence
What Allah would have them guard.
As to those women
On whose part ye fear
Disloyalty and ill-conduct,
Admonish them (first),
(Next), refuse to share their beds
(And last) beat them (lightly)
But if they return to obedience,
Seek not against them
Means (of annoyance):
For Allah is Most High,
Great (above you all).

SURAH AL NISA (4): VERSE 128

If a wife fears
Cruelty or desertion
On her husband's part,
There is no blame on them
If they arrange
An amicable settlement
Between themselves;
And such settlement is best;
Even though men's souls
Are swayed by greed.
But if ye do good
And practise self-restraint,
Allah is well-acquainted
With all that ye do.

SURAH HUJURAAT (49): VERSE 13

O mankind! We created
You from a single (pair)
Of a male and a female,
And made you into
Nations and tribes, that
Ye may know each other
(Not that ye may despise
Each other). Verily
The most honoured of you
In the sight of Allah
Is (he who is) the most
Righteous of you.
And Allah Hath full Knowledge
And is well acquainted (With all things).

SURAH AL TAHRIM (66): VERSE 12

And many the daughter
Of Imran, who guarded
Her chastity; and We
Breathed into her (body)
Of Our spirit; and she
Testified to the truth
Of the words of her Lord
And of his Revelations,
And was one of the
Devout (servants).

SURAH AL BAQARAH (2): VERSE 228

Divorced women
Shall wait concerning themselves
For three monthly periods.
Nor is it lawful for them

To hide what Allah
Hath created in their wombs,
If they have faith
In Allah and the Last Day.
And their husbands
Have the better right
To take them back
In that period, if
They wish for reconciliation.
And women shall have rights
Similar to the rights
Against them, according
To what is equitable;
But men have a degree (of advantage) over them.
And Allah is Exalted in Power, Wise.

SURAH AL NISA (4): VERSE 35

If ye fear a breach
Between them twain,
Appoint (two) arbiters,
One from his family,
And the other from hers;
If they wish for peace,
All ah will cause
Their reconciliation:
For Allah hath full knowledge,
And is acquainted
With all things.

SURAH AL BAQARAH (2): VERSE 229

A divorce is only
Permissible twice: after that,
The parties should either hold
Together on equitable terms

Or separate with kindness.
It is not lawful for you,
(Men), to take back
Any of your gift (from your wives)
Except when both parties
Fear that they would be
Unable to keep the Limits
Ordained by Allah.
If ye (judges) do indeed
Fear that they would be
Unable to keep the Limits
Ordained by Allah,
There is no blame on either
Of them, if she give
Something for the freedom.
These are the limits
Ordained by Allah;
So do not transgress them.
If any do transgress
The limits ordained by Allah,
Such persons wrong
(themselves as well as others).

SURAH AL BAQARAH (2): VERSE 230

So if a husband
Divorces his wife (irrevocably),
He cannot, after that,
Remarry her until
She has married
Another husband and
He has divorced her.
In that case there is
No blame on either of them
If they reunite, provided

They feel that they
Can keep the limits
Ordained by Allah,
Which He makes Plain
To whose who understand.

SURAH AL BAQARAH (2): VERSE 232

When ye divorce
Women, and they fulfill
The term of their (*Iddat*),
Do not prevent them
From marrying
Their (former) husbands,
If they mutually agree
On equitable terms.
This instruction
Is for all amongst you,
Who believe in Allah
And the Last Day.
That is (the course Making for) most virtue
And purity amongst you,
And Allah knows,
And ye know not.

SURAH AL BAQARAH (2): VERSE 241

For divorced women
Maintenance (should be provided)
On a reasonable (scale).
This is a duty
On the righteous.

SURAH AL BAQARAH (2): VERSE 236

There is no blame on you

If ye divorce women
Before consummation
Or the fixation of their dower;
But bestow on them
(A suitable gift),
The wealthy
According to his means,
And the poor
According to his means
A gift of reasonable amount
Is due from those
Who wish to do the right thing.

SURAH AL NISA (4): VERSE 129

Ye are never able
To be fair and just
As between women,
Even if it is
Your ardent desire:
But turn not away
(From a woman) altogether,
So as to leave her (as it were)
Hanging (in the air).
If ye come to a friendly
Understanding, and practise
Self-restraint. Allah is
Oft-Forgiving. Most
Merciful.

SURAH AL NISA (2): VERSES 2– 3

(2) To orphans restore their property
(When they reach their age),
Nor substitute (your) worthless things
For (their) good ones; and devour not

Their substance (by mixing it up)
With your own. For this is
Indeed a great sin.

(3) If ye fear that ye shall not
Be able to deal justly
With the orphans,
Marry women of your choice,
Two, or three, or four.
But if ye fear ye shall not
Be able to deal justly (with them),
Then only one, or (a captive)
That your right hands possess.
That will be more suitable,
To prevent you
From doing injustice.

SURAH AL NISA (4): VERSE 11

Allah (thus) directs you
As regards your children's
(Inheritance): to the male,
A portion equal to that
Of two females: if only
Daughters, two or more,
Their share is two-thirds
Of the inheritance;
If only one, her share,
Is a half.
For parents, a sixth share
Of the inheritance to each,
If the deceased left children;
If no children, and the parents
Are the (only) heirs, the mother
Has a third; if the deceased
Left brothers (or sisters)

The mother has a sixth.
(The distribution in all cases is) after the payment
Of legacies and debts.
 Ye know not whether
Your parents or your children
Are nearest to you
In benefit. These are
Settled portions ordained
By Allah: and Allah is
All-knowing, All-Wise.

SURAH AL BAQARAH (2): VERSES 180-182

(180) It is prescribed,
    When death approaches
    Any of you, if he leave
    Any goods, that he makes a bequest
    To parents and next of kin,
    According to reasonable usage:
    This is due
    From the God-fearing.
(181) If anyone changes the bequest
    After hearing it,
    The guilt shall be on those
    Who make the change.
    For Allah hears and knows
    (All things).
(182) But if anyone fears
    Partiality or wrongdoing
    On the part of the testator,
    And makes peace between
    (The parties concerned),
    There is no wrong in him:
    For Allah is Oft-Forgiving,
    Most Merciful.

SURAH AL BAQARAH (2): VERSE 221

Do not marry
Unbelieving women
Until they believe:
A slave women who believes
Is better than an unbelieving woman.
Even though she allure you.
Nor marry (your girls)
To unbelievers until
They believe:
A man slave who believes
Is better than an unbeliever
Even though he allure you.
Unbelievers do (but)
Beckon you to the fire.
But Allah beckones by His Grace
To the Garden (of Bliss)
And Forgiveness,
And makes His Signs
Clear to mankind:
That they may
Receive adminition.

SURAH AL NUR (2): VERSE 3

Let no man guilty of
Adultery of fornication marry
Any but a woman
Similarly guilty, or an
Unbeliever:
Nor let any but such a man
Or an Unbeliever
Marry such a woman:
To the Believers such a thing
Is forbidden.

SURAH AL MA'IDAH (5): VERSE 5

This day are (all) things
Good and pure made lawful
Unto you. The food
Of the people of the book
Is lawful unto you
And yours is lawful
Unto them.
(Lawful unto you in marriage)
Are (not only) chaste women
Who are believers, but
Chaste women among
The people of the Book,
Revealed before your time
When ye give them
Their due dowers, and desire
Chastity, not lewdness
Nor secret intrigues.
If anyone rejects faith,
Fruitless is his work,
And in the Hereafter
He will be in the ranks
Of those who have lost
(All spiritual good).

SURAH AL MUMTAHINAH (60): VERSE 10

O ye who believe!
When there come to you
Believing women refugees,
Examine (and test) them:
Allah knows best as to
Their faith: it ye ascertain
That they are Believers,
Then send them not back

To the Unbelievers.
They are not lawful (wives)
For the Unbelievers, nor are
The (Unbelievers) lawful (husbands)
For them. But pay
The Unbelievers what they
Have spent (on their dower).
And there will be no blame
On you if ye marry them
On payment of their dower
To them. But hold not
To the guardianship of
Unbelieving women: ask
For what ye have spent
On their dowers, and let
The (unbelievers) ask for
What they have spent
(On the dowers of women
Who come over to you)
Such is the command
Of Allah: He judges
(With justice) between you.
And Allah is full of
Knowledge and Wisdom.

SURAH AL MUMTAHINAH (60): VERSES 11 – 12

(11) And if any
    Of your wives deserts you
    To the Unbelievers,
    And ye have an accession
    (By the coming over of
    A woman from the other side),
    Then pay to those
    Whose wives have deserted

The equivalent of what they
Had spent (on their dower).
And fear Allah,
In Whom ye believe.

(12) O Prophet!
When believing woman come
To thee to take the oath
Of fealty to thee, that they
Will not associate in worship
Any other thing whatever
With Allah, that they
Will not steal, that they
Will not commit adultery
(Or fornication), that they
Will not kill their children,
That they will not utter
Slander, intentionally forging
Falsehood, and that they
Will not disobey thee
In any just matter
They do thou receive
Their fealty, and pray to Allah
For forgiveness (of
Their sins): for Allah is
Oft-Forgiving, Most
Merciful.

SURAH AL NISA (4): VERSE 4

And give the women
(On marriage) their dower
As a free gift; but if they
Of their own good pleasure
Remit any part of it to you

Take it and enjoy it
With right good cheer.

SURAH AL NUR (24): VERSES 2-4

(2) The woman and the man
     Guilty of adultery or fornication
     Flog each of them
     With a hundred stripes;
     Let not compassion move you
     In their case, in a matter
     Prescribed by Allah, if ye believe
     In Allah and the Last Day:
     And let a party
     Of the Believers
     Witness their punishment.

(3) Let no man guilty of
     Adultery or fornication marry
     Any but a woman
     Similarly guilty, or an
     Unbeliever:
     Nor let any but such a man
     Or an Unbelievers
     Marry such a woman:
     To the Believers such a thing
     Is forbidden.

(4) And those who launch
     A charge against chaste women
     And produce not four witnesses.
     (To support their allegation),
     Flog them with eighty stripes;
     And reject their evidence
     Ever after: for such men
     Are wicked transgressors;

SURAH AL NISA (4): VERSE 15

If any of your women
Are guilt of lewdness,
Take the evidence of four
(Reliable) witnesses from amongst you
Against them; and if they testify,
Confine them to houses until
Death do claim them,
Or Allah ordain for them
Some (other) way.

SURAH AL NUR (24): VERSES 6-9

(6) And for those who launch
A charge against their spouses,
And have (in support)
No evidence but their own,
Their solitary evidence
(Can be received) if they
Bear witness four times
(With an oath) by Allah
That they are solemnly
Telling the truth.

(7) And the fifth (oath)
(Should be) that they solemnly
Invoke the curse of Allah
On themselves if they
Tell a lie.

(8) But it would avert
The punishment from the wife,
If she bears witness
Four times (with an oath)
By Allah, that (her husband)
Is telling a lie;

(9) And the fifth (oath)

Should be that she solemnly
Invokes the wrath of Allah
On herself if (her accuser)
Is telling the truth.

SURAH AL NISA (4): VERSE 16

If two men among you
Are guilty of lewdness,
Punish them both.
If they repent and amend,
Leave them alone; for Allah
Is Oft-Returning, Most
Merciful.

SURAH AL NUR (24): VERSE 33

Let those who find not
The wherewithal for marriage
Keep themselves chaste, until
Allah gives them means
Out of His grace.
And if any of your slaves
Ask for a deed in writing
(To enable them to earn
Their freedom for a certain sum),
Give them such a deed
If ye know any good
In them: yea, give them
Something yourselves
Out of the means which
Allah has given to you.
But force not your maids
To prostitution when they desire
Chastity, in order that ye
May make a gain

In the goods of this life.
But if anyone compels them.
Yet, after such compulsion,
Is Allah Oft-Forgiving,
Most Merciful (to them).

SURAH AL NISA (4): VERSE 25

If any of you have not
The means wherewith to
Wed free believing women,
They may wed believing
Girls from among those
Whom your right hands possess:
And Allah hath full knowledge
About your faith.
Ye are one from another:
Wed them with the leave
Of their owners, and give them,
Their owners, according to what
Is reasonable: they should be
Chaste, not lustful, nor taking
Paramours: when they
Are taken into wedlock,
If they fall into shame,
Their punishment is half
That for free women
 This (permission) is for those
Among you who fear sin;
But it is better for you
That ye practise self restraint:
And Allah is Oft-Forgiving,
Most Merciful.

SURAH AL NISA (4): VERSE 15

If any your women
Are guilt of lewdness,
Take the evidence of four
(Reliable) witnesses from amongst you
Against them; and if they testify,
Confine them; and if they testify,
Confine them to houses until
Death do claim them,
Or Allah ordain for them
Some (other) way.

SURAH AL NISA (4): VERSE 16

If two men among you
Are guilty of lewdness,
Punish them both.
If they repent and amend,
Leave them alone; for Allah
Is Oft-Returning, Most
Merciful.

SURAH AL NISA (4): VERSES 17–19

(17) Allah accepts the repentance
Of those who do evil
In ignorance and repent
Soon afterwards; to them
Will Allah turn in mercy:
For Allah is full of knowledge
And wisdom.

(18) Of no effect is the repentance
Of those who continue
To do evil, until Death
Faces one of them, and he says,

"Now have I repented indeed.,"
Nor of those who die
Rejecting Faith; for them
Have we prepared
A punishment most grievous.

(19) O Ye who believe!
Ye are forbidden to inherit
Women against their will.
Nor should you treat them
With harshness, that you may
Take away part of the dower
Ye have given them – except
Where they have been guilty
Of open lewdness.
On the contrary live with them
On a footing of kindness and equality.
If ye take a dislike to them
It may be that ye dislike
A thing, and Allah brings about
Through it a great deal of good.

SURAH AL BAQARAH (2): VERSE 282

O ye who believe!
When ye deal with each other,
In transactions involving
Future obligations
In a fixed period of time,
Reduce them to writing.
Let a scribe write down
Faithfully as between
The parties; let not the scribe
Refuse to write: as Allah
Has taught him,

So let him write.
Let him who incurs
The liability dictate,
But let him fear
His Lord Allah
And not diminish
Aught of what he owes.
If the party liable
Is mentally deficient,
Or weak, or unable
Himself to dictate,
Let his guardian
Dictate faithfully.
And get two witnesses,
Out of your own men,
And if there are not two men,
Then a man and two women,
Such as ye choose,
For witnesses
So that if one of them
Errs, The other can remind her.
The witnesses
Should not refuse
When they are called on
(For evidence).
Disdain not to reduce
To writing (your contract)
For a future period,
Whether it be small
Or big: it is jester
In the sight of Allah, More
Suitable as evidence,
And more convenient
To prevent doubts

Among yourselves
But if it be a transaction
Which ye can carry out
On the spot among yourselves
There is no blame on you
If ye reduce it not
To writing.
But take witnesses
Whenever ye make
A commercial contract;
And let neither scribe
Nor witness suffer harm.
If ye do (such harm),
If would be wickedness
In you. So fear Allah;
For it is Allah
That teaches you.
And Allah is well acquainted
With all things.

SURAH AL BAQARAH (2): VERSE 222

They ask thee
Concerning women's courses.
Say: They are
A hurt and a pollution:
So keep away from women
In their courses, and do not
Approach them until
They are clean.
But when they have
Purified themselves,
Ye may approach them
In any manner, time, or place
Ordained for you by Allah.

For Allah loves those
Who turn to Him constantly
And He loves those
Who keep themselves pure and clean.

SURAH AL BAQARAH (2): VERSE 223

Your wives are
As a tilth unto you
So approach your tilth
When or how you will;
But so some good act
For your souls beforehand;
And fear Allah,
And know that ye are
To meet Him (in the Hereafter),
And give (these) good tidings
To those who believe.

SURAH AL BAQARAH (2): VERSE 25

But give glad tidings
To those who believe
And work righteousness,
That their portion is Gardens,
Beneath which rivers flow.
Every time they are fed
With fruits therefore,
They say: "Why, this is
What we were fed with before,"
For they are given things in similitude;
And they have therein
Companions pure (and holy);
And they abide therein (forever).

SURAH AL NAHL (16): VERSE 72

And Allah has made for you
Mates (and Companions) of
Your own nature,
And made for you, out of them,
Sons and daughters and grandchildren.
And provided for your sustenance
Of the best: will they
Then believe in vain things,
And be ungrateful for
Allah's favours?

SURAH AL NUR (24): VERSES 30 – 31

(30) Say to the believing men
     That they should lower
     Their gaze and guard
     Their modesty: that will make
     For greater purity for them:
     And Allah is well acquainted
     With all that they do.
(31) And say to the believing women
     That they should lower
     Their gaze and guard
     Their modesty; that they
     Should not display their
     Beauty and ornaments except
     What (must ordinarily) appear
     Thereof; that they should
     Draw their veils over
     Their beauty except
     To their husbands, their fathers,
     Their husbands' fathers, their sons,
     Their husbands' sons,
     Their brothers or their brothers' sons,

Or their sisters' sons,
Or their women, or the slaves
Whom their right hands
Possess, or male servants
Free of physical needs,
Or small children who
Have no sense of the shame
Of sex; and that they
Should not strike their feet
In order to draw attention
To their hidden ornaments.
And O ye Believers!
Turn ye all together
Towards Allah, that ye
May attain Bliss.

SURAH AL AZHAB (33): VERSE 59

O prophet! Tell
They wives and daughters,
And the believing women
That they should cast
Their outer garments over
Their persons (when abroad):
That is most convenient,
That they should be known
(As such) and not molested.
And Allah is oft-Forgiving,
Most Merciful

BIBLIOGRAPHY

A.R. Desai (1993), *Social Background of Indian Nationalism*, Popular Prakashan Private Limited, Bombay.

Agnivesh, Swami (2005), *Hinduism In The New Age*, Hope India Publications, Gurgaon.

Anupama Rao (2003), *Gender & caste*, Kali for Women, New Delhi.

Char S.V. Desika (1993), *Caste Religion And Country*, Orient Longman Limited, Hyderabad.

Flavia Agnes (2004), *Women & Law in India*, Oxford University press, New Delhi.

Janaki Nair (1996), *Women and Law in Colonial India*, Kali for Women, New Delhi.

Jatava D.R. (2001), *Sociological Thoughts of B.R. Ambedkar*, ABD Publishers, Jaipur.

K. Antonova, G. Bongard-Levin, G. Kotpvsky (1979), *A History of India*, Progress Publishers, Moscow.

Karat, Brinda (2005), *Survival and Emancipation-Notes From India Women's Struggle*, Three Essays Collective, New Delhi.

Kumkum Roy, Kunal Chakrabarti, Tanika Sarkar (2005), *The Vedas, Hinduism, Hindutva*, Ebong Alap, Kolkata.

Puniyani Ram (2005), *Religion, Power And Violence-Expression of politics in Contemporary Times*, Sage Publication, New Delhi.

R.C. Majumdar, H.C. Raychaudhuri, K. Datta (1948), *An Advanced History of India*, Macmillan and Co. Limited, London.

Ram, R. P. (1981), *Secular Challenge to Communal Politics*,

Vikash Adhyayan Kendra, Mumbai.

Romila Thapar (1978), *Ancient Indian Social History*, Oriented Longman Limited, Hyderabad.

Romila Thapar (2000), *Cultural pasts-Essays in Early Indian History*, Oxford University press, New Delhi.

Uma Chakravarti (2003), *Gendering Caste–Through a Feminist Lens*, Street, Calcutta.

Gadkar Gajendra, P.B (1951), *Hindu Code Bill-Karnataka University Lectures*, Karnataka University, Dharvad.

Sarkar U.C. (1961), *Epochs in Hindu legal History*, *Vedic* Research Institute, Hoshiopur.

Julius Jolly, tr. by Ghosh Balakrishna (1928), *Hindu Law & Custom*, Greater India Society, Kolkata.

Dange S.A. (1949), *India From Primitive Communism to Slavery*, People Publication House, Mumbai.

Kosambi D.D. (1965), *The Culture & Civilisation Of Ancient India in Historical outline*, Vikas Publication Pvt. Ltd., Mumbai.

Joshi Tarkateertha Laxmanshashtri, tr. by Nene S.R. (2005), *Development of Indian Culture-Vedas to Gandhi*, Lokvagmayagruh, Mumbai.

Kant Anjani (2003), *Women and The Law*, APH Corporation, Mumbai.

Sharma K.L. (1998), *Caste, Feudalism & Peasantry-The Social Formation of Shekhawati*, Manohar Publisher.

Shabbir Mohammad (1991), *B.R. Ambedkar Study in Law and Society*, Rawat Publication, New Delhi.

Gadkari Jayant, *Hindu Muslim Jamatvadacha Siddhant*, D. DH. Kosambi Educational Trust, Mumbai.

Shah A.B. (1981), *Religion and Society In India*, Somaiya Publication Pvt. Ltd, Mumbai.

Devraja N.K., *Hinduism and Modern Age, Islam and Modern Age*, New Delhi.

Ambedkar, B.R. (1982), *Hindu Code Billasambhandddhi*, ed.

Vimalkirti, Pragativadi Prakashan, Nagpur.

Kulkarni, Vishnu (1952), *Hindu Code Bill, Kayade* Prakashan, Ahemadnagar.

Khermode, C. (1987), *Dr. Ambedkar and Hindu Code Bill,* Sugava Prakashn, Pune.

Kadate, S (1965), *Paramparic and Aadhunik Bharat,* Marathvada Vidyapith, Marathvada.

Upadhay, B.S. (1974), *Women in Rigveda,* S. Chanda and Company.

Sinha, Niroj (1999), *Women in Indian Politics,* Gyan Publication House.

Santhanam M.K (2000), *50 Years of Indian Republic,* Publications Division Ministry of India, New Delhi.

Jayant Godkari (1996), *Society & Religion From Rigveda to Puranas,* Popular Prakashan, Mumbai.

Kosambi D.D. (1956), *An Introduction To the Study of Indian History,* Popular Prakashan Mumbai.

Engels Frederick (1972), *The origin of the Family, Private Property, and the State,* Dathfinder Press, New York.

Bhartiya Janata Party (1998), *States Paper Common Civil Code Need of the Hour,* Mumbai.

Nivedita Menon, (2001), *Gender & Politics in India,* Oxford University Press.

Ghadially Rehana (ed) (1988), *Women in Indian Society,* Sage Publication, New Delhi.

Jaffrelot C. & Hansesn T. B. (ed), *Hindu Nationalism & Indian Politics,* Oxford University Press, New Delhi.

Gail Omvedt (1990), *Violence Against Women New Movements & New Theories In India,* Kali for women, Calcutta.

Madevshashtri A. (1988), *The Vedic Law of Marriage or The Emancipation of Women,* Asian Educational Services, New Delhi.

JOURNALS

Bulletin Of Asian Concerned Scholars, (Oct-Dec 1993).

Economic and Political Weekly, (April 12-18, 2003).

Economic and Political Weekly, (May31-June 6, 2003).

Communalism Combat, (September 2002).

Lawyers Collective, (February 2005).

Indian Currents, (25 september2005).